Business Interests and the Reform of Canadian Competition Policy, 1971-1975

Methuen: Canadian Politics and Government

Business Interests and the Reform of Canadian Competition Policy, 1971-1975

W. T. Stanbury
University of British Columbia

Carswell/Methuen
Toronto • Calgary • London • New York • Sydney

Canadian Cataloguing in Publication Data

Stanbury, W.T., 1943—
    Business interests and the reform of Canadian
competition policy, 1971-1975

ISBN 0-458-92890-9 bd. ISBN 0-458-92900-X pa.

1. Business and politics—Canada. 2. Competition,
Unfair—Canada. 3. Canada. Laws, statutes, etc.
Combines investigation act. 4. Pressure groups—
Canada. I. Title.

HD
3626
.C2
S78
1977 / 61, 419

Printed and bound in Canada

1 2 3 4 5   81 80 79 78 77

Contents

Acknowledgments

This study was financed largely by the Consumer Research Council. The first draft of the study was prepared while the author was on sabbatical from the University of British Columbia. To both institutions goes my gratitude for financial support. The Department of Consumer and Corporate Affairs was most helpful during 1975-76, when I spent about one-half my time in Ottawa. The department provided an office, telephone and typing services. Without the comprehensive clippings files of the departmental library and the Competition Policy Secretariat, this study could not have taken the form it did. Elaine Harrington, Charlotte St. Clair, Karen Olcen and Gilles Menard all went out of their way to be helpful. Katrin Horowitz offered useful editorial corrections as well as help in the library.

At U.B.C. my colleague Norm Schaefer reviewed the manuscript and offered his comments. Mabel Chan extremely competently and cheerfully typed the revised version of the manuscript in addition to her normal load. The Faculty of Commerce provided the money to enable me to hire Carolyne Smart to act as my research assistant for Chapter 2.

Professor G. B. Reschenthaler made a valuable contribution by writing Chapter 7, which describes the proposed Competition Act of 1971. I completely concur with his analysis of the ambitious, but ill-fated, Bill C-256.

A number of busy individuals were kind enough to read the first draft and offer perceptive comments. To Paul Gorecki, David McQueen, David Bond, Michael Trebilcock, Roy Davidson and particularly to Tex Enemark, go my warmest appreciation for their efforts.

Publication of the study in this form was made possible by financial support received from the Department of Consumer and Corporate Affairs. To the senior officials and the Minister, I express my sincere gratitude for their help in getting this book published quickly.

The staff of Nootka Graphics, who did the typesetting, worked on weekends under considerable pressure to get the book ready for the printer. Alfred Penz did the charts and pasted up the text most competently.

Finally, my appreciation to Michael Trebilcock and the staff of the Consumer Research Council who waited patiently, but encouragingly, for the final manuscript. I hope it is worth the delay. All opinions expressed and errors of omission or commission are the responsibility of the author.

W. T. Stanbury
University of B.C.
May 1977

Chapter 1

Introduction

This chapter is designed to fulfill three objectives: to describe the purpose of this study, to outline briefly the history of business-government interaction on competition policy in Canada in the period 1971-75 and to describe the structure of the study itself.

PURPOSE OF THE STUDY

This book is a detailed study of a turbulent process of business-government interaction over a major issue of public policy: Canadian competition legislation. What follows is an examination of the roles of business and consumers as interest groups in the Canadian political process.

The study concentrates on the period 1971 to 1975 in which a serious effort at fundamental reform of Canadian anti-combines legislation was undertaken by the federal government. The very large number of business and consumer interests affected by the proposed reforms and the extensive use of the printed media combine to provide a rare opportunity for insight into the process of interest group politics in Canada.

Because it is both well expressed and virtually identical to our own objectives, we adopt the statement made by Professor H. G. Thorburn at the beginning of his paper on the behaviour of pressure groups in respect of the 1960 amendments to the Combines Investigation Act.

> The role of interest groups in influencing policy decisions in Canada has received little close analysis, yet it is obviously important. Lobbying is inevitable when government regulations touch everyone's affairs; the only defence for those adversely affected is to seek to influence the government itself. Anti-combines legislation offers a particularly good example of this process because it is the case *par excellence* in which the interests of business, particularly big business, and those of the public, both as citizens concerned with freedom and as economically self-interested consumers, conflict.[1]

While the study is fundamentally a case analysis, its purpose is not simply to recount an episode of Canadian economic and political history. Indeed, its purpose is to more fully understand the process of interest group interaction where a fundamental conflict exists between consumers as an interest group on the one hand, and business as an interest group on the other. With this objective in mind, we draw on some of the most significant contributions in the rapidly expanding literature on the general nature and operation of interest groups to develop a framework for understanding interest group activity in a Canadian setting.

INTEREST GROUPS AND POLICY FORMATION

The process of public policy formation is not well understood in Canada. The gap between the rough and tumble action and reaction of interest groups within and without the government and the decorous descriptions in the political science textbooks is large indeed. Of particular importance is the benign, if not to say naive, view of interest group behaviour held by many Canadians. They are accorded such legitimacy and are perceived to be so functionally important to the process of policy formation and administration that many Canadians find it hard to imagine the way in which narrowly held, but intensely focused, interests of specific groups are able to obtain legislation favourable to their interests and unfavourable to literally millions of their fellow citizens. Just as important as the ability to obtain favourable legislation is the ability to block legislation which might curb the interest group's ability to enjoy the benefits of its existing, protected position. This was the situation in respect of attempts by the government to obtain a genuinely effective competition policy with the introduction of Bill C-256, the Competition Act in June of 1971.

It is important to study specific examples of business-government interaction because of the particular characteristics of the relationship between business interests and the government. One writer has identified four major characteristics of the policy and administrative struggle between business and government.[2] First, much of the interaction or struggle is *invisible* to observers external to the process. In fact, much of it may be invisible to all but a few of the participants themselves. The real political process is, to a large degree, informal. Although we have *Hansard, Minutes and Proceedings* published for House and Senate committees considering draft legislation and stacks of written briefs available to outsiders (or would-be participants), the real process of influence and accommodation may take place on a face-to-face basis of which no record is ever published. Consider the following description of the efforts of the Ottawa office of the Canadian Manufacturers' Association:

> . . . the overwhelming bulk of CMA input is, and will continue to be, in the form of unpublicized, informal discussions — the constant

interchange of visits between government officials and CMA staff and committee personnel.

In its relations with a number of Ottawa departments, this process of consultation has virtually eliminated the need for formal submissions, except for those cases in which it is appropriate to provide rather full documentation of research in support of a particular policy proposal.

The CMA has not followed the practice of requesting annual meetings with the federal Cabinet for the presentation of its views. Instead it has preferred the flexibility and timeliness of individual presentations, as the occasion demands, on specific subjects and to the cabinet minister and officials directly affected.[3]

In fact, interest groups are constitutionally nowhere to be found. Reality is more practical and flexible. Second, the process of business-government interaction is *continuous*. While the intensity of the relationship may ebb and flow, it never ceases. Business managers, who regularly make decisions for capital expenditures with an economic life of a decade or more, realize that staying power is important. Often their time horizon is far longer than that of elected officials constrained by the electoral cycle. While government goes on forever, the incumbent politicians and the senior bureaucrats appear to come and go with greater frequency than do senior business executives. In the case of competition policy, many of the most vocal critics of the Competition Act in 1971 were also loosing their salvos on the experts' reports for the second stage of reform in late 1976. In the meantime, the Department of Consumer and Corporate Affairs had gone through six ministers, four deputy ministers and two Directors of Investigation and Research.

Third, the *intensity* of the relationship between business and government *varies over time*. In Canada, the decade between 1965 and 1975 seemed to be a period of high intensity in the relationship as business had to grapple with a considerable number of major pieces of legislation, e.g., the Carter Commission and subsequent tax reform legislation, the "overhaul" of unemployment insurance, major revisions to the Canada Labour Code, a number of consumer protection bills and a new corporations act. The Competition Act in 1971 amounted to a large discontinuous change in policy which formerly had only a modest impact on business activity. It came at a time when business felt, and acted, beleagured in the face of the Liberal government's many legislative initiatives which could have a significant impact on business and producer interests. Coming when it did, and being as ambitious as it was, the Competition Act constituted a major threat to business.

Finally, the *site* of business-government interaction is *constantly shifting*. Within the legislative process, the locus of the interaction moves from senior civil servants and advisors, to the minister and his political compatriates, to the House and Senate committees considering legislation of interest to business, to backbenchers of both major parties and, finally, to the department which administers the legislation as enacted. But this list of sites grossly understates the places where business is able to interact with the government. For example, in the case of competition policy, business interests were able to utilize the media, particularly newspapers and the trade press, to communicate their views to the government. Business was also able to obtain widespread editorial support from the important newspapers and trade organs.While the Department of Consumer and Corporate Affairs mounted a considerable campaign on behalf of the legislation, it failed utterly to obtain favourable press coverage or effectively to disseminate to a wider audience the advantages to consumers that were inherent in the proposed legislation.

Because of the invisibility and multiplicity of sites of interaction of business and government in respect of competition policy, it is probably impossible to classify the various interacting forces on a completely adequate basis. While this study focuses on business as an interest or pressure group, it also seeks to describe the views and actions of other actors in the debate over competition policy. Until a fuller account of the process is available, this one should provide food for thought.

HISTORICAL OVERVIEW

Because the process of policy change was long and involved numerous reports, pieces of legislation and principal actors, it may be useful to take a synoptic look at what happened. The major documentary elements in our story are defined, and their date of occurrence is given in Figure 1-1. A far more detailed chronology of the major events is contained in Appendix A. Readers lost in the narrative or analysis may wish to sort themselves out by referring to it as the need arises.

Over a decade has passed since the Government of Canada requested the Economic Council of Canada to prepare a report on, among other things, "combines, mergers, monopolies and restraint of trade."[4] In July 1969 the council published its *Interim Report on Competition Policy*,[5] in which it proposed major revisions to the Combines Investigation Act. On June 29, 1971 the government introduced Bill C-256, the Competition Act, in the House of Commons and it was given First Reading. It was a large and complex bill — 106 pages containing 103 sections.[6] The Explanatory Notes, in what must be a classic understatement, stated that the proposed legislation did "not represent a major departure from established Canadian competition policy."[7] Harlow Unger, correspondent of the London *Sunday Times*, was nearer the mark when he described Bill C-256 as "the most sweeping anti-trust legislation in North American history" and "probably the toughest set of business regulations anywhere in the free world."

FIGURE 1-1

FIGURE 1

Major Steps in the Reform of Competition Policy in Canada, 1966-77

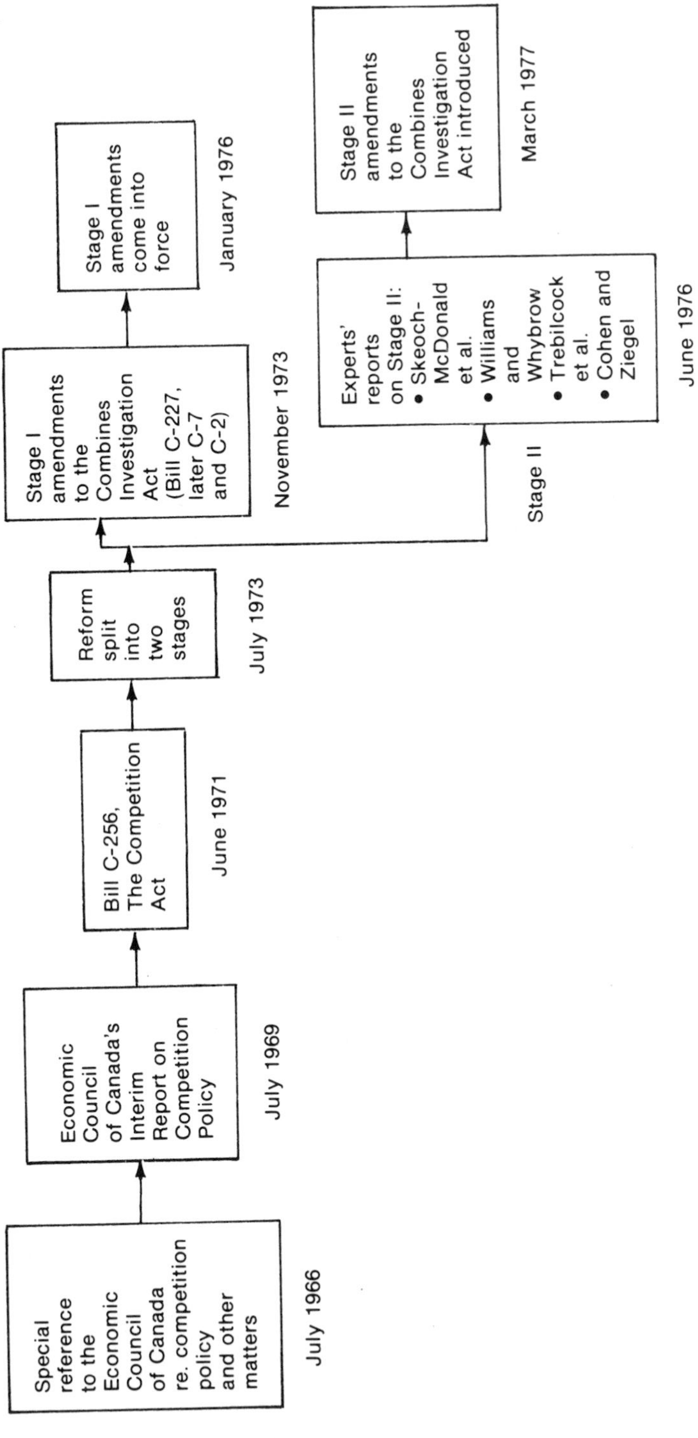

Special reference to the Economic Council of Canada re. competition policy and other matters

July 1966

Economic Council of Canada's Interim Report on Competition Policy

July 1969

Bill C-256, The Competition Act

June 1971

Reform split into two stages

July 1973

Stage I amendments to the Combines Investigation Act (Bill C-227, later C-7 and C-2)

November 1973

Stage I amendments come into force

January 1976

Experts' reports on Stage II:
• Skeoch-McDonald et al.
• Williams and Whybrow
• Trebilcock et al.
• Cohen and Ziegel

June 1976

Stage II

Stage II amendments to the Combines Investigation Act introduced

March 1977

Compared to the existing laws on restraint of trade, the Competition Act represented a large discontinuous change in the environment of Canadian businessmen. Their reaction was almost overwhelmingly negative. Five months after it was introduced, the *Financial Post* observed, "Not since the early days of the great tax debate has a single government proposal aroused the ire of the business community to the extent the Competition Act has."[8]

Early in 1972 the Minister of Consumer and Corporate Affairs, Ron Basford, was shifted to Urban Affairs, and Robert Andras, formerly Minister of Stte for Urban Affairs, took over responsibility for Consumer and Corporate Affairs. Within two months he announced that a revised bill would be reintroduced and that it would incorporate substantial changes in light of business' representations. He also indicated that a series of seminars would be held to allow businessmen and the public to communicate their views to the government.

On October 30, 1972 a federal general election was held and the Liberals, with only 109 seats to the Conservatives' 107, formed a minority government. A month later Herb Gray, formerly Minister of National Revenue, became the fourth Minister of Consumer and Corporate Affairs in five and one-half years. In the House of Commons on July 18, 1973 Mr. Gray announced that Canada's new competition policy would be implemented in stages. On November 6, 1973 a series of amendments to the Combines Investigation Act was given first reading in the House of Commons. This bill (C-227, later C-7 and C-2) was described as Stage I.[9]

On April 1, 1974 the Stage I amendments were sent to the House Standing Committee on Finance, Trade and Economic Affairs and the committee began its hearings on April 24.[10]

Another federal election occurred on July 8, 1974. The Liberals returned to majority government with 141 seats to the Conservatives' 95. One month later, Andre Ouellet, formerly Postmaster General of Canada, was appointed Minister of Consumer and Corporate Affairs. Herb Gray was dropped from the Cabinet.

By late March 1975 the House of Commons had received written submissions from seventy-seven organizations — primarily trade associations and business enterprises. As the *Globe and Mail* put it, "almost without exception, the briefs have been hostile. The members studying the bill in committee and the members of Parliament generally are feeling the heat."[11] The Standing Senate Committee on Banking, Trade and Commerce received about one-half that number, most of which were from trade asociations, individual firms. Only one was from a consumer organization, the Consumers' Association of Canada.[12]

The minister proposed thirty amendments to the original bill on December 3, 1974 and in the House Committee hearings the opposition was able to obtain a few of its own. It was June 3, 1975 before the Stage I amendments were reported out of the Commons committee. Only three days of debate in the Commons followed the committee's report and the bill received Third Reading on October 16, 1975. On December 10, 1975, after five days of additional hearings, the Senate committee reported the bill unamended to the Senate. The Stage I amendments to the Combines Investigation Act became effective January 1, 1976.

As Figure 1-1 indicates, the experts' reports with proposed legislation for Stage II were received in mid-1976. A bill incorporating the Stage II amendments to the Combines Act was introduced in the House of Commons in March 1977. The core of this study focuses on business-government interaction between June 1971 and the end of 1975. However, a chapter is devoted to the Economic Council's *Interim Report* and another to the earlier historical background.

STRUCTURE OF THE STUDY

The dominant political ethos of much of Western political science is pluralism. It is in pluralist theory (and reality) that interest groups become the focus of most important political activity. Chapter 2 examines the theory of pluralism and reviews the literature describing Canadian perceptions of the role of interest groups in the political process.

Chapter 3 examines some of the failures of pluralism in operational terms and also explains why consumers have never been an effective interest group. In Chapter 4 we present a framework of relationships between interest groups and the federal government. Particular emphasis is given to the role of busiess as a pressure group seeking to influence competition policy between 1971 and 1975.

To provide some historical perspective on Canadian attitudes and, more specifically, business and government's attitudes toward competition policy, in Chapter 5 we provide a brief review of the policy since its inception in 1889. Business hostility to an effective consumer-oriented competition policy is not new. Chapter 6 provides an analysis of the Economic Council's *Interim Report on Competition Policy* which was the principal basis for the legislation proposed two years later in 1971.

Chapter 7 describes in some detail the Competition Act introduced in Parliament in June 1971. Without an understanding of what was proposed it is not possible to appreciate how ambitious the government was being or appreciate the strong criticism (often inaccurate) levelled at the bill by business executives. Chapter 8 sets out the business and academic reaction to the Competition Act between the time it was introduced and the time the government made it clear that the legislation would be both amended significantly in light of business' views and introduced in stages. In addition to documenting business' evaluation of the act, Chapter 8 also indicates how the bill was seen by newspaper and trade press editorial writers.

In Chapter 9 we continue the story of business-government interaction as the government introduces the Stage I amendments to the Combines Investigation Act. While the battle continues to be fought in the media, much of the action shifted to the House and Senate committees which received scores of briefs and recorded hundreds of pages of testimony — primarily from the representatives of individual business firms and trade associations. This chapter covers the period November 1973 through December 1975 when the Stage I amendments (as amended) were given final reading in the House of Commons.

What did business gain for its efforts in opposing the competition policy legislation over this four-and-one-half-year period? In Chapter 10 we try to assess the impact business as a pressure group had in terms of the difference between the legislation originally proposed in the Competition Act and the legislation that went into force onJanuary 1, 1976. In the process we note the extent of the retreat from even what ws proposed in the Stage I legislation was introduced in November, 1973.

Finally, Chapter 11 seeks to tie up a number of loose ends; to provide a summary and some conclusions.

A CAVEAT ON GENERALIZATIONS

In this study we focus on the efforts of business and producer interests to prevent or severely weaken any reform of competition policy (as expressed in the Combines Investigation Act). During much of the study we will necessarily simplify and abstract from reality by refering to "business interests" as if the term properly described a single, unified, easily identified interest group. It is often the case that the "voice of business" can be more properly likened to the proverbial Tower of Babel as different industries, different regions and different sizes of firms express differing opinions on a policy issue. When this occurs, it is obvious that "business" can be as much of a kaleidoscope as the polity itself. However, on certain issues, although it is expressed by scores of trade associations and the executives or owners of hundreds of individually firms, "the voice of business" is effectively unified. In the case of the reform of Canada's competition policy between 1971 and 1975 this was the situation. With the exception of the less organized and less vocal representatives of small business, virtually all the trade associations and individual business leaders strongly opposed, in whole or in part, the Competition Act introduced in June of 1971 and its successor, the Stage I amendments to the Combines Investigation Act introduced in November 1973. For this reason, our collectivization of business interests in this study does only a small injustice to the facts.[13] In any event, the study is larded with the words of many individual participants who are identified by name and affiliation. Readers can judge for themselves whether the author has unfairly abstracted from significant differences in the views of individuals and specific trade associations.

A READER'S GUIDE

Readers impatient with theory, history and descriptive material and who just want to know how the story comes out should proceed directly to Chapter 10. Those interested in the details of the case study but who don't wish to wade through the more theoretical and earlier historical material should begin with Chapter 8 and read the two succeeding chapters. Academics, critics and serious students will doubtless have to read the entire study. I hope the rewards are comensurate with the costs of so doing.

NOTES

[1]H. G. Thorburn, "Pressure Groups in Canadian Politics: Recent Revisions of the Anti-Combines Legislation," *Canadian Journal of Economics and Political Science*, Vol. 30, No, 2, May 964, p. 157.

[2]Donald C. Blaisdell, assisted by Jane Greverus, *Economic Power and Political Pressures*, TNEC Monograph No. 26, Washington, D.C., USGPO, 1941, pp. 6-9.

[3]*Financial Post*, "Improve Business-Government Ties," October 7, 1972, p. 39.

[4]Press Release, Privy Council Office, July 22, 1966.

[5]Ottawa, Queen's Printer, 1969, 244 pp.

[6]The bill was accompanied by a 137-page volume entitled *The Competition Act: Explanatory Notes*, Ottawa, Department of Consumer and Corporate Affairs, 1971, mimeo.

[7]*Ibid.*, p. 1.

[8]December 11, 1971.

Bibliographical Note: A considerable number of newspaper references are used in this study. Many of the clippings files from which they were obtained gave only the name of the newspaper and the date of publication; no page number was indicated. It is for this reason that one does not appear in the footnotes.

[9]The original bill is contained in Department of Consumer and Corporate Affairs, *Proposals for a New Competition Policy for Canada, First Stage, 1973*, Ottawa, 1973.

[10]The Senate began its committee hearings on May 1, 1974 — some nineteen months *before* it formally received the bill after its passage in the Commons.

[11]William Johnson, "Proposed Competition Law Winning No Friends,"*Globe and Mail*, (Toronto), March 14, 1975.

[12]See Table 8-1, Chapter 8.

[13]It is also necessary in many places in the study to refer to "the government," implying a single-actor or unified entity. This, too, is a handy convention which both the writer and

the reader know to be a drastic simplification. However, in a number of places we specifically comment on the disparate views within the bureaucracy and among the elected officials. This should permit the use of the convention without drawing the ire of sophisticated critics.

Chapter 2

Interest Groups, Pluralism and Perceptions of Interest Groups in Canadian Political Processes

PLURALISM AND INTEREST GROUPS

One of the dominant themes of political science (particularly of American political science) has been the concept of pluralism, not simply as a political theory but as a political ideal. Political scientists, Theodore Lowi argues, have elevated "the pressure group from power to virtue."[1] We are told, "It goes without saying, then, that pressure groups are a natural phenomenon in social life, and that their abundance and vigour is the special glory of democratic society."[2] While they may be the "glory of democratic society," interest groups are constitutionally invisible. Blaisdell has pointed out that the political processes within which interest groups operate "is invisible . . . because citizen groups, the most energetic and purposeful of the working forces of government, are completely unprovided for by the written Constitution."[3]

Beginning with the writings of Arthur Bentley at the turn of the century,[4] many writers on politics came increasingly to accept the view that the group is the basic building block of political theory. This conclusion is preceded by the recognition (observation?) that "the chief social values cherished by individuals in modern society are realized by groups."[5] Organized groups constitute the structures of power "because they concentrate human wit, energy and muscle for the achievement of given purposes."[6] The concept of an interest group is broadly drawn. Truman defines it as "any group that, on the basis of one or more shared attitudes, makes certain claims upon other groups in the society for the establishment, maintenance or enhancement of forms of behaviour that are implied by the shared attitudes."[7]

Why do individuals organize into groups? The pluralist argument is that they do so "for the self-expression and security of the members that comprise them. . . . Self-expression and security, ideology and interest, are sought by the group members through control of the physical and social environment which surrounds each group. . . ."[8] In its strongest statements, pluralist theory denigrates the roles of the individual, who is described by Herring as "a mere cipher in a larger and emergent unit: the organized group."[9] The less extreme statements hold that the group is

11

simply a means by which individuals are able to fulfill their personal needs and express their values. This proposition presumes a complete mapping of individuals into groups — a rather strong proposition.

As a political ideal, pluralism is concerned with the diffusion of power among a wide variety of competing interests, multiple sources of initiative in both private and public policy and the recognition that each individual is the locus of a complex of overlapping and conflicting loyalties or roles.

> The goal of a pluralistic society is the diffusion of power into many organizations and groupings and thus the prevention of imbalances of power so that the freedom of the individual from the tyranny of the one, the few or the many is assured.[10]

The role of the state in pluralist theory is to assist in the resolution of conflict through the facilitation of bargaining, negotiation and compromise. "Theoretically, pressure groups compete with each other on equal terms, have equal bargaining power, with none enjoying an advantage over the other."[11] Citizens, when agrieved, make use of the right of petition and mobilize opinion. The state defines the rules of competition, and its executive rewards the rightful winner. Latham indicates that the legislature "referees the groups struggle, ratifies the victories of the successful coalitions and records the terms of the surrenders, compromises and conquests in the form of statutes."[12]

At any one time, "political reality can be grasped scientifically as a 'parallelogram of forces' among groups, and the public interest is 'determined and established' through the free competition of interest groups: 'The necessary composing and compromising of their differences is the practical test of what constitutes the public interest.'"[13]

Beyond theory and ideal, pluralism in its most recent form, a "vulgarized version," which Lowi describes as "interest-group liberalism," has become the "operative ideology of the American elite"[14] and the dominant public philosophy of our times. Neil Jacoby urges interest groups to assert their claims.

> In a pluralistic society, every institution has a right — if not a duty — to do what it can to survive. Pressure upon government for this purpose is a legitimate expression of a fundamental drive.[15]

Interest-group liberalism combines the concept of positive government intervention in social and economic affairs with the idea that the public interest is defined in terms of the organized interests in society.[16]

While the theory of pluralism does not countenance the absence of organized and effective consumer interest groups in public policy decision making, the reality of pluralistic society is different. This issue will be examined in Chapter 3.

PERCEPTIONS OF INTEREST GROUPS IN
CANADIAN POLITICAL PROCESSES

In the introduction to one of the few major studies of the operation of interest or pressure groups in Canada, Ronald W. Lang observes, "The study of pressure groups by political scientists in Canada in the past has been a sadly neglected area of the discipline."[17] He notes that the 1964 edition of R.M. Dawson's *The Government of Canada* has only one line on "interests": "The parties are the outstanding agents for bringing about cooperation and compromise between conflicting groups and interests of all kinds. . . ."[18] Presthus comments that the 1970 edition of Dawson's text "does not include in the index or the table of contents the terms 'interest groups,' 'pressure groups,' or 'lobbying.'"[19] His view is that Canadians have "a culturally determined orientation, semantical rather than substantive, which attempts to sublimate a process which seems functionally essential in any political system."[20] We shall return to this point later, but first we should point out there has been an increase in the number of studies of interest groups in the 1970s. Dawson's text may ignore interest groups, but Van Loon and Whittington's does not. It has a twenty-page-page chapter on "Interest Groups in Canadian Politics."[21] Presthus has published two major books based on interviews with bureaucrats, parliamentarians and interest group representatives (federal and provincial) in Canada and the United States.[22] Pross has recently collected a number of papers, conceptual and empirical, in a volume entitled *Pressure Group Behaviour in Canadian Politics*. The groups studied include a foreign policy pressure group, the mining industry and an environmental interest group.[23] In 1972 Kwavnick published his study of organized labour as a pressure group — focusing on the role of the Canadian Labour Congress.[24] Later he looked at the behaviour of the Quebec-based Confederation of National Trade Unions.[25] The Library of Parliament has also made a contribution to the literature in the form of a survey article.[26] Another reflection of this growing interest in pressure groups may be seen in the questioning by newspapers of the influence of interest groups in political decision making.[27]

Before going any further it may be useful to define what is meant by an interest or pressure group and by the term lobbying. Pross states, "pressure groups are organizations whose members act together to influence public policy in order to promote their common interest."[28] Milbrath defines lobbying as "the stimulation and transmission of a communication, by someone other than a citizen acting on his own behalf, directed to a governmental decision maker with the hope of influencing his decision."[29] For practical purposes, the phrases are co-terminous and we shall use them interchangeably.[30]

What are the important facets of the Canadian perception of interest groups in the political system? We shall try to summarize briefly the literature by answering this question in terms of the following points:

- Canadians have a positive view of interest groups in their political processes.

- Interest groups are accorded legitimacy in Canadian political processes.

- The functional nature of interest group activities is emphasized.

- The focus of lobbying activities in Canada is the bureaucracy and the Cabinet.

A POSITIVE VIEW OF INTEREST GROUPS

With very few exceptions, Canadians have a positive view of both the role and behaviour of interest groups in the domestic political system. Presthus writes, "Canada's political culture includes a generally affirmative perspective of interest groups, based largely upon a corporatist theory of society and a mildly positive appreciation of government's role and legitimacy. . . ." He notes that "neither government nor interest groups have enjoyed a similar legitimacy in the U.S."[31] Helen Dawson stresses the information input function of interest saying, "On the whole, Ministers welcome pressure group submissions as yet another source upon which to base decisions."[32] Perhaps trying to forestall the negative image of lobbyists among the untutored, Eggleston states: "Contrary to popular opinion, there is nothing sinister or derogatory about a lobbyist, as such. The lobbyist is a recognized part of our system of democratic government. He is recognized both in Britain and Canada by the rules of parliament."[33] Certainly his last statement can be challenged. In Canada there is no law in respect of lobbying activities at all, with the possible exception of the provisions regarding bribery of public officials. Kieran echoes Eggleston's point when he states:

> . . . if we are to understand this subject [lobbying] we must first dispose of the image of the cigar-chewing, bottle-passing political fixer and replace it with the image of responsible componentes of our society all diligently striving to get the best world possible for their constituents.[34]

Mr. Kieran is correct in that the representatives of effective interest groups hardly fit the description implicit in his words. Lobbyists are usually personally attractive people; they are well informed, well dressed and seldom crude in manner. That does not make them any more benign in their impact. A former Attorney General of Ontario is quoted as saying, "It is entirely proper to have this third level of government influencing us at the provincial and national levels."[35] His words are suggestive of at least an informal "estates general" in which the business, professional and other interests are directly represented in the political system. In his study of the Canadian Manufacturers' Association, published in 1938, S. D. Clarke made the same point when he said, "Cutting across the boundaries of constituencies and provinces to give representation to groups organized upon the basis of common interests, the lobbyists express, more completely than Members of Parliament, the diversified needs of the national community."[36]

Presthus presents data which indicates that Canadian elected officials "trust most lobbyists most of the time."[37] He asked the following question of 133 federal M.P.s: "Some observers have concluded that relations between a member and a lobbyists are based essentially upon mutual trust. Regarding lobbyists you have known, how much would you say you could rely upon them?" Some 19 percent replied "All of the time"; and 50 percent said "Most of the time"; only 28 percent said "Some of the time"; while 3 percent said "None of the time."[38]

The positive view of interest groups in the Canadian system is highlighted and reinforced by a somewhat pejorative view of lobbying in the U.S. Writing in the mid-1960s, McGillivray states that it is a myth that there is no lobbying in Canada, but he goes on to assure us that, "most of it is 'clean' lobbying presentation of a case without threats or bribes — rather than 'dirty' lobbying to use current American definitions."[39] The smug attitudes of Canadians on the issue of lobbying is evident in the following excerpt from a newspaper article in 1971:

> Whether Canadian "lobbyists" are less active than their American counterparts, or whether our legislators have a higher moral standard, the fact is that this country has been remarkably free of the sort of bribery and influence peddling scandals that have rocked successive U.S. administrations.[40]

What former M.P. Douglas Fisher called "such delightful fictions in Canada that lobbies don't really exist here, at least nowhere nearly as much in the United States,"[41] is evident in the following statement by Liberal M.P. Grant Deachman.

> This afternoon I went to the Parliamentary Library to look up some works on the subject of lobbying. Practically without exception all these books were written in the United States, because that is where lobbying has developed to a very high science, a much higher science than we find here. In the United States, particularly in respect of committees, there is very intense lobbying.
> Here the procedure is much simpler than in the United States Congress. Lobbying in the United States has developed to a very fine art compared with lobbying in Canada or even in Great Britain.[42]

In the same debate on a private member's bill to "provide for identification of lobbyists," a Liberal member from Quebec observed " . . . as far as I am concerned lobbying has not been a problem here in Canada. . . . On the other hand . . . the same does not apply in the United States. . . ."[43]

In April 1976, Conservative House Leader Walter Baker introduced another bill (a private member's bill) requiring the registration of individuals and groups attempting to influence legislation or the outcomes of administrative decisions within the responsibility of a Cabinet minister. The bill proposed a maximum fine of $5,000 for each week a lobbyist or his interest group evades the registry provisions.

While proposing a registration bill with significant penalties, Mr. Baker most usefully illustrates the positive view most Canadians hold of interest group and lobbying activities in an interview published in the Ottawa *Citizen.* Mr. Baker indicated "he doesn't think there's anything wrong with their work; he just wants people to see who they are. . . . He insists their efforts are a necessary part of the political process, but those efforts become somewhat tarnished as long as lobbyists are seen to operate furtively."[44] Mr. Baker is quoted as saying,

> Competing points of view and sources of information must be brought forward on important issues . . . otherwise decisions on matters of public policy will be made by a narrow group of politicians and bureaucrats, and those affected will be expected to cope helplessly with the effects.[45]

THE LEGITIMACY OF INTEREST GROUPS

Perhaps because interest groups are so deeply woven into the Canadian political fabric their legitimacy is not questioned. It is assumed that they have a variety of important functional roles to play in assisting government to carry out its tasks efficiently. To a degree at least, they are partners in terms of the political responsibilities they share.

Presthus obtained responses from 136 M.P.s on a number of questions which he describes as measures of legitimacy. He found the following percentages agreeing with these statements:[46]

- "Most legislators do not regard the activities of lobbyists as a form of improper pressure."   93 percent

- "Interest groups are necessary to make government aware of the needs of all the people."   85 percent

- "The information and services provided
  by interest groups are a necessary part
  of government policy making."   74 percent

- "Lobbyists are competent professionals
  who know their business."   73 percent

- "Lobbying as we know it today is healthy
  for democracy."   51 percent

The positive view of interest groups and the widespread assumption of their legitimacy in Canada, Presthus argues, is based on a corporatist theory of society. In this view, "social groups are fully equal to government in terms legitimacy, and . . . interest groups are a functional requisite of the governing process."[47] He points out that private groups will frequently be delegated public power through advisory councils and commissions.[48] One can go further and note that they will be used to administer certain public programs. When this occurs it makes apparent the symbiotic nature of the interest group-government relationships. Presthus states that it is a corollary of the corporatist or organic view of society that "government is not some alien apparatus which requires constant surveillance by private collectivities."[49] In other words, Canadians tend to be more trusting of public power and of the wielders of the power.[50] Put more critically, in the words of Northrop Frye, "The idea of a chain of command was built into this country from the beginning; the respect for authority."[51]

An illustration of the perceived legitimacy of Canadian interest groups is given by Laura W. Barr, executive director of the Registered Nurses' Association of Ontario (17,000 members) on becoming president of the Institute of Association Executives (800 dues paying non-profit, non-statutory associations): "The I.A.E. is a voice for specialists — of course it's a vested interest, Parliament does not easily lend itself to lobbying, but we are an important part of the checks and balances system of government."[52]

The contrast between Canada and the United States on the legitimacy of interest groups is described by Presthus:

> . . . whereas interest groups in the U.S. have often been regarded as exogenous, discontinuous and frequently illegitimate elements of the system, in Canada, from Confederation onward, they have been both normatively and symbiotically woven into the political fabric; indeed, the distinction between political and industrial leadership and interests are virtually imperceptible among the 'founding fathers' of Confederation.[53]

THE FUNCTIONAL NATURE OF INTEREST GROUPS

Canadian writers emphasize the functional nature of interest groups in the Canadian political system. First and foremost, interest groups are seen to provide information to policy makers.[54] Lobbyists provide decision makers and policy planners with information about the "real world," and in particular what the consequences of a policy change might be.

> For most civil servants, the (trade and professional) associations almost all represent a chance to make contact with the outside world on a regular basis. Together with the quiet lobbyists, they provide news and ideas that isolated government men in Ottawa need. . . .
> In the eyes of many senior civil servants, the risks of undue pressures or special interest are relatively minor compared to the danger of the vast government machine getting out of touch with the "real" world.[55]

The information provided is not always in the form of technical expertise; it is often in the form of feelings and attitudes of the members of various constituencies. As McGillivray puts it, interest groups "serve as a quick and handy indicator of the feelings of affected groups. . . ."[56]

Speaking as a Cabinet minister, Donald Macdonald stressed the value of information supplied by interest groups.

> In the process of preparing legislation and also in considering general policy changes, the government requires as much information as possible about the areas to be affected and the possible implications of any proposed changes. . . .
> What is of the greatest value is for the Minister to be apprised of the impact of the legislation from the particular viewpoint of the group concerned. Legislation must of necessity speak generally, but there may be special cases which persons in a particular industry or group might recognize more easily than can someone in government, surveying industry or the community generally.[57]

We have some more general empirical support for the provisions of "information" as a key to the functional aspects of interest group activities. Again we turn to Presthus,[58] who found that 40 percent of his sample of federal M.P.s ranked "providing information on pending legislation" as a "very important" or "fairly important" function of interest groups. Thirty-nine percent gave the same ranking to "helping me represent all community interests." Twenty-eight percent ranked "giving me attitudes of my constituents" as a "very" or "fairly important" function performed by interest group representatives. Obviously, the latter two functions deal with attitudinal information and political support rather than technical information about proposed legislation.

A number of writers have pointed out the symbiotic nature of interest group-government relations. While interest groups provide information (both technical and attitudinal), and organize and structure diffuse interests geographically[59] (and sometimes ideologically), they also are used to transmit information and even to administer government programs.

J. E. Anderson emphasizes the delegation by civil servants to interest groups of the setting of standards and regulations for trades and professions and also for the communication of government policy through trade and professional journals.[60]

M. G. Taylor takes the position that with respect to the medical profession in Canada, "no other group is as deeply involved in public administration . . . despite the fundamental antipathy between the healing arts and bureaucracy."[61] He points out that the self-governing professions safeguard the public interest without regulation by a public agency. He notes that the statutes under which the professions have turned the process of self-regulation into "miniature governments, conferring on them all of the types of power normally exercised by government."[62]

M. W. Bucovetsky points out that interest groups can perform the function of obtaining goal-consensus — so necessary to a government unit's growth. He states: "The symbiotic relationship between government agencies and their clientele is a well-known administrative phenomenon. In particular, the effective functioning and growth of a government bureau depends on its having a strong goal-consensus. The more homogeneous a bureau's clientele and the more clearly defined the clientele's interests, the more it will be to the bureau's own advantage to adopt goals that are harmonious."[63]

As Pross indicates, "it is not unusual for Canadian governments to create pressure groups in order to foster relations with 'special publics' and to promote a demand for policies which particular departments are anxious to adopt."[64]

In general, the functional approach to interest groups has much to commend it as a means of understanding their observed behaviour and rationalizing their role in the larger political system. Apparently government is of necessity dependent upon interest groups to assist it in shaping public policies that are both technically correct and politically acceptable to the constituent elements of society.

LOBBYING THE BUREAUCRACY AND THE CABINET

The focus of lobbying activity in Canada is the bureaucracy and the Cabinet, rather than the individual backbencher or members of parliamentary committees. The fact that interest group representatives devote the larger part of their energy to attempting to influence the policy makers in the bureaucracy is simply a reflection of the bureaucracy's power in the governmental process. When the famous bank robber Willie Sutton was asked why he robbed banks, reputedly he replied, "Because that's where the money is." In our own context Hugh Whalen makes the same point. "Notwithstanding our elaborate mythology on such subjects as parliamentary supremacy, ministerial responsibility and the rule of law, it is now clear that officials design and execute policy because of their technical skills, and because of the wider discretion that accompanies the growth of governmental functions."[65]

A senior civil servant, as quoted in an article in the *Financial Post*, described the locus for influencing government in the following way:

> People who really want to guide and influence government policy are wasting their time dealing with members of Parliament, senators and, usually, even ministers. If you want results — rather than just the satisfaction of talking to the prominent — you deal with us, and at various levels. . . . To produce results you need to see the key planners, who may be way down in the system, and you see them early enough to push for changes in policy before it is politically embarrassing to make them.[66]

The view that the crucial people to try to influence in Ottawa are the key civil servants is reiterated by "a highly successful lobbyist" in the same article:

> Really, most new ideas begin deep in the civil service machine. The man in charge of some special office. . . writes a memo suggesting a new policy on this or that. It works its way slowly up and up. At that stage civil servants are delighted, just delighted, to talk quietly to people like us, people representing this or that corporation or industry directly involved. That is the time to slip in good ideas. Later it oozes up to the politicians and becomes policy. By the time it is a government bill it is the very devil to change it. Then you have real trouble.[67]

Presthus provides some more general empirical support for the proposition that Canadian interest group representatives focus their efforts on bureaucracy, while their American counterparts expend their energy on individual legislators. He asked almost one thousand directors of interest groups, "Which three of the following elements in the political system receive the greatest amount of attention from you and your association?" In terms of the proportion of respondents ranking each target first, he obtained the following results:[68]

Target of Interest Group:	U.S.	Canada
Bureaucracy	21%	40%
Legislators	41	20
Legislative committees	19	7
Cabinet	4	19
Executive assistants	3	5
Judiciary	3	3
Other	9	6
N =	604	393

These results should not be surprising, given the different political structures of the two countries. The Canadian system of Cabinet government, characterized by the discipline of party-line voting, has resulted in the reduced influence of backbenchers. McGillivray quotes a lobbyist as saying, "the power of the individual member of Parliament or senator is just about zero."[69] Presthus states: "backbenchers are largely excluded from policy determination."[70] He quotes a federal M.P., "If they lobby, they lobby the Cabinet and deputy ministers. They know we have no power." A Quebec deputy is quoted as saying, "An ordinary member can't do enough to make it worthwhile for a lobbyist to see him. It occurs at a higher level."[71] Since power tends to seek power, interest groups devote their efforts to the Cabinet and the key figures in the bureaucracy. If this is true, why do legislators slightly outrank the Cabinet as the prime target of the interest groups activities? Presthus attributes it to the growing importance of committees in the Canadian legislative process. Of particular importance are certain members of committees, e.g., the chairman.[72] More important, says Presthus, is the apparent division of labour between the Cabinet and backbenchers. The former concentrates on substantive policy issues, while the latter deals with the demands of constitutents.[73] Since "a high proportion of Canadians feel considerable diffidence in approaching federal (and, by inference, provincial) officials,"[74] they use interest group representatives to intercede on their behalf. Apparently for some groups, or for some issues, backbenchers constitute the preferred point of access.

Backbenchers themselves provide other reasons why lobbyists try to influence individual members. Presthus's data "indicate the majority of members [in the sample] believe that lobbyists think, however wrongly, that if they can persuade a sufficient number of backbenchers to support a given policy, they may be able, in caucus, to change the mind of the relevant minister."[75]

Identifying the points of access to the policy formation process is much easier than trying to determine the effectiveness of various strategies vis-a-vis different participants. Van Loon and Whittington accurately summarize perceptions of the Canadian process: "The most effective presentations of interest groups views are the kind that the public never hears about, for they involve direct and informal contact between the bureaucracy and interest groups during the process of policy formulation."[76]

NOTES

[1]Theodore J. Lowi, *The End of Liberalism*, New York, Norton, 1969, p. 74.

[2]D. C. Corbett, "The Pressure Group and the Public Interest," in J. E. Hodgetts and D. C. Corbett (eds.), *Canadian Public Administration*, Toronto, Macmillan, 1960, p. 455.

[3]Donald C. Blaisdell, assisted by Jane Greverus, *Economic Power and Political Pressures*, Monograph No. 26, TNEC, Washington, DC., USGPO, 1941, p. 7.

[4]Arthur F. Bentley, *The Process of Government*, Bloomington, Ind., 1949 (originally published in 1908).

[5]Earl Latham, *The Group Basis of Politics*, Ithaca, N.Y., Cornell University Press, 1952, p. 1.

[6]*Ibid.* p. 12.

[7]David Truman, *The Governmental Process*, New York, Alfred A. Knopf, 1951. D.C. Corbett goes even further. He states, "Virtually all groups are pressure groups. The group pursues its interests by organizing its members to exert their concerted power on those who can help them or hurt them. The targets of this pressure may be individuals, other groups or the state" (*op. cit.* p. 454).

[8]Latham, *op. cit.*, pp. 28-29.

[9]E. Pendleton Herring, *Group Representation Before Congress*, Baltimore, Johns Hopkins University Press, 1936, pp. 5-6.

[10]Richard Eells and Clarence Walton, *Conceptual Foundations of Business* (3rd edition) Homewood, Ill., Richard D. Irwin, 1974, pp. 437-438.

[11]Blaisdell, *opt. cit.*, p. 13.

[12]Latham, *op. cit.*, p. 35.

[13]Wilfred Binkley and Malcolm Moos, *A Grammar of American Politics*, New York, Alfred A. Knopf, 1950, p. 7 as cited in Lowi, *op.cit.*, p. 75.

[14]Lowi, *op.cit.*, p. 84.

[15]Neil H. Jacoby, *Corporate Power and Social Responsibility*, New York, Macmillan, 1973, p. 150.

[16]Lowi, *op.cit.*, p. 71.

[17]Ronald W. Lang, *The Politics of Drugs*, Lexington Mass., Saxon House/Lexington Books, 1974, p. 5. Robert Presthus makes a similar point when he says "there has, in the main, been little critical scholarship in Canada which has traced the symbiotic role of [interest] groups." *Elites in the Policy Process*, London,Cambridge University Press, 1974, p. 14.

[18]Lang, *op.cit.*, pp. 6-7.

[19]Robert Presthus, "Interest Groups and the Canadian Parliament: Activities, Interaction, Legitimacy and Influence," *Canadian Journal of Political Science*, Vol. 4, December 1971, p. 446, footnote 5.

[20]*Ibid.*, p. 446.

[21]R. J. Van Loon and M.S. Whittington, *The Canadian Political System*, Toronto, McGraw-Hill, 1971, pp. 297-321.

[22]Robert Presthus, *Elite Accommodation in Canadian Politics*, Toronto, MacMillan, 1973, and *Elites in the Policy Process*, London, Cambridge University Press, 1974. See also Robert Presthus, "Interest Group Lobbying: Canada and the United States," *The Annals of the American Academy of Political and Social Science*, Vol. 400, 1972, pp. 44-57.

[23]A. Paul Pross (ed.), *Pressure Group Behaviour in Canadian Politics*, Toronto, McGraw-Hill Ryerson, 1975. See also two recent papers on other pressure groups Glyn R. Berry, "The Oil Lobby and the Energy Crisis," *Canadian Public Administration*, Vol. 17, No. 4, Winter 1974 and Carolyn J. Tuohy, "Pluralism and Corporatism in Ontario Medical Politics," in Rea and McLeod (eds.), *Government and Business in Canada* (2nd edition) Toronto, Methuen, 1976, pp. 395-413.

[24]David Kwavnick, *Organized Labour and Pressure Politics*, Montreal, McGill-Queen's University Press, 1972.

[25]David Kwavnick, "Pressure Group Demands and Organizational Objectives: the CNTU, the Lapalme Affair and National Bargaining Units," *Canadian Journal of Political Science*, Vol. 6, No. 4, December 1973, pp. 582-602.

[26]Canada, Library of Parliament, "Pressure Groups in Canada," *The Parliamentarian*, Vol. 51, No. 1, January 1970, pp. 11-20.

[27]See, for example, Clive Baxter, "Familiars in the Corridors of Power. Plainman's guide to the lobbyists, who now are legion in the nation's capita," *Financial Post*, July 12, 1975, p. 6. The role of former deputy ministers Simon Reisman and James Grandy as advisors to Lockheed Aircraft Corporation is discussed in James Ferrabee, "Ex-Mandarins' Business Links Raise Eyebrows in Parliament," *Citizen* (Ottawa), March 26, 1976, p. 6; Orland French, "Guides Could Cut Dealings with Government," *Citizen*, March 25, 1976, p. 1; Orland French, "Cooling off time on government contacts urged for ex-MPs," *Citizen*, March 26, 1976, p. 31. The role of Senator Salter Hayden, a vice-president and director of a major sugar producer, and also chairman of the Senate Standing Committee on Banking and Finance which was reviewing competition policy legislation was challenged by Senator David Croll. See Richard Cleroux, "Competition Act Study Raises Conflict Issue," *Globe and Mail*, (Toronto) February 12, 1975.

[28]A. P. Pross, "Pressure Groups: Adaptive Instruments of Political Communication," in A. Paul Pross (ed.), *Pressure Group Behaviour in Canadian Politics*, Toronto,McGraw-Hill, 1975, p. 2.

[29]Lester Milbrath, *The Washington Lobbyists*, Chicago, Rand McNally, 1963, p. 8.

[30]Not everyone agrees. H. H. Hannah, "The Interest Group and Its Activities," (*Proceedings of the 5th Annual Conference, Institute of Public Administration of Canada*, Toronto, 1953, p. 1972) states, "I think the spade and the club is, in my mind, the distinction between the interest group and the pressure group." There is another term, believed by Canadians to be less pejorative, for the lobbyist. It is "Parliamentary Agent." Such individuals are officially recognized. "Rules are set down for their conduct and they have to pay an annual fee of $25 for the privilege of being [a] registered agent. These agents are almost always Ottawa lawyers who appear before Senate and the Commons' committees to promote various private bills." Tissington distinguishes these persons from "the second unofficial group of influence wielders [who] come closer to the American view of a lobbyist." (Farmer Tissington, "'Parliamentary Agents' don't like the word Lobbyist," *Times-Journal*, (St. Thomas), July 7, 1971, p. 19).

In the U.S. recently Senator Abraham Ribicoff introduced a bill to change the provisions of the Regulation of Lobbying Act, passed in 1946. The proposed regulations would not only apply to anyone whose job involved lobbying as a substantial purpose but also to anyone who spent more than $250 a quarter or $500 a year "to influence the policy making process." It would also include anyone who talked, on separate occasions, to eight employees of Congress or the executive branch. (*Business Week*, June 9, 1975, p. 98). These regulations define the term lobbyist very broadly.

[31]Presthus, *Elites in the Policy Process, op.cit.*, p. 14.

[32]H. J. Dawson, "National Pressure Groups and the Federal Government," in Pross (ed.), *op.cit.*, p. 37.

[33]W. Eggleston, "The Cabinet and Pressure Groups," *Proceedings of the 5th Annual Conference, The Institute of Public Administration of Canada*, Toronto, PAC, 1953, p. 165.

[34]J. W. Kieran, "Lobbying," *Executive*, April 1969, p. 33.

[35]Quoted in Presthus, *Elite in the Policy Proces*, *op.cit.*, p. 33. Common Market officials joke, "We are a community of ten. The tenth is Unilever, with a veto substantially more useful than Luxembourg's," (Richard Body M.P., "Euro-Lobbying," *The Spectator*, April 12, 1975, p. 435). W. C. Osborn in his *Paper Plantation* (New York: Grossman, 1974) points out that Maine's reliance on "a group of highly paid, special interest lobyists," is such that they are referred to as the "third house," of the legislature, "The strength of this 'third house' derives from the weaknesses of the other two" (p. 228).

[36]S. D. Clarke, "The Canadian Manufacturers' Association," *Canadian Journal of Economics and Political Science*, Vol. 4, 1938, p. 522. See also S. D. Clarke, *The Canadian Manufacturers' Association: A Study in Collective Bargaining and Political Pressure*, Toronto, University of Toronto Press, 1939.

[37]Presthus, "Interest Groups and the Canadian Parliament," *op.cit.*, p. 444.

[38]*Ibid.*, p. 454 Table VII.

[39]Don McGillivray, "Lobbying at Ottawa," in Paul Fox (ed.), *Politics: Canada* (3rd edition), p. 163, (Originally a five-part series by Southam News Services, April 9-15, 1964).

[40]Tissington, *op.cit.*, p. 19. One wonders where Mr. Tissington was during the Hal Banks affair, the Gerda Munsinger affair (no pun intended), the Lamontagne acquisition of furniture scandal, the Raymond Denis-Lucien Rivard relationship and other embroglios concerning influence in high places.

[41]Cited in Lang, *op.cit.*, p. 7.

[42]*Ibid.*, p. 6.

[43]*Ibid.*, pp. 5-6.

[44]Orland French, "Lobbying's No Whisper Word to Baker," *Citizen* (Ottawa), April 9, 1976, p. 33. The same story also indicates that Mr. Baker will propose another bill "which would prohibit retired public servants from dealing with their former government departments on behalf of private interests." In part, Mr. Baker's bill was prompted by the critical comments concerning the role of the former Deputy Ministers of Finance and Industry, Trade and Commerce as consultants to the Lockheed Aircraft Corporation. Lockheed was involved in selling the federal government some $1.1 billion worth of long range patrol aircraft. See the references in note 27 above.

[45]*Ibid.*, p. 33. Mr. Baker's bill suffered the universal fate of opposition private members bills — it was defeated.

[46]Presthus, "Interest Groups and the Canadian Parliament, *op.cit.*, p. 455, Table VIII.

[47]Presthus, *Elites in the Policy Process, op.cit.*, p. 4.

[48]*Ibid.*, p. 33.

[49]*Ibid.* p. 211. In one of his other papers Presthus states this point as follows: "Because interest groups and their agents are integral parts of the system, lobbying is not required to ensure that government does its duty." ("Interest Group Lobbying, *op.cit.*, p. 45).

[50]Presthus describes a related phenomenon as the deferential style of Canadian politics. "Political leaders, including the higher bureaucracy, can and do define and seek the 'public interest' without much need for explanation of their actions or for participation by the general public." ("Interest Groups and the Canadian Parliament," *op.cit.*, pp. 455-456).

[51]Keith Ashford, "Frye Tackles Great 'Identity Crisis,'" *Citizen* (Ottawa), April 6, 1976, p. 63.

[52]Financial Post, August 9, 1975, p. 24.

[53]Presthus, *Elites in the Policy Process, op.cit.*, p. 9.

[54]This is also emphasized in the U.S. literature, e.g., "The government couldn't possibly function without the inputs provided by skilled advocacy of special interests, be they industrial or otherwise." Robert Fellmeth, *The Politics of Land*, New York, Grossman, 1973, p. 478.

[55]Baxter, *op.cit.*, p. 6.

[56]McGillivray, *op.cit.*, p. 164.

[57]Cited in J. E. Anderson, "Pressure Groups and the Canadian Bureaucracy," in W. D. Kernaghan (ed.), *Bureaucracy in Canadian Government*, Toronto, Methuen, 1969, p. 102.

[58]Presthus, Interest Groups and the Canadian Parliament, *op.cit.*, p. 448 Table II.

[59]See Kwavnick, *Organized Labour and Pressure Politics, op.cit.*

[60]Anderson, *op.cit.*

[61]M. G. Taylor, "The Role of the Medical Profession in the Formulation and Execution of Policy," *Canadian Journal of Economics and Political Science*, Vol. XXVI, No. 1, February 1960, p. 108.

[62]*Ibid.*, p. 111.

[63]M. W. Bucovetsky, "The Mining Industry and the Great Tax Reform Debate," in A. P. Pross (ed.), *op.cit.*, p. 107.

[64]A. P. Pross, "Pressure Groups: Adaptive Instruments of Political Communication," in A. P. Pross (ed.), *op.cit.*, p. 19. A possible illustration of this phenomenon is the funding of consumer interest groups by the Department of Consumer and Corporate Affairs. It was expected that such grants would total at least $600,000 in 1975/76. See "Government Grants for Advocacy," *Journal* (Ottawa), March 19, 1975, p. 38.

[65]Hugh Whalen, "The Peaceful Co-existence of Government and Business," *Canadian Public Administration*, Vol. IV March 1961, p. 2.

[66]Baxter, *op.cit.*, p. 6.

[67]Baxter, *op.cit.*, p. 6.

[68]Presthus, *Elites in the Policy Process, op.cit.*, p. 255, Table 8-3.

[69]McGillivray, *op.cit.*, p. 164.

[70]Presthus, "Interest Group Lobbying," *op. cit.*, p.46.

[71]Presthus, *Elites in the Policy Process, op.cit.*, p. 248. Van Loon and Whittington make the same point: "Parliament, therefore, is not an important focus of interest group activity. . . . the focus of interest group activity at the federal level is more likely to be the bureaucracy than the Cabinet." (*op.cit.*, p. 306). They quote an "experienced lobbyist": "when I see Members of Parliament being lobbied, it's a sure sign to me that the lobby lost its fight in the civil service and the Cabinet." (*op.cit.*, p. 306).

[72]Presthus *Elites in the Policy Process, op.cit.*, p. 244.

[73]*Ibid.*, p. 248.

[74]*Ibid.*, p. 248.

[75]*Ibid.*, p. 249-250.

[76]Van Loon and Whittington, *opcit.*, p. 311. The power of the bureaucracy as an independent force is emphasized by Lang. He argues that the interdepartmental committee on drug prices and patents, whose existence was unknown to the pharmaceutical industry lobby, was the key force in determining the policy outcome, in this case, compulsory patent licensing. (Ronald W. Lang, *The Politics of Drugs, op.cit.*, p. 136). A less sanguine view of the civil servants efforts is given by Hugh Winsor, "How Mandarins Worked to Foil the Drug Lobby," *Globe and Mail* (Toronto), October 28, 1975. This is a review of Lang's book.

Chapter 3

The Failures of Pluralism and the Ineffectiveness of Consumers as an Interest Group

We have examined the pluralist view of political processes and we have indicated the nature of Canadian perceptions of the role of interest groups in the political system. Because the latter part of this study is concerned with the effectiveness of business as an interest group, it is useful to examine why consumer interests have been poorly organized and largely ineffective in the public policy process. To put the problem of consumer interests in perspective, we shall first indicate some of the difficulties with pluralism in practice.

FAILURES OF PLURALISM

In practice, pluralism has a number of significant failings. First, not all significant interests manage to get organized and to compete actively with contending interests for a say in public policy information. As President John F. Kennedy pointed out, the voice of consumers "is not always loudly heard in Washington as the voices of smaller and better organized groups — nor is their point of view always defined and presented."[1] Neil Jacoby comes to the same conclusion: "The basic flaw in the distribution of political power among American institutions is that producer interests rather than consumer interests tend to dominate and shape the actions of government."[2] With respect to transportation policy in Canada and the Canadian Transport Commission, J. S. Grafstein states, "the regulatory policy has not cast its net wide enough to examine the effects of transport policies or carriers' activities on the consumer."[3] He argues that a consumer advocate should be built into the regulatory process. Harold Buchwald, a former chairman of the Canadian Consumer Council, makes a similar point: "The most effective way to begin to redress this imbalance and advance consumer interests at the government (and even industry) level is to have a strong consumer lobby, a consumer constituency supported by a strong consumer-oriented research facility." Buchwald asks, "Who will accept your proposal without researched and documented backup? Who will be persuaded to react without some ballot box influence?"[4] In general, less intense interests which are widely diffused are not adequately represented by organized interest groups as are the interests which are intensely important to a relatively few individuals or firms.

Lowi takes the view that interest-group liberalism amounts to "a conspiracy to shut out the public." He says that "one of the assumptions underlying direct group representation is that on the boards and in the staff and among the recognized outside consultants there will be regular countervailing checks, and balances. . . . [T]his would be expected to expand the 'scope of conflict.' But there is nothing inevitable about that, and the safer assumption might well be the converse."[5]

David Truman, the principal disciple of Arthur Bentley, recognized the existence of unorganized interest groups, but argued that their interests would be asserted by both appointed and elected officials in all branches of government. Alternatively, if segments of society were sufficiently disadvantaged, latent groups would become organized as a sort of "countervailing" force against those groups who were benefiting at their expense.[6] James Q. Wilson states that the conventional theory of interest-group politics holds that "any interest seriously threatened by a proposed policy could force supporters of the policy to bargain with it and make substantial concessions."[7] Glendon A. Schubert has described this facet of Truman's theory as "a vague but fervent transcendentalism";[8] certainly, most individual consumers and erstwhile consumer groups (e.g., the Consumers' Association of Canada or Consumers Union) would agree.[9]

A second major failing of pluralism is that the "socially optimum balance" may not result from the competitive behaviour of the multifarious groups. The market place for representative interest groups may suffer from the same problems as do economic markets. These are the problems of externalities, indivisibilities, economies of scale and so forth. In fact, except in terms of pluralism as a *process*, it seems impossible to define a social optimum in a pluralistic society. Since the pluralists specifically deny that there is an "interest of the nation as a whole, universally and invariably held and standing apart and superior to those of the various groups within it,"[10] the public interest is defined in terms of the balancing of group interests. The public interest "must necessarily represent a working compromise and be subject to continuous definition, as need arises, in the process of achieving an often delicate balance among conflicting interests."[11]

In terms of its impact on public policy, there are additional problems associated with pluralism. Lowi points out that "programs following the principles of interest-group liberalism create privilege." What makes this hard to bear is that such privilege is "touched by the symbolism of the state."[12] More than the spectre of the iron law of oligarchy is raised. One of the results of clear and effective representation of an interest by a group in the policy formation process is that membership in the group becomes implicitly less voluntary.[13] Furthermore, as organized groups become larger and are seen to "represent" defined interests, the greater the likelihood that their *internal* pluralism will be diminished.

One of the basic assumptions of the interest-group liberalism version of the pluralist model is that "organized interests are homogeneous and easy to define, sometimes monolithic." Furthermore, "any 'duly elected' spokesman for any interest is taken as speaking in close approximation for each and every member."[14] An example of the conflict between diminished internal pluralism and the appropriateness of this assumption would appear to be the American Medical Association or the Canadian Labour Congress.

Another of what Lowi calls the "costs of interest-group liberalism" is that "government by and through interest groups is in its impact conservative in almost every sense of that term."[15] In particular such a government is strongly resistant to change for officially recognized oxes refuse to be gored. Put another way, " . . . few if any programs organized on the basis of direct interest representation or group self-administration have ever been eliminated."[16]

In summary, pluralism in practice has significant failings in terms of the interests of consumers. The consumer interest is not manifested in the form of effective formal organizations. The reasons for this will be discussed below. Consequently, the impact of consumer interests on public policy is modest.[17] The idea of a social optimum (public interest) as the balancing of contending group interests is academic as far as consumers as an interest group are concerned. The impact of organized consumer interest groups in countervailing the pressures of producer interests range from the largely ineffectual to the non-existant. The effectively organized interests (notably producers) succeed over time in obtaining the sanction of public policy for the protection and advancement of their position. Administrative regulation by "independent regulatory agencies" has long provided a safe heaven from the vicissitudes of competition for the regulated firms. Latham argues that "the administrative agency of the regulatory kind is like an army of occupation left in the field to police the rule won by the victorious coalition."[18] The validation and entrenchment of existing interests make them extremely difficult to counteract in the event the consumer interest can be effectively organized to contend in the fray.

CONSUMERS: AN INEFFECTIVE INTEREST GROUP

Why are consumers unorganized and ill-represented in the corridors of power? Aren't all of us consumers? Isn't the protection and advancement of the interest of consumers a definable and legitimate interest?[19] Consumers are the "unrepresented commonality" in the sense that "everyone is a consumer" even if "no one is solely a consumer."[20]

Consumers do have identifiable interests yet they are not effectively represented by organized interest groups. As George Stigler has observed, there is "no historical example of a viable, continuing broad-based consumer political lobby."[21]

A number of explanations have been advanced for the failure of consumer interests to become effectively organized. Using role analysis, Loyns and Pursaga find, "The consuming role is not only one among many roles, but it also suggests it is not the most important." They argue that "this conclusion leads directly to the political paradox which states that, in spite of their pervasive commonality, consumer interests and concerns are likely to be underrepresented."[22] Put another way, the stronger commonality or dominant role for most individuals is "the productive characteristics of human endeavor."[23]

This point is also emphasized by Knox when he states:

> . . . for the great mass of the population it is both easier and, from their own point of view, more rational to concentrate on improving their position as producers rather than as consumers.[24]

As intuitively plausible as these explanations are, they are somewhat lacking in rigour. Mancur Olson's book, *The Logic of Collective Action*,[25] provides a more analytically pleasing explanation of why there is no broad-based consumer political lobby. Olson first sets out the basic premise of those political scientists who see the group as the basis of politics. "Groups of individuals with common interests are expected to act on behalf of their common interests much as single individuals are often expected to act on behalf of their personal interests. . . . The idea that groups tend to act in support of their group interests is supposed to follow logically from [the] widely accepted premise of rational, self-interested behaviour."[26] It is the burden of Olson's thesis that this premise is incorrect unless the number of individuals in a group is quite small, or unless there is coercion. He argues that quite frequently " . . . *rational self-interested individuals will not act to acieve their common or group interests.*"[27] The reason for this is the achievement of a common goal involves the creation of a public good for all those having a similar interest. The esential characteristics of such public goods are: (1) Once they are created they are available to all and the consumption by one individual in no way reduces the amount available to others. Because of their "jointness in supply" such goods are not divisible and appropriable by individuals; (2) No one can be excluded from the benefits of such goods (or it is uneconomic or socially unacceptable to do so).[28] Suppose an individual or a small group of individuals is able to persuade the Canadian Transport Commission to reduce airfares between Toronto and Vancouver. This benefit is available to all who fly this route, whether they participated in the action or not. They have no incentive to participate in financing the representation so long as they can receive the benefits for free. Public goods will only be provided if the benefit to an individual or a small group is greater than the estimated cost of generating the public good. The larger the group, Olson points out, the less likely the benefit to any individual will be sufficiently large to have that person finance the cost of creating the good rather than go without.[29]

Large, unorganized groups, even those such as consumers, who do have a real economic interest, will remain as latent groups unless (1) members of the group can be *coerced* into paying dues to finance the lobbying or other representational activities, or (2) group membership and financial support are necessary to obtain some other non-collective benefit. This Olson calls the "by-product" theory of large pressure groups.[30] One example he cites is the American Medical Association, which provides malpractice defence, technical publications and other individual benefits to doctors along with its very extensive lobbying activities against "socialized medicine."[31]

Lowi is talking about the by-product theory, although he does not call it that, when he says:

> Interest groups do compete and coalesce, as political scientists say. Yet they also possess an important administrative dimension. They would have no "staying power" at all if they did not have an efficient bureaucracy.[32]

Lowi argues that "the trade association is basically an administrative structure whose most important mission is regularizing relations among participants in the same industry, trade or sector. . . . Trade associations have been widely defined erroneously as pressure groups first and foremost. While they are ubiquitous in Washington and the state capitals, their basic function is administering to their members."[33]

Returning to the point that benefits to consumers represent public goods, we should point out that it is a well-worn axiom of public finance that in the absence of a government which levies compulsory charges (e.g., taxes) on all citizens (or at least most), the quantity of public goods with which a society will provide itself will be suboptimal.[34] Consumers as an interest group face an analogous problem, but they lack the means to solve it. Any voluntary scheme will fail if each individual rationally pursues his own self-interest. As Leone points out, "despite public acceptance of the 'product' of public interest advocacy, few are willing to pay the costs of production.'" He concludes that "the resource constraint ultimately will end the current round of public interest advocacy."[35]

What are the implications when we recognize that advancement of the consumer interest involves the production of a public good in the technical sense?[36] Provided that the social benefits outweigh the social costs, citizen consumers should feel free to insist that the government finance a variety of formal organizations whose objective is to represent "the consumer interest." There is no need for government to undertake this activity directly by incorporating it within its own organization. Rather, it may adequately finance private voluntary organizations dedicated to advancing the consumer interest on a wide variety of fronts. In doing so, the state is using its taxing power (an involuntary levy to prevent "free riders") to ensure that a greater quantity of a public good is provided than would be the case if the matter were left entirely in the hands of individuals. Citizen consumers in pressing for government intervention are acting to improve the allocation of resources in our society.

NOTES

[1]Cited in "Report of the Consumer Advisory Council," in David A. Aaker and George S. Day (eds.), *Consumerism: Search for the Consumer Interest*, New York, The Free Press, 1971, p. 25.

[2]Neil H. Jacoby, *Corporate Power and Social Responsibility*, New York, Macmillan, 1973, p. 158. Jacoby can't seem to make up his mind about the power of producer interests. One page earlier he says, "The notion that corporate enterprise 'dominates' or unduly influences the American government simply does not withstand examination."

[3]J. S. Grafstein, "Some Issues in the Development of Regulatory Policies: Who Is Regulating What?" in K. W. Studnicki-Gizbert (ed.), *Issues in Canadian Transport Policy*, Toronto, Macmillan, 1974, p. 348.

[4]Canadian Consumer Council, *Annual Report, 1972*, Ottawa, Information Canada, 1973, p. 21.

[5]Theodore J. Lowi, *The End of Liberalism*, New York, Norton, 1969, p. 87.

[6]David B. Truman, *The Governmental Process*, New York, Alfred A. Knopf, 1951, pp. 448-449.

[7]James Q. Wilson, "The Politics of Regulation," in James W. McKee (ed.), *Social Responsibility and the Business Predicament*, Washington, D.C., Brookings, 1974, p. 165.

[8]Glendon A. Schubert Jr., "'The Public Interest' in Administrative Decision Making: Theorem, Theosophy or Theory?" *American Political Science Review*, Vol. 51, June 1957, p. 359.

[9]Daniel Bell, in his "The Revolution of Public Entitlements" (*Fortune*, April 1975, p. 185) reminds us that there are two special requirements for equity in "a representative republic." First, all interests must be represented and, second, all issues must be viewed as negotiable. Real world pluralism satisfies neither requirement.

[10]Truman, *op.cit.*, p. 443.

[11]A. J. Boudreau, "Public Administration and the Public Interest," *Canadian Journal of Economics and Political Science*, Vol. 16, 1950, p. 371.

[12]Lowi, *op.cit.*, pp. 87, 88.

[13]*Ibid.*, p. 88.

[14]*Ibid.*, p. 71.

[15]*Ibid.*, p. 89.

[16]*Ibid.*, p. 84.

[17]The long term impact of Ralph Nader and his associates is hard to predict. Some of the major studies done under his direction are: Edward F. Cox *et al.*, *The Nader Report on the FTC*, New York, Baron Publishing 1969; Robert C. Fellmeth, *The Interstate Commerce Omission*, New York, Grossman, 1970; James S. Turner, *The Chemical Feast: Report on the Food and Drug Administration*, New York, Grossman, 1970; and Mark J. Green *et al.*, *The Closed Enterprise System*, New York, Grossman, 1972.

A critical view of Nader's work is contained in Ralph de Toledano, *Hit and Run: The Rise — and Fall? of Ralph Nader*, New Rochelle, N.Y., Arlington House, 1975. A review of the efforts to make the consumer interest felt in the U.S. is contained in Mark V. Nadel, *The Politics of Consumer Protection*, New York, Bobbs-Merrill, 1971. In Canada, the Canadian Consumer Council sponsored a number of studies in 1972-73 which received only limited circulation. The studies include the following: Michael J. Trebilcock, *The Case for A Consumer Advocate* (62 pp.); Edward Belobaba, Jack Berkow, Marc Denhez, Ellen Macdonald, *On the Question of Consumer Advocacy — A Working Paper* (241 pp.); C. Lloyd Brown-John, *The Canadian Transport Commission Experiment* (100 pp.); David R. Cayne, *Consumer Representation Before Quebec Regulatory Agencies* (88 pp.); Donald A. Dawson, *The Canadian Radio-Television Commission and the Consumer Interest* (111 pp.); Paul B. Huber, *Study of the Consumer Interest and Regulatory Commissions in New Brunswick, Nova Scotia, Prince Edward Island and Newfoundland* (100 pp.); John McDougall, *The National Energy Board and the Candian Consumer* (15 pp.); John C. McManus, *Federal Regulation of Transport in Canada* (47 pp.); John Palmer, *Taxation by Regulation? The Experience of Ontario Trucking Regulation* (14 pp.); John Palmer, *Empirically Testing the Effects of Provincial Trucking Regulation: A Further Analysis* (20 pp.); John Palmer and John Erkkila, *The Role of the Consumer in Affecting the Decisions of the Hydro-Electric Power Commission of Ontario* (16 pp.); Gilbert B. Reschenthaler, *The Performance of Selected, Independent Regulatory Commissions in Alberta, Saskatchewan and Manitoba* (218 pp.); Ellen Richardson, *Consumer Interest Representation, Three Case Studies: I. The Tariff Board, II. The Anti-Dumping Tribunal, III. The Textile and Clothing Board* (49 pp.); W. T. Stanbury, *The Consumer Interest in Public Utility Regulation* (68 p.); W. T. Stanbury, *The B.C. Public Utility Commissioners and Their Work* (70 pp.); The above two items were part of a larger study entitled *The British Columbia Public Utilities Commission and the Consumer Interest* prepared for the Canadian Consumer Council.] Martin W. Westmacott, *The Canadian Transport Commission, Freight Rates and the Public Interest* (75 pp.); The results of these studies are summarized in Canadian Consumer Council's *Report on the Consumer Interest in Regulatory Boards and Agencies*, Ottawa, June 1973 (mimeo).

Revised versions of C. Lloyd Brown-John's and Martin Westmacott's papers were published in Karl M. Ruppenthal and W. T. Stanbury (eds.), *Transportation Policy: Regulation, Competition and the Public Interest*, Vancouver, Centre for Transportation Studies, University of British Columbia, 1976, pp. 157-170 and pp. 49-91 respectively.

[18]Earl Latham, *The Group Basis of Politics*, Ithaca, N.Y., Cornell University Press, 1952, p. 38.

[19]See Jacob S. Ziegel "The Future of Canadian Consumerism," *Canadian Bar Review*, Vol. LI, 1973, pp. 191-206.

[20]R. M. A. Loyns and Alex J. Pursaga, "Economic Dimensions of Consumer Interest," paper prepared for the Canadian Consumer Council, June 1973, mimeo, p. 5. Persia Campbell in her *Consumer Representation in the New Deal* (New York, Columbia University Press, 1940, p. 31) relates an amusing story. At meetings between consumer and producer representatives, the chairman, a retired general, was given to shouting, "Who is the consumer? Show me a consumer!"

[21]Manuel F. Cohen and George J. Stigler, *Can Regulatory Agencies Protect Consumers?*, Washington, D.C., American Enterprise Institute, 1971, p. 49. In Canada, one could argue that the owners of pigs are better represented than people in their role as consumers. The *Directory of Associations in Canada*, lists ten associations under the title "Consumer Protection" while listing thirty-one federal or provincial associations under the heading of "Swine." See Brian Land, *Directory of Associations in Canada*, Toronto, University of Toronto Press, 1974, pp. 24, 87, 88. An association is defined to be "a voluntary non-governmental, non-profit organization composed of personal or institutional members, with or without federal or provincial charter, formed for some particular purpose or to advance a common cause, especially of a public nature" (p. vii).

[22]Loyns and Pursaga, *op.cit.*, p. 30.

[23]*Ibid.*

[24]F. Knox, *Consumers and the Economy*, London, Harrap, 1969, p. 84.

[25]Mancur Olson Jr., *The Logic of Collective Action*, Cambridge, Harvard University Press, 1965.

[26]*Ibid.*, p. 1.

[27]*Ibid.*, p. 2 (emphasis in the original).

[28]For a brief discussion see John F. Due, *Government Finance: Economics of The Public Sector* (4th edition), Homewood, Ill., Richard D. Irwin, 1968, pp. 8-9. For a more comprehensive discussion see John G. Head, "Public Goods and Public Policy," *Public Finance*, Vol. XVII, No. 3, 1962, pp. 197-219.

[29]Olson, *op.cit.*, pp. 33-36.

[30]*Ibid.*, p. 132.

[31]*Ibid.*, p. 140.

[32]Lowi, *op.cit.*, p. 39.

[33]*Ibid.*, p. 36.

[34]See Richard A. Musgrave, *The Theory of Public Finance*, New York, McGraw-Hill, 1959, pp. 6-12.

[35]Richard C. Leone, "Public Interest Advocacy and the Regulatory Process," *The Annals of the American Academy of Political and Social Science*, Vol. 400, May 1972, p. 56.

[36]This passage is taken from my paper "Consumer and Coalition Reform — A Political View," in Claude Masse (ed.), *Rapport de la Conference Canadienne Sur le Droit et la Consommation* (Sept. 26-28, 1975), Montreal, Faculte de Droit, Universite de Montreal, 1976, p. 366.

Chapter 4

A Framework for Interest Group Behaviour:
The Case of Business and Competition Policy

As we have noted in Chapter 2, interest groups in Canadian politics may seek to influence policy outcomes in a wide variety of ways. It is usually argued that the principal constituencies of the effective interest group are the civil servants (key policy advisors) and the members of the Cabinet. Of lesser importance, it is asserted, are backbenchers (of both the government and opposition parties), administrative agencies, political parties, "grass roots" voters and the media. In looking for evidence that an interest group has been able to influence government policy significantly, we are forced to proceed indirectly. While we can observe changes in legislation between the time it is introduced and the time it becomes law[1] (or what actually occurs in practice), it is difficult to connect cause and effect.

In the case of the Competition Act, business was able to obtain widespread coverage of its views in the media (principally in newspapers and the trade press) and to obtain widespread editorial and columnist *support* for its position. The volume of writing by academics on the act was small and by no means entirely strongly supportive of the legislation.[2] Unlike the case of the 1960 amendments to the Combines Investigation Act,[3] academics were not organized in support of stronger anti-combines legislation, nor were they much in evidence as individual advocates of the legislation proposed.[4] Much of the evidence relied upon in the remainder of the study was provided by newspapers and the trade press (in the form of both their news and editorial columns) and by academic publications. To the extent that the press accurately depicts (and often editorially reflects) the mood of the business community, of Parliament and the larger community, it is a reliable source in an investigation of how business interests were able to alter significantly the provisions of the Competition Act. All the details of the "inside story" may never be told. So soon after the events (the extensions of which are still going on as this is written in early 1977) we have to rely on the evidence that is available externally. Causal links will have to be inferred, rather than directly observed. Our "explanation" will undoubtedly be incomplete.

By gaining widespread support among newspaper and trade press editors and columnists, business was able to *reinforce* its written submission and direct face-to-face contacts with policy makers. As we have noted, one of the basic functions of interest groups is to provide policy makers with information. As we shall see in Chapters 8 and 9 of the study, civil servants and Cabinet members were repeatedly told by interest group representatives that their draft legislation amounted to untested theory, developed in any ivory tower. It was continually emphasized that their formulations were out of touch with the "real world." The views of business were consistently reiterated in the editorial positions of most of the daily newspapers and trade press.[4A] The combined effect of these sympathetic vibrations made the pro-competition, pro-consumer proposals advanced by the government untenable. It takes a strong civil servant or minister, certain of both the intellectual validity and the political reality of his position, to resist for long the combined onslaught of cleverly prepared briefs, passionate face-to-face arguments and hostile newspaper editorials and comment. Policy advisors and Cabinet members who supported a strong pro-competition policy did not have a large and vocal "clientele" providing an independent source of information and ideological support. Consumers, who would have been the principal beneficiaries of a strong pro-competition policy, were not effectively organized, for reasons we have already discussed. Academics provided little effective public support.

Business as an interest group appeared to be highly successful in making the policy makers' key external reality source (newspapers) closely reflect its position. As a result, policy makers experienced strong cognitive dissonance in comparing their original ideas for the reform of competition policy to "reality." They learned, perhaps painfully, that the *technical quality* of a policy solution is only one part of the problem. Policy solutions must also be *acceptable* to the dominant participants in the policy environment. Acceptability and technical quality may be independent or even opposed to each other.

As detailed in Chapter 8, the initial responses of many of the major papers to Bill C-256 were positive. The *Financial Times,* one week after the Competition Act was introduced, welcomed the proposed legislation. Two months later it described C-256 as "a badly botched bill" and as "a dangerous bill. . . ."[5] After the hostile views of business became known editorialists and columnists came to reflect views similar to business. Why? Is it a question of the newspapers and trade press desiring to avoid cognitive dissonance? Perhaps there are more fundamental forces at work.

First and foremost, newspapers are big *businesses* themselves. If profit is not an objective, it is certainly a constraint on their desire to serve the public interest. Even the smaller papers are usually part of large chains, e.g., Thomson Newspapers, F.P. Publications, Southam Press, K.C. Irving, etc. About three-quarters of a daily newspaper's revenues come from advertising. The bulk of this comes from other business enterprises. Second, the newspaper business, and the media in general, is a highly concentrated industry. In 1970, some 77 of 116 daily newspapers were members of multi-paper groups. F.P. Publications had eight, the Southam group had eleven, Thomson Newspapers had thirty, a Quebec group had four and K.C. Irving had five. Senator Davey, chairman of the Special Senate Committee on Mass Media[6] which reported in 1970, indicates that in late 1974 chain ownership had risen to account for 80 percent of the daily newspapers in Canada.[7] When it comes to the trade press, one firm, MacLean-Hunter, totally dominates the field.[8]

Second, multi-media ownership is also very common in Canada. For example, in 1970 the Demarais, Paresien, Francoeur group owned four daily papers, twelve weeklies, five weekend papers, two radio stations, and one T.V. station.[9] K.C. Irving owned five daily papers, one radio station and two T.V. stations, all in New Brunswick.[10] This is not to mention Mr. Irving's enormous industrial holdings in the province.[11]

When it comes to issues such as mergers, resulting in high concentration in most media markets in Canada, and monopoly (a significant number of daily newspapers are monopolies in their urban centre), newspaper publishers are hardly in a strong position to cast the first stone.

Third, whatever their official party label, the editorial view of most of the newspapers and trade press in Canada is small *c* conservative. One is unlikely to find strong press support for policies which might constrain traditional business practices — particularly when the support for such policies is not well organized and vocal. For all of these reasons, the probability of Canadian newspapers and the trade press adhering to a position on competition policy and the regulation of restraints of trade which is significantly different from the announced views of the business is low.[12]

Charles Lynch of the Southam News Service raises an issue seldom mentioned in discussion of the relationship between the media and interest groups. Some of the part-time lobbyists may actually be found in the parliamentary press gallery. Lynch states that such lobbying is "a continuing problem. It's always been assumed over the years that the press gallery is used in this way by certain people, but it is very difficult to police."[13] Obviously, evidence of this sort of activity by journalists is very difficult to obtain. The extent to which it actually occurred in the competition policy debate is now known.

In Figure 4-1 we describe a framework which may be useful in understanding interest group activities and the role of business as an interest group in influencing competition policy between 1971 and 1975. We define the key foci of the interest group's attentions to be the civil service (in particular, the important policy advisors), the Cabinet, backbenchers (including the opposition), the political parties, parliamentary committees and administrative agencies. In terms of importance, the first three, in that order, greatly outrank the others on most issues. The interest group makes direct, face-to-face representations to the policy advisors in the bureaucracy with a view of influencing proposed legislation *before* it is taken to the Cabinet by the relevant minister. If they have not been able "to get their oar in" at this stage (as was true in the Competition Act case), they try to obtain government-sponsored amendments. Many of the changes business was able to persuade the government to make *after* Stage I was announced took the form of amendments proposed by the Minister of Consumer and Corporate Affairs. As noted above, the parliamentary system of government places a premium of access and influence *early* in the policy development process. Once a bill is introduced, it tends to be official government policy and harder to change.[14] In the case of the Competition Act, the government announced at the time of First Reading of Bill C-256 in June 1971 that it wished to hear the representations of business interest groups and others and would amend the bill in light of such representations. In tone and spirit, the bill was offered more as an "exposure draft" than as a regular bill. Business did not believe Mr. Basford's words on this point and reacted violently to the change in the *process* implicit in the government's actions. They seemed convinced that the new policy would be put into law without their being able to give effect to their views.

In our framework, as indicated in Figure 4-1, all the actors will exist in the environment of the communications media. While it is not true in every case, it is our contention that the interest group seeks to obtain both widespread dissemination of its views and favourable reinforcement of them by the opinion segment of the media. Blaisdell points out that interest groups, by soliciting general approval for their aims, raise them to the status of public problems.[15] We have tried to illustrate the desire for widespread dissemination of the interest group's views by solid lines emanating directly from the interest group which create a host of reflections (dashed lines) which form part of the environment of the actors the interest group wishes to influence. What is said in the media and by the media (i.e., their editorial stance) is an important part of the "reality" of most decision makers.

In the case of competition policy, the genesis of the policy changes was apparently in the government's reference to the Economic Council in July 1966, requesting it to prepare a report on, among other things, "combines, mergers, monopolies and restraint of trade."[16] Three years later the council produced its *Interim Report on Competition Policy*.[17] Very little comment on the report was forthcoming from business. Only a few published articles appeared by academics.[18] Apparently without advance consultation with those most affected by its provisions, policy advisors in the Departments of Consumer and Corporate Affairs and Justice

FIGURE 4-1

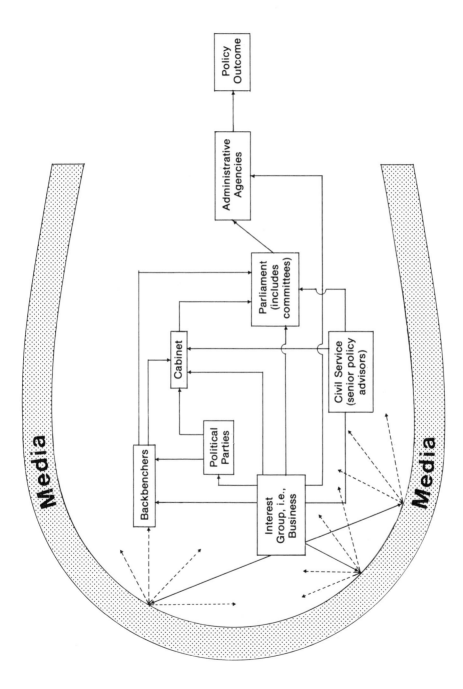

produced draft legislation in June 1971. These procedures made the government, and bureaucratic officials, in particular, vulnerable to charges that their proposals were "too theoretical," that they were drawn up in an "ivory tower" by civil servants and academics who "never met a payroll." This theme was stressed repeatedly by the bill's opponents and by newspaper editorial writers and columnists.

Business interest groups made strong direct oral and written representations to those responsible for the legislation, to the parliamentary committees to which the bill was referred, and to the Cabinet. It also seems apparent, from comments regarding contributions to the Liberal Party before the election as a result of which the Trudeau administration was able to retain power only as a minority government, that the party was made aware of business' views. Backbenchers also received representations from business interests. Perhaps because of their previous positions or because of their personal views, selected opposition members were enlisted in the cause and worked hard to amend the bill radically.

Business-government interaction over competition policy provides strong support for Clarke's point that "the major changes in government policy have been brought about through the mobilization of public opinion rather than through the application of technical counsel."[19] Members of Presthus' sample of 134 federal M.P.s were asked to rank the effectiveness (from the interest group's point of view) of various activities carried on by interest groups. Fifty-six percent of the M.P.s ranked "mobilizing public opinion" as the most effective activity. Some 23 percent ranked "personal contact with the Cabinet" and 20 percent ranked "appearance before committees" as the second and third most effective weapons respectively.[20]

With respect to competition policy, business was able to mobilize public opinion in the form of the support for its position by the newspapers and the trade press. Not only were the representations of business interest groups widely reported, but the editorial stance of the papers, in the great majority of cases, was favourable to business' views. Even though the public officials defending the legislation might be sure that what was being said in the media did not represent the interests of "the silent majority,"[21] they were hardpressed to stick to their position. If they refuse to be moved when all around them are saying they were misguided or wrong, they would be labelled as intransigent. Resistance to the pressure of special interests is much easier when there are counter pressures exerted by competing interests or where that interest is unable to obtain media coverage and support of its position. With respect to competition policy, neither was present. Business interest groups were able to obtain widespread reinforcement for their hostile attitudes toward C-256 and Stage I from newspapers and the trade press. In doing so they were able to change the civil servants' and the key politicians' perceptions of what was realistic and politically acceptable to those most directly affected by the proposed changes. The aggressive representations of business, together with the sympathetic environment of the media, created a "new reality" for the proponents of more far-reaching legislation aimed at restraints of trade in Canada.

NOTES

[1]Chapter 10 of this study tries to identify the "gains and losses" accruing to business and the government as the main actors in process of forming Canada's new competition policy.

[2]L. A. Skeoch (ed.), *Canadian Competition Policy*, Kingston, Ont., Industrial Relations Centre, Queen's University, 1972 (papers by Skeoch, English, Arthurs, Reuber and Grover); The Conference Board in Canada, *Canada's Competition Policy*, Ottawa, 1972 (papers by Moore and McQueen); Norman P. Goldman, "Canadian Competition Law and Unfair Trade Practices," *Boston College Industrial and Commercial Law Review*, Vol. XIII, No. 6, June 1972, pp. 1303-1329; Dale F. Orr, "The Competition Act and Its Application to the Service Sector," *B.C. Studies*, No. 13, Spring 1972, pp. 100-109; W. A. Neilson, "The Competition Act and the Public," *Canadian Forum*, Jan-Feb., 1972, pp. 2-3; G. B. Reschenthaler, "A New Competition Act: Moving to an Effectively Competitive Economy," in McFadyen, Reschenthaler and Shaffer (eds.), *Industrial Organization in Canada*, (2nd edition) Edmonton, University of Alberta, pp. 298-308; H. E. English article on C-256 in *Canadian Consumer*, December 1972, pp. 237-238. See also A. Milton Moore, "The Competition Act — Objectives, Rationale and Justification" and Dale F. Orr "What the Competition Act Doesn't Do," papers presented to the Faculty of Commerce and Business Administration, University of British Columbia, Continuing Education Seminar, November 19, 1971.

[3]H. G. Thorburn, "Pressure Groups in Canadian Politics: Recent Revisions of the Anti-Combines Legislation" (*Canadian Journal of Economics and Political Science*, Vol. 30, No. 2, May 1974) has stated: "While it is unusual for academics to engage in vigorous lobbying campaigns, twenty-eight of the country's university economists and five political scientists registered their protest against the government's proposals . . ." [which would have weakened the act]. They wrote eight individual letters to the Minister and sent him seven memoranda. Their criticisms were generally severe and some were very detailed, extending in one case to twenty typewritten pages. A number of prominent academics (Professors Skeoch, Rosenbluth and English) prepared briefs and appeared before the House Banking and Commerce Committee. Professor Britnell and other members of the Department of Economics of the University of Saskatchewan submitted a brief. Thorburn indicates "all of these opposed the government's proposals vigorously and some explained in detail the misconceptions in the government's bill" (p. 168). Also see G. Rosenbluth and H. G. Thorburn, *Canadian Anti-Combines Administration, 1952-60*, Toronto, University of Toronto Press, 1963, Chapter 8.

[4]Professors D. L. McQueen of Glendon College, York University, and J. S. Ziegel of the University of Toronto appeared the Senate Banking, Trade and Commerce Committee for the Consumers' Association of Canada. See *Proceedings of the Committee*, December 18, 1974, pp. 19-25. Professor Donald N. Thompson submitted a brief to the House Committee on Finance, Trade and Economic Affairs in 1974.

[4A]The press, in at least one instance, went considerably further than expressing its editorial stance against the proposed competition legislation. Ian Urquhart, now with *Maclean's*, was formerly a reporter with the Toronto *Star*. He wrote the author as follows: I promised to relate to you my experience with the Toronto *Star*. It started with a story I did in 1974 for the *Star* on the competition bill lobby. The story ran in the back pages before either the publisher (Beland Honderich) or the editor (Martin Goodman) had seen it. I understand they were displeased with it. Then the Canadian Daily Newspaper Publishers Association, of which the *Star* is a prominent member, presented their brief to Herb Gray, then Minister of Consumer Affairs, in April, 1974. I was given a copy of the brief in advance with instructions from Goodman to do a story on it. I was somewhat miffed by these instructions because we had not bothered to do individual stories on any other brief although, as you point out, there were lots of them. But I went ahead and wrote the story (I really had no choice). My story was quite critical, pointing out the discrepancies in the publishers' brief, which was written by J. J. Robinette. To my considerable surprise, the story actually ran for one edition in the *Star* before Honderich spotted it. He was furious, ordered the story killed, and dictated a new story himself that said the competition bill was a threat to a free press. I believe that, but for the protection afforded me by my union (the Newspaper Guild), I would have been fired. At any rate, I decided to take the offensive and launched a grievance against Honderich and the *Star* for not consulting me before rewriting my story. Prior consultation is a requirement in the Guild's contract with the *Star*. I lost the grievance, however, on the grounds that the story was not rewritten but killed and replaced with an entirely new story. The grievance did serve its purpose, however, of discouraging *Star* management from taking any retaliatory action against me. But I was told to write another story on the competition bill detailing the arguments against the bill. This I did in as objective a manner as possible under the circumstances. But the story never ran because the July 8, 1974 election intervened and the competition bill died on the parliamentary agenda. (Letter to the author, May 3, 1977.)

[5]A series of five articles on Bill C-256 in the *Financial Times* in August and September of 1971 was reprinted as *Financial Times of Canada Guide to the Competition Act*, Toronto, 1971. Editor and publisher Michael Barkway hints at an explanation in his Introduction to the *Guide* when he says, "The draft Competition Act is admitted even by Ottawa officials to be 'convoluted'. The longer I worked on it, the more clearly I realized the impossibility of tracing down the consequences it could have on different business" (p. 1).

[6]Report of the Special Senate Committee on Mass Media, *Words, Music and Dollars*, Vol. II, Ottawa, Queen's Printer, 1970, Part I.

[7]"Davey wants newspaper chains broken up," *Sun*, (Vancouver) November 14, 1974, p. 65.

[8]Report, Vol. II, pp. 90-94.

[9]Report, Vol. II, p. 83.

[10]Report, Vol. II, p. 89. On October 3, 1972 a number of Irving companies were indicted on several counts of merger and monopoly between 1948 and 1971. During this period Irving acquired control of all five English language daily newspapers in New Brunswick. The Irving companies were convicted by trial judge (see *R. v. K. C. Irving Ltd. et al.* 16 C.C.C. (2d) 1974 pp. 49-126). However, this verdict was reversed by the Appeal Court (see 62 D.L.R. (3d) 1975 pp. 157-192). This decision was upheld in the Supreme Court of Canada in unanimous decision of all nine judges on November 16, 1976. (as yet unreported). The Court ruled that while the mergers had given Irving a monopoly, the Crown had not established that the monopoly had or was likely to operate "to the detriment or against the interest of the public." A comprehensive review of this decision is given in G. B. Reschenthaler and W. T. Stanbury, "Benign Monopoly: Canadian Merger Policy and the K. C. Irving Case," *Canadian Business Law Journal*, forthcoming, 1977.

[11]Report, Vol. II, p. 88. See also R. Hunt and R. Campbell, *K. C. Irving: The Art of the Industrialist*, Toronto, McClelland and Stewart, 1973.

[12]An outstanding counter example was provided by the *Free Press* (Winnipeg) during November and December, 1949. See *The McGregor Controversy and the Combines Act, Free Press*, (Winnipeg) Pamphlet No. 29, 1949.

We should, perhaps, qualify the phrase "views of business." It represents a high level of abstraction. On matters of competition policy, the views of small business often differ from those of "big business." Thorburn (*op.cit*. pp. 160-165) outlines the differences in the case of the 1960 amendments. As we shall point out in Chapter 9, John Bullock of the Canadian

Federation of Independent Business saw the Stage I amendments as beneficial to small business.

[13]Quoted in Orland French, "Lobbying's No Whisper Word to Baker," *Citizen* (Ottawa), April 9, 1976, p. 33.

[14]Brian E. Owen ("Business Managers' Influence [Or lack of Influence] on Government," *Business Quarterly*, Vol. 41, No. 3, 1976 attributes part of the failure of Manitoba business interests to have much impact upon the Automobile Insurance Act, Manitoba drug substitution legislation and the province's mining policy to the fact that "actions by business managers were concentrated at the later stages of the process of government policy formulation," i.e., legislative consideration and reglations (p. 67). Owen continues, "neglecting action at early stages [i.e. 'societal need,' 'recognition of need,' 'articulation of demand' and 'decision to proceed with legislation' in his terminology] may allow situations which could possibly be handled without major system changes to get out of hand" (p.67). Manitoba businessmen also chose to direct their activities at politicians rather than civil servants. "The implications of this can be undesirable for business managers because civil servants did substantial analytic work and provided decision options to politicians. They were also responsible for moving the process of government policy formulation from stage to stage. If a good relationship is established with the civil service, greater potential for influence exists" (p. 68).

[15]Donald C. Blaisdell, assisted by Jane Greverus, *Economic Power and Political Pressures*, Monograph No. 26, TNEC, Washington, D.C., USGPO, 1941, p. 47.

[16]Press Release, Privy Council Office, July 22, 1966.

[17]Ottawa, Queen's Printer, July 1969, 244 pp.

[18]These points will be examined in more detail in Chapter 6.

[19]S. D. Clarke, "The Canadian Manufacturers' Association," *Canadian Journal of Economics and Political Science*, Vol. 4, 1938, p. 522.

[20]Robert Presthus, "Interest Groups and the Canadian Parliament: Activities, Interaction, Legitimacy and Influence," *Canadian Journal of Political Science*, Vol. 4, December 1971, p. 450, Table III.

[21]In this context I am referring to the interests of consumers broadly defined.

Chapter 5

Canadian Attitudes Toward Competition Policy: The Historical Climate

The attitudes of Canadian businessmen which led to the "massive flight from competition in the 1880s and 1890s"[1] remain unchanged in the 1970s. There does not exist in Canada any fundamental belief in the virtues of competition as the method of allocating scarce resources and of diffusing economic and political power. Our more structured and authoritarian society takes business power for granted and seeks only to restrict *undue* restraints on trade or those which operate to the public detriment. It does not seek to strike down per se the wide variety of restrictive trade practices characteristic of discretionary market power in the hands of business enterprises. The socially approved pursuit of "a living profit," together with large-scale intervention by government in the nation's economic life has resulted in a combination of economic affairs uniquely suited to ensure the dominance of producer interests over consumer interests - high tariffs,[2] high concentration,[3] productive inefficiency[4] and extensive foreign ownership.[5]

Anti-combines policy in Canada finds almost no support among businessmen. This is different from the situation in the United States. David McQueen contrasts the two when he says,

> American business men are prepared, in the final analysis, to live with anti-trust, in part because of their still strongly held private-enterprise ideology. The same is not true here. . . . Many Canadian business men still appear to regard competition policy as not in any way supportive of markets and private enterprise. They speak of it largely as an intrusion on enterprise; they lump it with every other sort of unwanted government intervention in the market; and they do not accept that they ought — in their own, best longer-term interest — to live with anything more than the frailest, most deceptive shadow of a competition policy.[6]

At the time of the passage of the original anti-combines legislation in 1889 "an exhaustive list of the combinations mentioned in the trade journals or claimed to exist by newspapers would extend into every nook and cranny of the Canadian business world."[7] Competition, rather than being viewed as "the life of trade," was almost universally condemned by businessmen as "the death of trade." Michael Bliss notes that

"Professor W. J. Ashley of the University of Toronto . . worried that worship of the consumer led people to forget 'the worry and laceration of the spirit' (as well as 'the vulgarization of business') involved in perpetual competition."[8]

From the very beginning businessmen and their representatives have strongly influenced anti-combines legislation in Canada. Lloyd Reynolds indicated that opponents of the original legislation in 1889 moved that it be referred to the Committee on Banking and Commerce. "Large lobbies of manufacturers and trades descended on Ottawa to oppose the bill, and were heard by the committee."[9]

Mr. N. Clarke Wallace of Toronto, who drafted the original bill, described the lobbyists as "those men who have formed those illegal combines." They were able to come down "in great force to defeat the bill." He went on to observe that "they came down before the Banking and Commerce Committee at its last meeting, with a great array of lawyers from Montreal and Toronto and with amendments carefully considered, to legislate this bill out of existence."[10] Reynolds states:

> Apparently as a result of this business pressure, the original measure was withdrawn while still in committee, and a startlingly different bill was substituted. The clause which forbade the securing of special concessions was dropped, as was also the provision concerning forfeiture of the corporate charter. The insertion of the word "unlawfully" greatly weakened the effect of the measure, for it carried a clear implication that only acts previously unlawful at common law were to be unlawful under the new act. Another new clause cast considerable doubt on the legal status of trade unions. Mr. Wallace reluctantly accepted the new act, which passed the House and went to the Senate. It came back from the Senate in still more emasculated form, for that body inserted the words "unduly" or "unreasonably" in each of the subsections.[11]

Reynolds concluded that "a more half-hearted statute can scarcely be imagined,"[12] for members of a combine could not be convicted unless the Crown proved they were "unlawfully" arranging to "unduly prevent or lessen competition."

Bliss argues that Mr. Wallace's entire effort was "no more than a political sham", for Wallace "deliberately watered down his own bill until it was ineffectual. . . . He did not object when the Senate reinserted the various 'undulys' and the 'unreasonably' in amendments to his bill."[13] The purpose of this "fraudulent political posturing" was designed to enhance Wallace's popular reputation as the scourge of the combines and "also as part of a calculated Conservative manoeuvre to deflect criticism from the combine-creating effects of the protective tariff."[14]

In 1892 the original act was transferred to the Criminal Code and became S520. In 1899 the statute was amended and the words "unduly" and "unreasonably" were deleted. In 1900 it was amended again and "unduly" was reinserted but the word "unlawfully" was dropped.[15] The change may have been accidental, but it was absolutely necessary to give the statute any effect at all. Gosse states, "The intentions of the House in making the change are not apparent from the debates. If there were any discussions on the section, they took place in committee and there is no record of them."[16] Bliss indicates the change was accidental. "Incredible as it seems, this happened by accident when a senator who prided himself on his drafting ability suggested omitting the word [unlawfully] in order to get rid of the 'surplusage' in the section wording which 'as a matter of art, ought not to prevail.'"[17] Bliss claims that no one in Parliament realized what the amendment implied.[18] It was not until 1903 that business began to feel the weight of the amendment when a prosecution was launched. Before the amendment of 1900, only one prosecution had occurred and it was unsuccessful.[19]

For the period 1889-1910 the legislation has been described as "insignificant and ineffectual, it did not reflect a serious desire by legislators to resist economic consolidation or restore the forces of the free market."[20] Little wonder, the act of 1889 made no provisions for federal enforcement; cases were to be brought by the provincial attorneys general. Between 1900 and 1910 only seven cases were tried, five of which resulted in convictions.[21]

In response to considerable public pressure to take further action against combines, Laurier's Minister of Labour, W. L. Mackenzie King, brought in new legislation in 1910 — the Combines Investigation Act. King's attitude is reflected in his statement, "I would like the House to understand that in introducing this legislation no attempt is being made to legislate against combines, mergers and trusts as such. . . ."[22] The legislation would permit the examination of firms "where there is reason to believe that a combine is operating to an undue disadvantage of the public."[23] Note that King's language assumes that combines will operate to the disadvantage of consumers; restraints will be imposed (perhaps) only if the disadvantage becomes *undue*. King stated, "The one end and purpose of this legislation is to prevent the mean man from profiting in virtue of his meanness."[24] Very early in the history of competition policy in Canada a distinction was made between "good" and "bad" combines and between "reasonable" and "unreasonable" restraints on competition.

In contrasting the U.S. Sherman Act of 1890, which declared unlawful "Every contract or combination . . . in restraint of trade . . .," to the Combines Investigation Act of 1910, Professor James E. Boyle noted that the latter "contains no prohibitions of any kind. It accepts the economic philosophy of the twentieth century and suffers monoolies to dwell in peace, as long as the monopolistic benefits are distributed fairly."[25] Boyle's approbation of the Canadian law stemmed from his general view of competition and monopoly. As he saw it, "competition is self-annihilating over most of our industrial field, monopoly is inevitable and is likewise desirable."[26]

While the act of 1910 did provide a new mechanism for federal enforcement, it was cumbersome. Rather than hale business executives before the courts following a regular criminal investigation, King proposed that six citizens could make application to a judge for an order directing an investigation into the alleged combine, which at that time included mergers, trusts and monopolies as well as the more common horizontal conspiracies.

> If, after a hearing, the judge found the situation to warrant an inquiry he could issue an order to that effect. The Minister of Labour was then to appoint a board of three commissioners, one selected by the applicants, one by the parties against whom the application was made and the third, the chairman who was to be a judge, nominated by the other two members. A board had power to compel the attendance of witnesses, examine them under oath, require the production of documents and general incidental powers to carry out a full inquiry.
>
> A board had wide powers of report, it could make "such findings and recommendations as, in the opinion of the board, are in accordance with the merits and requirements of the case." Reports were to be transmitted to the Minister at the conclusion of any inquiry and to be published in the *Canada Gazette*.[27]

An American writer, Professor Boyle, described these procedures as "simple, swift and free from technicalities."[28]

The publicity attendant to the investigation, and, in particular, the publication of the report, was to effect the necessary remedy. King was a strong believer that "light is the sovereign antiseptic and best of all policemen."[29] He believed that the machinery outlined above would "enable an intelligent public opinion to be formed and focused on a particular evil which you are endeavouring to stamp out. Penalties are frequently of no service toward that end."[30] King was not alone in his view that publicity was the best remedy for combines offences. Professor Boyle asserted, "Publicity and the fear of publicity is doubtless the strongest remedy. . . . The pressure of informed public opinion is irresistible."[31] After reviewing the *United Shoe Machinery* investigation,[32] the first one following the legislation of 1910, Boyle concluded, "the first lesson is the soundness of the principle of efficient publicity."[33]

Only one investigation was conducted under the 1910 legislation before the greater concerns of W.W. I manifested themselves.[34] Inflation during the war resulted in an investigation by a special House of Commons committee which, in turn, recommended more far-reaching legislation. In 1919 the Board of Commerce Act and the Combines and Fair Prices Act were passed. The board had extensive powers of investigation, either upon its own initiative or upon application by an individual. It could make cease-and-desist orders where it found the Combines and Fair Prices Act had been violated. The members of the Board of Commerce took their duties seriously and made use of their powers — particularly those concerning high prices caused by excess profits. In 1920, the constitutionality of the new acts was challenged. The Supreme Court of Canada was equally divided on the question. Upon appeal, the Privy Council in 1921 held that, because of the administrative features of direct control embodied in the legislation, it was ultra vires of the federal government and the acts were without force.

Between 1910 and 1923, when a new Combines Investigation Act was introduced, only one prosecution was launched. It was conducted by the Attorney General of Ontario under the Criminal Code and it was unsuccessful.[35] As with the act of 1910, Mackenzie King's words again characterized the dominant Canadian attitude toward restraints of trade, "The legislation does not seek in any way to restrict just combinations or agreements between business and industrial houses and firms, but it does seek to protect the public against possible ill effects of these combinations."[36] Again King extolled publicity as the remedy for combines. "The power of a well-informed public opinion and the power of Parliament to deal with any situation of which it may have accurate and concrete knowledge — that is, the power which this legislation brings into being."[37] As King saw it, investigations conducted by a new permanent federal official (the registrar) would disclose information "in order that the framers of public opinion throughout the country, whether they be in parliament, on the platform, of the press or in whatever form public opinion cares to express itself, may have an opportunity to help redress a public wrong."[38] King saw this as "the greatest power which it is possible to give."[39] Just in case publicity and informed public opinion did not deter the price fixers, the act of 1923 provided for fines of up to $25,000 for corporations and up to $10,000 or two years' imprisonment for individuals.

Expenditures on administration and enforcement, which could be considered an index of the government's belief in the legislation, were small. Between 1924-25 and 1940-41, with exception of two years, annual expenditures on the administration of the act were in the range of $13,200 to $59,600. In 1925 there were only three permanent staff members engaged in the administration of the act; in 1941 the number had increased to eight.[40] However, the number of prosecutions increased. Between 1923 and 1942 fourteen cases were prosecuted (see Table 5-1) and twelve convictions were sustained. The bulk of these (ten cases with nine convictions) occurred before 1935 when the Conservatives brought in the Dominion Trade and Industry

TABLE 5-1

Activities Under the Combines Investigation Act, 1889-1975

Period	Combines Cases Launched by The Crown[2]	Misleading Advertising Charges laid	Cases sent directly to Attny-General, Commissioner's or RTPC Reports not prosecuted[1]	Discontinued Inquiries Per Annual Report	Discontinued Inquiries Other	Complaint Files Opened (excluding misleading advertising)
1889-1900	1	} not applicable ⑤	n.a.	n.a.	n.a.	} ⑥
1901-1910	7		n.a.	n.a.	n.a.	
1911-1923	1		n.a.	n.a.	n.a.	
1924-1944	14[3]		7	n.a.	n.a.	
1945/46-1949/50	1		2	n.a.	n.a.	
1950/51-1954/55	9		3	23	n.a.	542
1955/56-1959/60	20[4]		6	30	n.a.	456
1960/61-1964/65	18	15	10	72	5	816
1965/66-1969/70	25	75	0	77	6	579
1970/71-1974/75	48	483	4	76	18	963[7]
1975/76	13	108	0	14	n.a.	158[7]

NOTES: (n.a. = not available)

[1] Excludes the six general research inquiries. Left hand column RTPC reports, right hand column is for cases sent directly to AG, but not prosecuted.

[2] 1889-1959/60 dated by the day of the trial judgment, thereafter dated by the date an Indictment preferred. The earliest date was chosen. Excludes purely procedural cases, constitutional cases, misleading advertising cases (see column 2) and private cases. A number of private cases (Wampole v. Karn (1906); Weidman v. Shragge (1912); Dominion Supply v. Robertson (1917) resulted in important interpretations of the law.

[3] Includes R. v. Symington et al. in which convictions were obtained under the Secret Commissions Act and charges under the Criminal Code and Combines Act were withdrawn. (Supreme Court of B.C., March 13, 1926).

[4] Includes 4 cases decided in 1960 after the end of fiscal 1959/60 and one decided in 1961. These were not counted in the period 1960/61-1964/65 as charges were laid before April 1/60.

[5] Sec. 36 (formerly 33A) became effective in 1960 and Sec. 37(33B) in July 1969 (it was formerly S.306 of the *Criminal Code*).

[6] J. A. Ball, (*Canadian Anti-trust Legislation*, Baltimore, Williams and Wilkins, 1934, p. 95) indicates that between 1910 and early 1934 that "over three hundred preliminary inquiries into complaints have been conducted".

[7] Changes in the method of recording complaints probably reduced the 1974/75 and 1975/76 counts by about 100.

Commission Act. Administration of the Combines Act came under the three-man commission. The new act permitted the commission to recommend approval of N.R.A.-type restrictions on competition where it found that "wasteful or demoralizing competition existed in an industry" and that the agreements in the industry "would not unduly restrain trade or operate against the public interest."[41] Approval of such agreements by the Cabinet was a bar to prosecution under the Combines Investigation Act or the Criminal Code S.498 or S.498A, except as approved by the commission. A constitutional reference to the Supreme Court of Canada in 1936 established that S.14 of the Act of 1935, which gave the commission the power to approve agreements limiting competition was ultra vires of the federal legislative power.[42] In 1937, new legislation abolished the registrar (administrator of the act since 1923) and created a permanent commissioner, together with provisions for special commissioners to conduct investigations if the permanent official was already busy.

While the number of prosecutions increased between 1923 and 1942 over the previous period (see Table 5-1), the number averaged less than one per year. More importantly, the level of fines following convictions was very low. The average fine per *firm* was $2,722 and was $843 for *individuals*.[43] Virtually all cases were conducted under the Criminal Code rather than the Combines Act. The maximum fine under the code during this period was $10,000 for a corporation and $4,000 or two years' imprisonment for an individual. In only two of the convictions between 1923 and 1942[44] was the maximum fine levied. The average fine per *case* (all firms and all individuals involved) was only $15,809. In contrast, the average in the U.S. under the Sherman Act was $51,204 (see Table 5-2). This was despite the fact that the maximum fine under the Sherman Act was $5,000 until 1955.

Before moving to the post-W.W. II era, we should note that a significant change was made when the Combines Investigation Act was amended in 1935. It is described in the Economic Council in its 1969 report as follows:

> The Combines Investigation Act of 1923 did, in fact, appear to include most, if not all, services in the definition of a combine, but because most prosecutions during this period were based on the section of the Criminal Code prohibiting combinations rather than on the Combines Investigation Act, the position with regard to services was never clarified by the courts. In the process of amending the act in 1935, the Bennett government originally introduced a bill which contained the same definition of a combine as did the 1923 act. Following an unrecorded discussion by the Senate Banking and Commerce Committee, however, the Senate returned to the House, and the House eventually accepted, an amended bill which restricted the scope of the act to activities pertaining to articles and the price of insurance.[45]

The power of the Senate committee, well-populated by men sympathetic to business, was obvious. Services were exempted from the act until the beginning of 1976 following the coming into force of the Stage I amendements.[46]

In his review of the important decisions under the Combines Investigation Act and the Criminal Code published in 1948, S. F. Sommerfeld indicates the ambivalence of successive Canadian governments toward the rights of consumers:

> The legislature has bent over backwards in trying to be absolutely fair to everybody by stipulating that the combination must operate or be likely to operate "to the detriment or against the interest of the public, whether producers, consumers or others". This is no doubt commendable. But it has also succeeded in clouding the issue; namely what meaning is to be ascribed to those words.[47]

In an attempt to assess the "general public attitude toward the desirability and the possibility of preserving competition" in the early 1950's, Professor V. V. Bladen is forced to put the situation in negative terms, "One can say with confidence that no government could repeal the legislation nor nullify for long its administration."[48]

It was, in fact, the nullification by the Minister of Justice, of a provision of the act which led to the 1951 and 1952 amendments to the Combines Investigation Act. On December 29, 1948, Mr. F. A. McGregor, Commissioner of the Combines Investigation Act since 1925, handed in his report *Flour-Milling Industry: Investigation into an Alleged Combine in the Manufacture, Distribution and Sale of Flour and Other Grain-Mill Products.*[49] Although the Combines Investigation Act contained a provision requiring the Minister responsible (then the Minister of Justice) to make such reports public within fifteen days, the Minister did not issue the report until November 7, 1949. He did so because Mr. McGregor handed him his resignation on October 9, 1949 and it was announced in the House of Commons on November 4, 1949. The resignation and the belated publication of the report, which concluded that from 1936 to 1947, the major milling companies in Canada had operated an elaborate price-fixing cartel, resulted in the appointment of the MacQuarrie Committee to study anti-combines legislation in Canada on June 27, 1950. On October 1, 1951 the four-man committee presented an interim report to the Minister (on resale price maintenance) and its final report on March 8, 1952.[50]

Following the interim and final reports, a series of amendments to the Combines Investigation Act were introduced. These included the establishment of the Restrictive Trade Practices Commission, the abolition of the ceiling on fines, provision for prohibition orders and the prohibition of resale price maintenance.[51] The number of prosecutions rose. Nine cases were decided between 1950-51 and 1954-55 and twenty

Average Fine Per Case, 1889-1975 Combines Investigation Act[4] and Sherman Act

Period[1]	Canada				U.S.
	Conspiracy Cases	Merger and Monopoly Cases	RPM Cases	All Combines Investigation Act Cases	All Sherman Act Cases[2]
1889-1910	$ 5,188 n = 4	–	–	$ 5,188 n = 4	$ 19,989 n = 11 (1890-1909)
1911-1925	–	–	–	–	$ 29,129 n = 45 (1910-1924)
1926-1942	$ 15,809 n = 11[5]	–	–	$15,809 n = 11	$ 51,204 n = 159 (1925-1944)
1943-1949	–	–	–	–	$ 35,802 n = 50 (1945-1949)
1950-1954	$ 87,667 n = 6	$85,000 n = 1	–	$87,286 n = 7	$ 18,711 n = 64
1955-1959	$ 47,423 n = 11[6]	–	$ 502 n = 3	$37,368 n = 14	$ 50,074 n = 86
1960-1964	$ 58,050 n = 6	–	$ 900 n = 2	$43,763 n = 8	$126,557 n = 62
1965-1969	$ 54,120 n = 15	–	$1,694 n = 9	$34,460 n = 24	$116,622 n = 46
1970-1975	$248,956 n = 8	$40,000 n = 1	$4,953 n = 16	$68,662[3] n = 26[3]	data not available

NOTES: [1]Canadian cases are dated by the period in which the fine was levied. U.S. cases are dated by the period in which the charge was laid.
[2]Offences include conspiracy, monopolization, RPM, vertical integration, exclusive dealing, price discrimination, boycotts and labour cases.
[3]Includes the one price discrimination case in which a fine of $15,000 was levied in 1974.
[4]Includes cases under the Criminal Code also
[5]For the purpose of computing the average fine per case R. v. Singer and R. v. Belyea and Weintraub were combined as they resulted from the same investigation.
[6]For the purpose of computing the average fine per case R. v. Gair et al. and R. v. Bathurst Pulp and Paper et al. were combined as they resulted from the same investigation.

SOURCES: Derived from W. T. Stanbury, "Penalties and Remedies Under the Combines Investigation Act, 1889-1976," *Osgoode Hall Law Journal*, Vol. 14, No. 3, 1976, Tables 3, 4, 5, 6 and Richard A. Posner, "A Statistical Study of Antitrust Enforcement," *Journal of Law and Economics*, Vol. 13, No. 1, April 1970.

were decided in the succeeding five years. In addition, three and six reports respectively in the two periods were published by the RTPC which did not lead to prosecution (see Table 5-1).

Between 1950 and 1959 a total of 147 firms in conspiracy cases were fined an average of $7,046 each. Both the average fine and the number of individuals convicted decrased over the previous period. Because of the increase in the average fine per firm and in the average number of firms involved per case, the average fine in Canadian conspiracy cases between 1950 and 1954 substantially exceeded that in the U.S. (see Table 5-2).

In the succeeding five-year period, the average fine per conspiracy case in Canada fell below the U.S. level. The fines in the few resale price maintenance cases between 1955 and 1959 averaged only $502 per case.

Revisions to the Combines Investigation Act in 1960 provided another opportunity to see the solicitude for producer interests and their influence upon legislation. With respect to the committee hearings preceeding the 1960 amendments, "the lawyers and business executives were heard with great respect. Their submissions were often followed by fulsome votes of thanks. . . . Many members [of the Committee] revealed a conception of the role of government as that of pleasing substantial interests. The objections of the economists (and consumers) were thus not taken seriously by government members."[52] The thrust of the Conservative government's proposed amendments was severely to weaken the legislation. Economist Stefan Stykolt stated that the government's amendments appeared designed to destroy the effectiveness of Canada's anti-combines policy by making successful prosecutions . . . much more difficult than under existing legislation, if not altogether impossible." Another economist, H. C. Eastman, foresaw the effects of the amendments as "higher prices, more numerous small producers, lower productivity and a lower standard of living in Canada."[53]

The result was that "the government accepted some of the suggestions that business had been pressing for years [following the 1952 amendments], while protesting that the changes were devices to protest small business or were merely clarifications of the existing law . . .[54] the government was not prepared openly to destroy the effectiveness of the Combines Investigation Act."[55]

The uniquely Canadian propensity to frame a moderately pro-competition statute, coupled with carefully crafted loopholes, is seen in the 1960 amendments. The prohibition against resale price maintenance was retained, but sellers were provided with four defences which made it all but impossible to obtain a conviction. As James Gillies points out, "either through intention or oversight, no Canadian government has ever formulated a well-thought-out program for promoting competition or, conversely, for fostering monopoly."[56] In adopting the policy that

TABLE 5-3

Combines Prosecutions, Excluding Misleading Advertising, By Type of Offence, 1950/51-1975/76[1]

Type of Offence	1950/51-1954/55	1955/56-1959/60[4]	1960/61-1964/65	1965/66-1969/70	1970/71-1974/75	1975/76
Conspiracy (e.g., price fixing)	6	15	7	16	18	4
Merger and/or Monopoly	1	2	0	1	4	0
Predatory pricing or price discrimination	0	2	2	0	2	0
Resale price maintenance and/or refusal to supply	2	1	8	8	18	9
OTHER	0	0	1[2]	0	6[3]	0
TOTAL	9	20	18	25	48	13

NOTES:

[1]Cases in period 1950/51-1959/60 dated by day of trial judgment, later cases dated by day Information was laid.

[2]RPM, refusal to deal and discriminatory advertising allowances.

[3]Two conspiracy and monopoly cases, one RPM and discriminatory advertising allowances case, one monopoly and predatory pricing case, and two conspiracy and RPM cases.

[4]Includes four cases decided in 1960 after the end of fiscal 1959-60 and one decided in 1961. These were not counted in the period 1960/61-1974/75 as charges were laid before April 1, 1960.

SOURCE:

P. K. Gorecki and W. T. Stanbury, "The Administration and Enforcement of the Combines Investigation Act," (study in progress, University of British Columbia, Faculty of Commerce and Business Administration, 1977).

combines are criminal conspiracies perpetrated only by a small minority of avaricious businessmen, Thorburn points out that such a policy "tends to leave undisturbed the large and often monoplistic concentration of economic power, but enables the government to satisfy the demands of the consuming public by making a show of its criminal statute and list of prosecutions."[57]

The number of combines cases (conspiracy, merger, monopoly, resale price maintenance and price discrimination) in the period 1960-61 to 1964-65 was *smaller* than in the preceeding five-year period, although the number of investigations increased as can be seen from the number of RTPC reports which did not result in prosecution and the number of discontinued inquiries shown in Table 5-1. More importantly, only seven conspiracy cases were prosecuted between 1960-61 and 1964-65 as compared with fifteen in the previous five-year period (see Table 5-3). The total number of combines prosecutions rose to twenty-five between 1965-66 and 1969-70; the number of discontinued inquiries increased very slightly; and the number of complaint files opened decreased compared with the previous five-year period (see Table 5-1). One third of the prosecutions in the late 1960s were RPM (resale price maintenance) and/or refusal to supply cases. In the next five-year period (1970-71 to 1974-75) the number of such cases more than doubled and equalled the number of conspiracy cases (see Table 5-3). The total number of combines prosecutions almost doubled between 1970-71 to 1974-75 and 1965-66 to 1969-70. Of particular note is the fact that four merger and monopoly cases were brought to court. However, the number of misleading advertising cases prosecuted in the first half of the 1970s was ten times the number of combines cases and seven times the number of misleading advertising cases in the previous five years.

In 1975-76 the number of RPM/refusal to supply cases was more than double the number of conspiracy cases. The number of misleading advertising cases was eight times the total number of combines cases (see Table 5-1).

In summary, we should note that 104 of the 157 combines prosecutions since 1889 have taken place in the last 16 years and that 61 of these have occurred in the last 6 years. With respect to conspiracy cases, sixty-six of the eighty-nine since 1889 were prosecuted between 1950-51 and 1975-76. Thirty-four such cases were in one ten-year period, 1965-66 to 1974-75.

It is against this background and in this context that the battle over the reform of Canada's competition policy has taken place during the 1970s.

NOTES

[1]Michael Bliss, *A Living Profit*, Toronto, McClelland and Stewart, 1974, p. 34.

[2]James W. Melvin and Bruce Wilkinson, *Effective Protection in the Canadian Economy*, Special Study No. 9 for the Economic Council of Canada, Ottawa, Queen's Printer, 1968; B. W. Wilkinson and K. Norrie, *Effective Protection and the Return on Capital*, Economic Council of Canada, Ottawa, Information Canada, 1975.

[3]Department of Consumer and Corporate Affairs, *Concentration in the Manufacturing Industries of Canada*, Ottawa, Information Canada, 1971; Statistics Canada, *Industrial Organization and Concentration in the Manufacturing, Mining and Logging Industries*, 1970, Ottawa, Information Canada, 1975.

[4]H. C. Eastman and S. Stykolt, *The Tariff and Competition in Canada*, Toronto, Macmillan, 1967; D. J. Daly, B. A. Keys and E. J. Spence, *Scale and Specialization in Canadian Manufacturing*, Staff Study No. 21, Economic Council of Canada, Ottawa, Queen's Printer, in 1968; Paul K. Gorecki, *Economies of Scale and Efficient Plant Size, in Canadian Manufacturing Industries*, Bureau of Competition Policy Research Monograph No. 1, Ottawa, Information Canada, 1976.

[5]Government of Canada, *Foreign Direct Investment in Canada*, Ottawa, Information Canada, 1973; Statistics Canada, *Corporations and Labour Unions Returns Act*, Catalogue 61-210 Annual, Ottawa.

[6]David L. McQueen "Tribunals and Take-Overs in Canada," in The Conference Board in Canada, *Canada's Competition Policy*, Ottawa, 1972, p. 55.

[7]Bliss, *op. cit.*, p. 40.

[8]*Ibid.*, p. 45.

[9]Lloyd G. Reynolds, *The Control of Competition in Canada*, Cambridge, Mass., Harvard University Press, 1940, p. 134.

[10]*Hansard*, April 22, 1889. A more detailed discussion of the original bill can be found in John A. Ball, *Canadian Anti-Trust Legislation*, Baltimore, Williams and Wilkins, 1934, Ch. 1, 2 and in Richard Gosse, *The Law on Competition in Canada*, Toronto, Carswell, 1962, Ch. III.

[11]Reynolds, *op.cit.*, p. 134.

[12]*Ibid.*

[13]Michael Bliss, "Another Anti-Trust Tradition: Canadian Anti-Combines Policy, 1889-1910," *Business History Review*, Vol. 47, No. 2, Vol. 47, No. 2, Summer 1973, p. 182.

[14]*Ibid.*, pp. 182-183.

[15]F. N. MacLeod "Combines Investigation Act — Detriment," unpublished paper, Ottawa, Department of Justice, n.d., C.1972, mimeo, pp. 62, 63.

[16]Gosse, *op.cit.*, p. 77.

[17]Bliss, "Another Anti-Trust Tradition," pp. 183-184.

[18]*Ibid.*, p. 184.

[19]See *R. v. The American Tobacco Company of Canada, La Revue de Jurisprudence* Vol. 3, 1897, pp. 453-464.

[20]Bliss, "Another Anti-Trust Tradition," p. 177.

[22]See W. T. Stanbury, "Penalties and Remedies Under the Combines Investigation Act 1889-1976," *Osgoode Halle Law Journal*, Vol. 14, No. 3, 1976, Table 3.

[22]Cited in L. A. Skeoch (ed.), *Restrictive Trade Practices in Canada*, Toronto, McClelland and Stewart, 1966, pp. 23, 24.

[23]*Ibid.*, p. 24.

[24]*Ibid.*, p. 26.

[25]James E. Boyle, "Canada's Combines Investigation Act: A Lesson for the United States," *Quarterly Journal of the University of North Dakota*, Vol. III, No. 2, January 1913, p. 164.

[26]*Ibid.*, p. 166.

[27]*Report of the Committee to Study Combines Legislation,* Ottawa, Queen's Printer, 1952, p. 10.

[28]Boyle, *op.cit.,* p. 167.

[29]Cited in L. A. Skeoch (ed.), *op.cit.,* p. 26.

[30]*Ibid.,* p. 26. If the three-man board found that the persons under investigation had done any of the acts set out in S.498 of the Criminal Code and the persons investigated did not cease such acts within ten days after the publication of the report, they were liable for a penalty of up to $1,000 per day.

[31]Boyle, *op.cit.,* p. 168.

[32]*United Shoe Machinery Co. of Canada* v. *Laurendeau et al. and Drouin et al.,* 2 D.L.R. 77-84 (1912).

[33]Boyle, *op.cit.,* p. 170.

[34]The discussion which follows is taken from the *Report of the Committee to Study Combines Legislation, op.cit.,* p. 11.

[35]*Attorney General for Ontario* v. *Canadian Wholesale Grocers Association* 52 O.L.R. 536 (1923) — the trial decision; 53 O.L.R. 627 (1923) — the appeal decision.

[36]Cited in L. A. Skeoch (ed.), *op.cit.,* p. 30.

[37]*Hansard,* May 8, 1923, p. 2605.

[38]*Ibid.*

[39]*Ibid.*

[40]V. W. Bladen, *An Introduction to Political Economy,* Toronto, University of Toronto Press, 1941, p. 211, footnote 19.

[41]*Report of the Committee to Study Combines Legislation, op.cit.,* pp. 12-13.

[42]Reference re.Dominion Trade and Industry Commission Act, 1935 [1936] S.C.R. 379; 3 D.L.R. 607. A very useful discussion of the origin of the Dominion Trade and Industry Commission Act is given in D. F. Forster, "The Politics of Combines Policy: Liberals and the Stevens Commission," *Canadian Journal of Economics and Political Science,* November 1962, pp. 511-526.

[43]Stanbury, *op.cit.,* Table 5.

[44]*Ibid.,* Table 3. Throughout the entire period a maximum was in effect in only 36 percent of all conspiracy cases was it imposed on one or more firms.

[45]Economic Council of Canada, *Interim Report on Competition Policy,* Ottawa, Queen's Printer, 1969, p. 141.

[46]The Economic Council (*Ibid.,* p. 141) states, "In 1949, the question of including services surfaced again, but the then Minister of Justice, Mr. Garson, opposed the move."

[47]S. F. Sommerfield, "Free Competition and the Public Interest," *University of Toronto Law Journal,* Vol. 7, 1948, p. 446.

[48]V. W. Bladen, "Monopoly and Competition in Canada," in E. H. Chamberlin (ed.), *Monopoly, Competition and Their Regulation,* London, International Economic Association, 1954, p. 19. Bladen exhibits his general satisfaction with Canadian combines legislation in his "Competition and Monopoly and Their Regulation: Submission to the Royal Commission on Canada's Economic Prospects," Toronto, January 25, 1956.

[49]This account is taken from the Winnipeg *Free Press, The McGregor Controversy and the Combines Act,* Winnipeg *Free Press* Pamphlet No. 29, 1949, 31 pp. See also G. Rosenbluth and H. G. Thorburn, *Canadian Anti-Combines Administration, 1952-60,* Toronto, University of Toronto Press, Chapter 2, "The Flour Milling Report," pp. 10-16.

[50]*Report of the Committee to Study Combines Legislation and Interim Report on Resale Price Maintenance,* Ottawa, Queen's Printer, 1952, 72 pp.

[51]For more details see Rosenbluth and Thorburn, *op.cit.* Chapter 3, "The MacQuarrie Committee," pp 17-25.

[52]H. G. Thorburn, "Pressure Groups in Canadian Politics: Recent Revisions of the Anti-Combines Legislation," *Canadian Journal of Economics and Political Science,* Vol. 30, No. 2, May 1964, p. 171.

[53]*Ibid.*, p. 167.

[54]*Ibid.*, p. 169.

[55]*Ibid.*, p. 173.

[56]James Gillies, *A Review of the Economic Council's Interim Report on Competition Policy*, Montreal, Private Planning Association of Canada, 1969, p. 10.

[57]Thorburn, *op.cit.*, p. 158.

Chapter 6

Immediate Background to the Competition Act: The Interim Report on Competition Policy

The chronology of the Competition Act and its successors should probably begin in 1966. On July 22, 1966 the Economic Council of Canada was asked to prepare a report on the responsibilities of the Department of the Registrar General which was established by the Government Organization Act, given royal assent on June 19, 1966.[1] The terms of reference given the council were, "in light of the government's long-term economic objectives, to study and advise regarding":

1. The interests of consumers particularly as they relate to the functions of the Department of the Registrar General.
2. Combines, mergers, monopolies and restraint of trade.
3. Patents, trademarks, copyrights and registered industrial designs.[2]

The reference to the Economic Council followed a speech by the prime minister on May 24, 1966 on Second Reading of the bill which created the Department of the Registrar General.[3]

Within twelve months the council produced the first of its three "interim reports," which became its final reports. This one concerned item (a) in the terms of reference of July 22, 1966.[4]

On December 21, 1967, royal assent was given to the bill which transformed the Department of the Registrar General into the Department of Consumer and Corporate Affairs. The Office of the Director of Investigation and Research, Combines Investigation Act, which had moved from the Department of Justice to the Department of the Registrar General, was now incorporated into the Department of Consumer and Corporate Affairs. On June 25, 1968 the Liberal government with Pierre Trudeau at its head was returned to office with 155 seats to the Progressive Conservatives' 72. In July, Ronald Basford of Vancouver was made Minister of Consumer and Corporate Affairs, replacing John Turner who became Minister of Justice. One year later, the Economic Council brought forward its *Interim Report on Competition Policy*[5], which addressed item (b) in the terms of reference of July 22, 1966. It was to be the intellectual father of the Competition Act.

It is evident that at the time of the reference to the Economic Council in July 1966 the government anticipated a fairly major revision of Canadian competition policy. This is apparent from a press release issued on behalf of the Registrar General, Guy Favreau, in July of 1966:

> With particular reference to proposals for amendments to the Combines Investigation Act that have been the subject of discussion in Parliament and the press, and of submissions by individuals and groups, the minister stated it is most important that this legislation should not be amended piecemeal. Any amendments to the legislation ought to be in keeping with its fundamental philosophy and in furtherance of it. When consideration is being given to reviewing the general structure and philosophy of the act, it would be very unwise to enact immediate temporary and piecemeal amendments to correct particular situations. At a time when a general review is in contemplation, such particular measures ought to be taken up and considered in the context of the whole review and any revision that may take place in the light of the findings and recommendations of the Economic Council.[6]

When the council's *Interim Report* was published, "the minister [Mr. Basford] revealed that he had already initiated a complete revision of the Combines Investigation Act. He noted that there is a wide range of views on competition policy and said the government would consider every aspect with care. He asked individuals, organizations and companies interested in the *Report* and the combines law to make their views known to him by the middle of October 1969, by briefs and letters or otherwise."[7] Although the Director of Investigation and Research described the Economic Council's *Interim Report* as "the important study [of Canadian competition policy] of the current century . . ."[8] the volume and intensity of response to it was not great. Academics produced less than a handful of articles on the *Report*.[9] Parliamentary debate was all but non-existant.[10] The number of briefs, sent in response to the Minister's request was small and, predictably, almost entirely from business. Between January 1, 1969 and May 5, 1970 the Department of Consumer and Corporate Affairs received letters or briefs from the following:[11]

- Canadian Manufacturers' Association
- National Grain (1968) Limited and McCabe Grain Company Limited
- Retail Council of Canada
- Canadian Bankers' Association
- Consumers' Association of Canada
- National Automotive Trades Association of Canada
- Canadian Chemical Producers' Association
- Canadian Chamber of Commerce
- Retail Merchants' Association of Canada
- Canadian Liquid Air Limited

- Bakery Council of Canada
- Dominion Stores Limited
- Imperial Oil Limited
- Canadian Chiropractic Association
- Canadian Pulp and Paper Association
- Gulf Oil Canada Limited
- Canadian Association of Real Estate Boards
- Canadian Electrical Manufacturers' Association
- Canadian Consumer Council
- D. G. Hemple
- Ivey and Dowler
- Darling, Warner, Thompson and Anderson
- Warren Allman

Bruce C. McDonald, then professor of Law at Queen's University, offered an explanation for the modest response the *Interim Report* provoked:

> The virtual absence of publicized reaction . . . is not due to a lack of interest in the *Report* but rather to the fact that the *Report* is so general on many critical points that until specific legislation is introduced there is little to react to. . . . The single most striking feature of the *Report* is the generality with which it deals with central substantive issues.[12]

The reason for this may reside in the nature of the council itself. The *Interim Report* was one of its "concensus documents", rather than one of its staff studies where authorship is clearly identified. Speaking in September 1971, Arthur J. R. Smith, chairman of the council at the time the *Interim Report* was prepared, remarked,

> it represents a concensus among twenty-eight people reflecting a very broad cross-section of views and interests in different parts of the country and different sectors of the economy. It is not a scholar's report. It is not an economist's report. It is not an expert's report. It is a concensus report among a group consisting very largely of decision makers.[13]

The *Interim Report* stated that the objective of competition policy legislation "should be the promotion of dynamic efficiency, flexibility and good all-around performance in the Canadian economy."[14] A few pages later in their discussion the council refined its position saying:

> Essentially, we are advocating the adoption of a single objective for competition policy: the improvement of economic efficiency and the avoidance of economic waste. . . .[15]

James Gillies, then an academic and perhaps unaware of the details of business opinion he was later to learn as a Conservative M.P. and shadow Cabinet minister, wrote,

> . . . no one can disagree with this objective. Moreover it is a pleasant
> relief to find the objective of policy stated in such clear and
> unemotional terms.[16]

In adopting its position, the council pointed out it did not wish to disparage other objectives such as a more equitable distribution of income or the diffusion of economic power. Rather, it felt that a competition policy concentrated on a single objective "is likely to be applied more consistently and effectively," and that the tax-transfer system was better equipped to deal with these other objectives.[17] The council also pointed out that the pursuit of multiple goals (e.g., efficiency and the diffusion of power) may result in a conflict of objectives, and that the pursuit of efficiency and the reduction of economic waste could also result in furthering other objectives.

Before we examine the specifics of the council's policy proposals, a number of other features of the *Interim Report* should be noted. The council indicated a clear recognition of the need for the coordination of the government's economic policies (e.g., tariffs, taxes, procurement, trade, intellectual and industrial property). The council's appreciation of the dynamic factors in economic growth (technological change and innovation) extended to a recognition of the need for regular review and reassessment of the objectives and administration of competition policy.

Defining three broad types of social control over industrial activities, competition policy aimed at the market sector, regulation and public ownership, the council recognized the importance of the latter two. It proposed that the Director and a new tribunal be given the power to study government-regulated and government-owned enterprises, even though other clauses in the legislation may not, in practice, be applicable to these activities.

SPECIFIC PROPOSALS IN THE INTERIM REPORT[18]

The council proposed that five restrictive practices "be subject to essentially per se prohibition under criminal law"[19]: collusive arrangements to fix prices including bid rigging; collusive arrangements to allocate markets; collusive arrangements to prevent entry of new firms or restrict expansion of existing ones; resale price maintenance; and misleading advertising.

It is important to note that the council "waffled" on the issue of whether "unduly" should be retained in S.32 of the act or whether collusive agreements should be prohibited per se as is the case in the United States.[20]

The council recommended that misleading advertising and inadequate servicing be dropped as defences against refusal to supply (used to enforce resale price maintenance). With respect to loss leader selling, also a defence against refusal to supply, the council recommended "that this matter be subjected to an early general inquiry by the civil tribunal. . . ."[21]

With the transfer of S.306 of the Criminal Code to the Combines Act as S.33D (later S.37) in July of 1969 and the similar per se prohibition of misleading price advertising under S.33C (later S.36) the council saw no need to change the law in this area.

Administratively, the council recommended that cases involving the five per se prohibitions be sent directly to the Attorney General by the Director rather than routing them through the proposed new tribunal to replace the Restrictive Trade Practices Commission.

The council recognized that Canada's merger policy had been completely ineffective under the criminal law and that mergers must be evaluated on a case-by-case basis to determine their potential economic consequences. The council recommended the establishment of a specialized tribunal to rule on mergers and other restraints of trade made subject to the new civil procedures it proposed. "The basic reasons for seeking to place some of the federal government's competition policy on a civil law basis would be to improve its relevance to economic goals, its effectiveness and its acceptability to the general public. The greater flexibility afforded by civil law is especially to be desired in those areas of the policy that do not lend themselves to relatively unqualified prohibitions and that may in addition call for some case-by-case consideration of the likely economic effects of particular business structures or practices."[22]

The council saw the functions of the new tribunal as similar to an ordinary civil court. It would hear cases, make adjudications and impose remedies. "In addition, however, it would engage in economic analysis and in the issuance of reports similar to many of those now issued by the Restrictive Trade Practices Commission."[23]

The proposed Competitive Practices Tribunal would do the following:[24]

1. Evaluate mergers brought before it and impose or recommend remedies.

2. Evaluate proposed intercompany export agreements and specialization agreements and "register" such agreements if they are deemed to be in the public interest.

3. Examine certain trade practices and determine whether, on balance, the use of such practices is or is not in the public interest. These trade practices would include: refusal to deal, including those under franchise agreements but excluding those associated with reale price maintenance; basing point pricing; exclusive dealing and tying arrangements; market access arrangements; predatory practices; price

and advertising allowance discrimination; and consignment selling. None of these practices would be an offence in general — only where it was shown to have a deleterious effect in a specific case.

4. Sponsor and report on general inquiries as currently provided for in S.42 (later S.47) of the Combines Investigation Act

Cases going before the tribunal would, in general, originate with the new Director of Legal Proceedings (who would replace the Director of Investigation and Research).[25] The tribunal would have the power to impose both temporary and permanent injunctions where it found a merger or referrable trade practice against the public interest. Detailed criteria were specified by the council indicating what the tribunal should consider in examining mergers and trade practices.[26]

The council did not propose changes in the law specifically to deal with monopoly and dominant firm situations. Rather, it proposed that such problems be dealt with in their incipiency and their actuality through the criteria specified for the evaluation of mergers and referrable trade practices.[27]

One of the most important proposals of the Economic Council's *Interim Report* concerned the service industries. It recommended:[28]

1. that the per se provisions of the revised Combines Investigation Act be made applicable to all commercial activities, including services provided in connection with the sale or rental of land and buildings and the unregulated activities of "regulated industries."

2. that the purview of the proposed Competitive Practices Tribunal embrace all economic activities, whether goods-producing or service-producing. . . .

ACADEMIC REVIEWS OF THE INTERIM REPORT

The private Planning Association of Canada commissioned James Gillies, then the dean of the Faculty of Administrative Studies at York University, to prepare a review of the *Interim Report*. His review was generally favourable: "By and large, this commentator hopes the policy recommendations of the *Interim Report* are adopted, since he believes that efforts to reach the goals that the various Economic Council *Annual Reviews* espouse for the Canadian economy would be helped by the adoption of the recommendations in the *Interim Report*. It seems reasonable to suppose that Canadian industry could operate more effectively within the framework of such a policy."[29]

A theme running through Gillies review is that we really are unable to estimate what the effect of the previous and current policy has been, nor are we able to predict what will be the impact of the council's recommendations.

the significant thing is not the fact that the legislation exists, but the question of whether it has any effect on the operation of Canadian firms and on the well-being of the Canadian economy. . . .[30]
Since we do not know . . . certain basic facts about the Canadian economy [e.g., importance of economies of scale, the relationship between concentration and economic performance etc.] . . . we clearly cannot be confident that we know with any certainty what the results of the reforms suggested in the *Report* would be.[31]

Gillies was critical of the council's failure to distinguish between mergers involving the foreign ownership of Canadian industry. He pointed out that "almost every country in the world appears to be experiencing an increase in mergers"[32] and that Canada is no exception. He continued, "Does it make any difference to Canadian competition policy whether or not merging firms involve foreign corporations? From the point of view of the [*Interim*] *Report* apparently not, since there is essentially no reference to this situation."[33] Gillies was disturbed by this omission; contending that "it is difficult to accept the idea that any policy for competition in Canada can ignore the implications of foreign ownership."[34]

He was also critical of the Economic Council for ignoring the quality of management as a variable in the study of industrial organization:

The *Report* is lacking in any serious analysis of mangement in Canadian industry. Surely the driving force today in Canadian firms, as has been the case throughout history in all countries, is management. Perhaps a study of management is as important as a study of other economic factors in an evaluation of the operation of industry and markets. A simple dismissal of Galbraith's thesis as probably not applying to Canada is far from satisfactory.[35]

Gillies was mildly critical of the *Interim Report* on two other points. He questioned whether the administration of competition policy should be located in the Department of Consumer and Corporate Affairs, yet he did not propose a specific alternative.[36] Second, he questioned the council's suggestion that the abolition of tariffs would result in greater competitive pressures in some Canadian industries. He said there was no evidence to support this claim and argued further, that it contrasted with the council's recommendations that export agreements be permitted on the grounds they would increase the capability of domestic firms in penetrating foreign markets.[37]

Carl H. Fulda, professor of Law at the University of Texas and visiting professor at the Osgoode Hall Law School in 1970, described the *Interim Report* as "an important document of proposed law reform."[38] He concluded that "the recommendations of that *Report* represent a judicious adaptation to Canadian conditions of European and U.S. methods dealing with similar problems. They point the way in the right direction for any future attempt to strengthen the present Canadian law."[39]

Fulda specifically supported the proposed civil law procedures, noting, "no other country uses criminal punishment as the only sanction for violation of its anti-monopoly and competition policy."[40] He was critical of the Economic Council's unwillingness to press for a pure per se ban on price-fixing and market-sharing agreements. He found the council's arguments for retaining "unduly," "not convincing." He pointed out, "Enforcement authorities in all countries have limited staffs and budgets and, therefore, are not likely to squander their resources on trivial cases. Moreover, it is difficult to determine when price-fixing agreements are 'minor' or 'major.' Consumers would always be victimized."[41] Fulda argued that "unduly" must be eliminated if the legislation against price-fixing is to be effective.

After reviewing the proposals of the *Interim Report* in respect of specialization agreements and the law on this issue in the European Economic Community, Fulda stated that such agreements "should not be used to strengthen existing oligopolies, but, as the European examples show, to permit 'medium-size' firms to compete more effectively against large firms, some of which are foreign-owned."[42] With respect to mergers, Fulda noted that the *Interim Report* apparently disregards the incipiency theory which is prominent in U.S. merger jurisprudence, in contending that only mergers in "rather highly concentrated industries" should be subjected to a "public interest examination."[43] he stated that between 1945 and 1961 there were 118 mergers in Canadian industries where 8 or fewer firms accounted for 80 percent of total shipments[44]

Bruce C. McDonald, who was to become the co-author of one of the major studies[45] leading up to the Stage II revisions of the Combines Act in 1977, wrote a decidedly mixed review of the *Interim Report.* He preceeded his criticisms of the *Report* by acknowledging some of its virtues.[46] He welcome (1) the articulation of a specific goal for competition policy, (2) the assumption that civil procedures are possible in federal competition policy, (3) the council's recognition of the need to coordinate various economic policies, (4) the council's recommendation of continuing reassessment of the goals and administration of competition policy and (5) the proposal to limit the use of criminal law and the courts "to cases where the essential issue is whether a certain type of practice, a priori undesirable, existed in fact."[47]

McDonald also approved of the inclusion of services within the Combines Act, the provision for specialization agreements, the proposed strengthening of the research function and the legislation relating to exclusive dealing, tying and other market access arrangements.[48]

On the other side of the ledger, McDonald, as we have noted, was critical of the "generality with which [the *Report*] deals with central substantive issues." He wanted the *Report* to go beyond "uncontroversial generalities or the statement of obvious problems, which cannot be criticized for being wrong but are useless in the absence of a more detailed attempt to be constructive. . . . in places the *Report* reads more like a padded undergraduate essay than the result of a three-year government research effort."[49]

McDonald stated that "the single most serious defect of the *Report* is its failure to come to grips with the competitive implications of fewness."[50] He noted that the proposed per se ban on horizontal agreements did not recognize the legal difficulties of tacit collusion, conscious parallelism, price leadership and the far more general relationship between market structure and economic performance. Like others[51] McDonald asked, "Should businessmen who act rationally in a tight oligopoly be subject to criminal penalties?"[52]

McDonald argued that the *Interim Report* does not deal adequately with the activities of trade associations, "another case where a unique commercial context demands unique legal rules . . . particularly . . . for information collection and dissemination."[53]

Advertising as a barrier to entry, McDonald felt, was not treated adequately in the *Interim Report*. Nor had the Economic Council come to terms with the conflict between making competition policy decisions make economic sense and the need to preserve a workable system of judicial administration and enforcement.[54] Having listed a number of specific factors to be taken into account in merger cases, McDonald noted that the council "at the same time [said] some of them may not be relevant and others, not listed, may be relevant?" He wondered whether the list of factors is designed "to satisfy lawyers by creating the appearance of specific standards while preserving full flexibility for the economists?"[55] While observing that the *Interim Report* did not distinguish between horizontal, vertical and conglomerate mergers, and that the council's approach to mergers may leave something to be desired, he concluded that "it nevertheless represents a healthy step toward sensible merger control."[56] McDonald is more critical of the council's failure to devote any attention "to general issues of bigness and diversification as such."[57] He is similarly critical of the council's approval of "the practice of 'suggesting' prices both horizontally and . . . vertically."[58] The council's avoidance of the loss leading issue McDonald described as "an escape as irritating as it is surprising."[59]

With respect to enforcement and remedies McDonald found the *Report* "somewhat unimaginative," indicating its failure to recognize the role of private initiative in the total enforcement effort.[60] Civil actions on behalf of the public were not considered. He noted that daily fines, the incidence of fines and the greater use of imprisonment are not discussed in the *Report*. The mechanics of enforcing the tribunal's injunctions were not considered.[61]

McDonald characterized the council's treatment of the five per se criminal offences (apparently in favour of per se illegality, but then significantly qualifying its position) as "highly unsatisfactory and verges on the irresponsible."[62] He concluded his review by saying, "there are enough recurring elements of unrealism, deliberate avoidance of central issues, naivete or error in the *Report* to shake one's confidence in the document."[63] Yet McDonald goes on to add, "in most basic ways it represents an excellent step forward in the development of Canadian competition policy."[64]

THE INTERIM REPORT AS PARENT OF THE COMPETITION ACT

The details of the Competition Act, introduced in the House of Commons in mid-1971, are described in Chapter 7. In reading that chapter it is important to recognize in the proposed act a number of features which were proposed by the Economic Council in 1969. These include:

- The inclusion of services under the purview of competition legislation.
- The establishment of civil procedures, including the Competitive Practices Tribunal, to deal with mergers; ten restrictive trade practices (e.g., price discrimination, tied selling, delivered pricing etc); registered agreements with respect to exports, franchises and specialization arrangements; and interlocking directorates.
- The establishment of a list of offences declared to be illegal per se e.g., price fixing, bid rigging, agreements to prevent entry.
- An increase in the severity of maximum penalties (fines and imprisonment).
- The continuation of the administration of competition policy within the Department of Consumer and Corporate Affairs.

During his vacation in the summer of 1969, the Minister of Consumer and Corporate Affairs, Mr. Basford, took the Economic Council's *Interim Report* with him and read it carefully. Even at that time Basford was personally committed to advocacy of the consumer interest in the Cabinet and the government more generally. When he returned from his vacation he told his officials he approved of the *Interim Report* and wanted new legislation to reflect its recommendations. From the start the minister set an ambitious schedule to get the new bill before Parliament. On March 3, 1970 he described the department's work on the bill as "a top priority item" and indicated that it was ready for interdepartmental discussions within the government.[65] He went on to say,

Although the schedule for producing a new bill is very tight, I am still aiming to bring a new bill down before the summer [of 1970] so that it will be available for study before the summer recess.[66]

The Director of Investigation and Research noted in his *Annual Report* for 1969-70, "Although every effort was made, this expectation could not be realized, but the revision continues to receive a very high priority in the department."[67]

To speed up the process of Cabinet approval, the bill was sent in pieces to Cabinet committee — yet it took a year to go through. It was only seen in toto a week before it was tabled in the House of Commons. The Cabinet was believed to be split on the bill and it was said that Basford only got approval by prevailing upon the prime minister to push it through the Cabinet.

NOTES

[1]The new department was assigned the administration of (1) combines, mergers, monopolies and restraint of trade; (2) patents, copyrights and trade marks; (3) bankruptcy and insolvency; and (4) corporate affairs. The Government Organization Act, 1966 was proclaimed on October 1, 1966 and the Honourable Guy Favreau, Q.C. was appointed Registrar General of Canada. As President of the Privy Council Mr. Favreau had been responsible for these matters since December 1965.

[2]From *Report of the Director of Investigation and Research, Combines Investigation Act,* year ended March 31, 1967, Ottawa, Queen's Printer, 1967, p. 8.

[3]*Ibid.,* p. 8. On April 4, 1967 John N. Turner, Minister Without Portfolio was appointed Registrar General of Canada.

[4]Economic Council of Canada, *Interim Report on Competition Policy,* Ottawa, Queen's Printer, 1969. It was not until January 1971 that the Economic Council published its *Report on Intellectual and Industrial Property.* (Ottawa, Information Canada, 1971) in response to item (c) in the terms of reference of July 22, 1966.

[6]*Report of the Director* year ended March 31, 1967, p. 9. The original source for this is the Press Release of July 22, 1966 by Guy Favreau, President of the Privy Council and the minister responsible for combines.

[7]*Report of the Director,* year ended March 31, 1969, p. 21.

[8]David H. W. Henry, "Current Trends in Canadian Antitrust Enforcement," *Antitrust Law Journal,* Vol. 40, No. 4, 1971, p. 783.

[9]James Gillies, *A Review of the Economic Council's Interim Report on Competition Policy,* Montreal, Canadian Economic Policy Committee, Private Planning Association, 1969; Carl H. Fulda, "Proposed Changes in Canadian Combines Legislation: Some Comparative Comments on the 'Interim Report on Competition Policy,'" *Osgoode Hall Law Journal,* Vol. 8, No. 3, December 1970, pp. 415-429; Bruce C. McDonald, "Canadian Competition Policy: Interim Report of the Economic Council of Canada," *Antitrust Bulletin,* Vol. 15, Fall 1970, pp. 521-546.

[10]A brief flurry was created when David Orlikow (NDP, Winnipeg-North) pressed the government to release copies of the forty briefs presented to the Economic Council with respect to the terms of reference given to it on July 22, 1966. See *Commons Debates,* January 21, 1971, pp. 2634-2640. Only one page was devoted to an analysis of the *Interim Report.*

[11]Reply to Motion for the Production of Papers No. 299 and 299A, April 29, 1970 and May 5, 1970 by the President of the Privy Council.

[12]Bruce C. McDonald, op.cit., pp. 522, 529.

[13]The Conference Board in Canada, Canada's Competition Policy, Ottawa, 1972, pp. 86-87.

[14]Interim Report, op.cit., p. 5.

[15]Ibid., p. 19.

[16]Gillies, op.cit., p. 13.

[17]Interim Report, op.cit., p. 20.

[18]These are set out in Chapter 6 of the Interim Report, op.cit., pp. 99-131.

[19]Interim Report, op.cit., p. 102.

[20]Ibid., pp. 102-103.

[21]Ibid., p. 105.

[22]Ibid., p. 109.

[23]Ibid., p. 110.

[24]Ibid., pp. 112, 122.

[25]Ibid., Chapter 10.

[26]Ibid., pp. 116, 123.

[27]Ibid., pp. 128-129.

[28]Ibid., pp. 147-148. With respect to 1. the Council recommended that the exemption for bona fide trade union activities be continued.

[29]Gillies, op.cit., p. 3.

[30]Ibid., p. 7.

[31]Ibid., p. 40. Gillies points out that "these deficiencies are perhaps more a criticism of the state of economic research in Canada than they are of the Report" (p. 41).

[32]Gillies, op.cit., p. 22.

[33]Ibid., p. 23.

[34]Ibid.,

[35]Ibid., pp. 40-41.

[36]Ibid., pp. 42-43.

[37]Ibid., p. 43.

[38]Fulda, op.cit. p. 429

[39]Fulda, op.cit., p. 429

[40]Ibid., p. 416

[41]Ibid., p. 420.

[42]Ibid., p. 426.

[43]Ibid., p. 427.

[44]Ibid.

[45]L. A. Skeoch with B.C. McDonald, in consultation with M. Belanger, R. M. Bromstein and W. O. Twaits, Dynamic Change and Accountability in A Canadian Market Economy, Ottawa, Supply and Services Canada, 1976.

[46]McDonald, op.cit., pp. 522-525.

[47]Ibid., p. 524.

[48]Ibid., p. 527, 528-529.

[49]Ibid., p. 529.

[50]Ibid., p. 531.

[51]W. T. Stanbury and G. B. Reschenthaler, "Oligopoly and Conscious Parallelism: Theory, Policy and the Canadian Cases," Osgoode Hall Law Journal, Vol. 15, No. 3, 1977 (forthcoming).

[52]McDonald, *op.cit.*, p. 531.

[53]*Ibid.*

[54]*Ibid.*, p. 533.

[55]*Ibid.*, p. 534.

[56]*Ibid.*, p. 535.

[57]*Ibid.*

[58]*Ibid.*, p. 537.

[59]*Ibid.*, p. 538.

[60]*Ibid.*

[61]*Ibid.*, p. 540.

[62]*Ibid.*, p. 542.

[63]*Ibid.*, pp. 543-544.

[64]*Ibid.*, p. 544.

[65]*Report of the Director*, year ended March 31, 1970, p. 10.

[66]*Ibid.*

[67]*Ibid.*

Chapter 7

The Proposed Competition Act of 1971: Ascendency of the Consumer Interest*

On June 29, 1971 the Liberal government introduced to Parliament for First Reading a new anti-combines law;[1] if passed, it would have represented the first major change in the Canadian combines legislation since 1960. Essentially the bill provided for enactment of the recommendations made by the Economic Council of Canada in its *Interim Report on Competition Policy* in 1969.[2] However, in many respects the proposed legislation went beyond the *Interim Report* in pursuit of its professed aim of serving the interest of the Canadian consumer.

SUMMARY OF BASIC POLICY

While the proposed legislation was basically an extension of previous policy, major changes were proposed. These changes in policy were outlined by the government as follows:[3]

1. The exclusive reliance on the criminal courts that previously prevailed is broadened to include the civil law to permit creation of an independent tribunal which can rule on certain economic and business matters. This greatly modifies the emphasis of the old legislation on the "punishment" of individuals and corportation.
2. A list of practices subject to outright prohibition (Sections 16-26) is left to the courts to deal with. This removes from the main portion of the law the concept of "undueness" in the limitation of competition. The overall effect is that of conferring much greater clarity on competition law.
3. Through the agency of the Competitive Practices Tribunal, an expert body will be available to determine the relative advantages and disadvantages of mergers, and to rule on the acceptability of specialization and export agreements, trade practices, and other aspects of competition policy in accordance with criteria established in the act.

---

*This chapter was written by Professor G. B. Reschenthaler of the Faculty of Business Administration, University of Alberta.

4. A major new ingredient of the proposed Competition Act is the extension of competition policy to service industries. With the exception of certain aspects of the insurance industry, the present Combines Investigation Act applies only to those industries that actually produce, transport, store, distribute or sell physical articles, whether it is a ton of iron ore or a toothbrush.

PER SE CRIMINAL OFFENCES

The proposed bill listed ten offences which were to be considered directly by the courts as criminal violations under the Criminal Code (see Figure 7-1). These per se offences specified in S. 16(1) included agreements between two or more parties:

1. To fix prices
2. To allocate markets
3. To limit production or supply
4. To limit facilities for production or distribution
5. To lessen or limit quality, grades or kinds of products
6. To limit channels of distribution
7. To prevent market entry or expansion
8. To cause withdrawal from a market
9. To boycott buyers or sellers-refusal to sell
10. To rig tenders

The proposed bill treated these offences as illegal per se; consequently, the courts would only be required to make a finding of fact that an offence occurred for the government to obtain a conviction.

The proposed legislation [S. 16(1) and (2)] proscribed agreements to rig tenders and would have permitted the courts in examining price conspiracies in the form of identical tenders to accept as evidence of conspiracy the submission of identical bids provided the service or commodity being tendered was not normally sold on the basis of a regular or ordinary price. Unfortunately, this provision would not have prevented formula bidding, which accounts for many instances of identical bids.

Most of the foregoing offences were prohibited under the existing Combines Investigation Act (S. 32) when they could be demonstrated to be lessening competition "unduly." Being a criminal offence, price-fixing conspiracies had to meet a high standard of proof (beyond a reasonable doubt) that competition had been lessened unduly.

The bill also provided certain exemptions from the sweeping nature of the per se offences. These exemptions included the following agreements [S. 16(3)]:

FIGURE 7-1

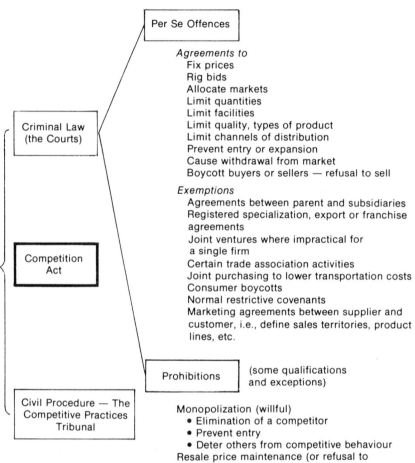

Per Se Offences

Agreements to
Fix prices
Rig bids
Allocate markets
Limit quantities
Limit facilities
Limit quality, types of product
Limit channels of distribution
Prevent entry or expansion
Cause withdrawal from market
Boycott buyers or sellers — refusal to sell

Exemptions
Agreements between parent and subsidiaries
Registered specialization, export or franchise
agreements
Joint ventures where impractical for
a single firm
Certain trade association activities
Joint purchasing to lower transportation costs
Consumer boycotts
Normal restrictive covenants
Marketing agreements between supplier and
customer, i.e., define sales territories, product
lines, etc.

Criminal Law
(the Courts)

Competition
Act

Civil Procedure — The
Competitive Practices
Tribunal

Prohibitions   (some qualifications
                 and exceptions)

Monopolization (willful)
• Elimination of a competitor
• Prevent entry
• Deter others from competitive behaviour
Resale price maintenance (or refusal to
sell if not accept RPM)
Professional and amateur sports
Misleading advertising — "credulous man" test
• Price
• Guarantees/warranties
• Performance/life
• Other materially misleading facts
Tests and testimonials
Pyramid selling (where misleading)
Referral selling
Bait-and-switch selling
Selling above advertised prices
Games/Lotteries and similar product promotions
• Disclosure of value by area and chances
of winning
• No undue delay in distribution
• Random distribution by area

Mergers
Restrictive trade practices
• Price discrimination
• Promotional allowances
• Tied sales
• Directed selling
• Exclusive dealing
• Reciprocal buying
• Entrenching a
monopoly power
• Delivered pricing
• Refusal to deal
Registered agreements
• Export
• Franchise
• Specialization
Interlocking directorates

1. Agreements between officers of a parent company and its sub-sidiary
2. Registered specialization, export and franchising agreements
3. Joint ventures where it was economically impractical for a single firm to proceed alone
4. Certain trade association activities

   - Collection and publication of industry statistics
   - Establishment of product standards
   - Exchange of credit information
   - Definitions of commercial terminology
   - Cooperation in research and development
   - Restrictions on industry advertising
   - Agreements on sizes and shapes of containers

5. Joint purchasing agreements to reduce transportation costs
6. Consumer boycotts
7. Normal restrictive covenants limited to reasonable time and place limitations between a seller and buyer of an established business wherein the seller agreed not to compete
8. Agreements to permit normal market arrangements between a supplier and customer in such matters as defining sales terri-tories and product lines

These proposed exemptions did not represent a departure from the existing legislation. The exemptions were either formally recognized in the old S.32 or had not been the subject of successful prosecutions.

The failure of the government to define the conditions under which it would be "impractical" for a single firm to develop a product, thus necessitating a joint venture, was unfortunate. The government clearly had in mind cases of financial stringency and situations where single firms lack technical know-how. However, given the limitations which were proposed for mergers, the formation of many joint ventures would have been likely had Bill C-256 been enacted.

The exemption of agreements between buyers and sellers defining sales territories and product lines needed rewording to insure that it applied only to manufacturer sales representatives and *new* firms.

The wording of this exemption is taken from the *Explanatory Notes;* the bill itself was far more ambiguous. Part II, S.16, ss.(3)(g) simply exempted "a restrictive practice as defined in ss.40(1) between a supplier and his customer. But ss.40(1) refers exclusively to restrictive practices so the reference must be to S.40(2), (c) and (d) which permitted directed selling and exclusive dealing agreements where "the practice is reasonably necessary in order to facilitate the entry or introduction of a new firm or a new commodity or service into a market and is not carried on for period of time that is longer than is reasonable for such a purpose." Exclusive dealing arrangements were also to be permitted where "the practice is reasonably necessary in order to facilitate the entry or introduction of a new firm or a new commodity or service into a market and is not carried on for period of time that is longer than is reasonable for such a purpose." Exclusive dealing arrangements were also to be permitted where "the practice is incidental to, and reasonably necessary for, the purpose of enabling two or more persons to carry on business under a common trade description or designation and is not significantly restrictive of competition."

OTHER INDICTABLE OFFENCES
(see Figure 7-1)

Monopolization (S.17)

The proposed legislation included significant provisions prohibiting willful monopolization. Specifically, "No person . . . shall for the purpose of completely or substantially controlling a market, willfully engage in behaviour that is intended :

- To eliminate a competitor
- To prevent entry into a market
- To deter or prevent another person from engaging in competitive behaviour

While the Government maintained[4] that evidence of predatory practices was required for action under this section, the offence was so generally and vaguely worded that it might have been possible to prosecute almost any dominant firm for any action which adversely affected a competitor, including direct and general price competition. Furthermore, while the courts could impose fines and issue orders of prohibition, there was no provision for remedial steps which would lead to the restoration of competition in industries where it had ceased to be a significant force.

Resale Price Maintenance (S.18)

These prohibitions were broadened and the existing defences for price maintenance which had been enacted in 1960 were eliminated.[5] Suggested selling prices could only be affixed to wrappings or used in advertisements if it was made clear that the product could be sold at a lower price.

The outright prohibition on resale price maintenance through refusal to sell promised to end the practice. A general prohibition with no defences would have protected the manufacturer's interest since he had no need to fear discriminatory action by retailers. In effect, the proposed legislation recognized the right to buy of a wholesaler or retailer.

The only loss to a manufacturer was the threat to implicit price-fixing arrangement in oligopolistic industries. The relative price stability which might be possible when only a handful of manufacturers dominate an industry might be undermined by price competition at the retail level. However, it is difficult to see any way in which this increased price competition between manufacturers could fail to serve the public interest in terms of its effect on prices, employment and productivity.

Misleading Advertising (S.20)

These offences were broadened. The courts were to determine whether or not an advertisement was "materially"-misleading. The test provided for in the legislation was whether a *credulous* man would be misled. The bill detailed specific types of misleading advertising and outlined many abuses at length; as well, attention was directed to misleading price claims, performance tests and fictitious testimonials. This, no doubt, reflected the increased strength of the consumer movement in Canada. The proposed bill, by adopting the credulous man standard, promised to ease the standard of evidence necessary for conviction considerably in comparison to the prevailing "reasonable" man standard under which few cases involving other than price advertising had been won.

The existing (1971) law on misleading advertising prohibited not only misleading price advertising (S.36), but also advertising which made misleading claims or statements of fact (S.37). The types of activities which the Bureau of Competition Policy viewed as constituting misleading advertising under the existing S.37, which had become law in July 1969, included:[6]

- A misleading statement of fact in an advertisement. Example: "Below our cost" when the selling price is, in fact, higher than the delivered price of the article to the retailer.
- A statement of performance not supported by an adequate test. Example: Rope advertised as "2,000-pound test" where no adequate and proper test of the rope has been made.
- Deceptive use of contests.
  Example: "You are the lucky winner of our grand award" when, in fact, the "award" was not exceptional in that many people received the identical mailing piece.
- "Free" offers that are not, in fact, free.
  Example: Receipt of the "free" gift is contingent on the purchase of another article or articles which could be purchased through conventional channels at lower prices.
- Bait-and-switch operations where the item used as bait was not in fact, held for sale by the advertiser. This is the practice of advertising an article at an exceptionally low price with the intention not of selling that article, but of switching customers to other goods.

- Contests purporting to award prizes where such prizes are not, in fact available.

  Example: An advertiser announces planned distribution of $25,000 in prizes but, in fact, does not provide for the distribution of prizes.
- The "stuffed flat."

  Example: An advertiser using the classified section purports to be selling his household furniture whereas, in fact, he is selling goods from other sources.
- Clip-and-paste solicitations.

  Example: A direct mail device in which, typically, the customer is invited to verify a listing in a directory but which, when signed and returned, amounts to an order for which he may be invoiced.
- Misrepresentation of origin

  Example: A manufacturer encloses a foreign-made article in a display package marked "made in Canada."

More important to consumers than the changes in the proposed bill was the number of prosecutions undertaken by the Department of Consumer and Corporate Affairs in 1969, 1970 and 1971. With the increased emphasis on consumer interests, the government assembled the machinery and people necessary for detection and prosecution. For the year ended March 31, 1970 two convictions for false and misleading advertising under S.33D (now S.36) were obtained. For the year ended March 31, 1971 there were fifteen convictions. In 1969-70 there were twenty-five convictions for misleading price advertising under S.33C (now S.37) and in 1970-71, there were twenty-eight convictions. The government won convictions in about 70 percent of the cases taken to court in the years 1969 and 1970.[7]

Unfortunately, the direct penalties imposed in these cases probably did not serve as a significant deterrent. Of the thirty fines imposed for misleading advertising convictions in the period August 1, 1969 to November 30, 1970, only one exceeded $1,000 and that was a fine of $3,000 levied against Imperial Tobacco. In each case, orders of prohibition were issued. Excluding the Imperial conviction, the average fine per charge on conviction was $147. In most cases the attorney fees exceeded the fines. Business complained loudly over alleged ambiguities in the phrase "misleading" and also over the conviction rate. There was a fear that businesses would be assumed guilty whether convicted or not.[8] Bill C-256 provided for substantially larger fines than those imposed before 1971.

Under the proposed law certain other marketing practices were also treated as indictable offences under the Criminal Code.

Pyramid Selling (S.22)

This practice was prohibited unless the sponsors disclosed to a potential entrant the gains he might expect to earn on the basis of the level the scheme had reached in his likely sales area.

Referral Selling (S.23)

These types of marketing arrangements were prohibited.

Bait-and Switch Selling (S.24)

It would become an offence to advertise a product at a bargain price unless reasonable quantities of the advertised product were available in terms of a normal response to the advertisement or the availability of a limited quantity was specifically stated. Unfortunately, there is probably no effective way to eliminate this trade practice completely since the proposed conditions could easily be met and bait-and-switch tactics still be utilized.

Selling at Higher Than Advertised Prices (S.25)

A merchant would be required to offer an advertised commodity for sale at the advertised price or less.

Games, Lotteries and Similar Product Promotion Schemes (S.26)

These were to be permitted only when they conformed to specified ground rules. The new requirements included:

- Fair disclosure of the number, value, geographic area and distribution of prizes and the chances of a contestant winning a prize.
- No undue delay in distribution of prizes.
- A random distribution of prizes as to time and area of allocation.

COMPETITIVE PRACTICES TRIBUNAL

The most important innovation in Bill C-256 was a proposal to enact *civil* procedures respecting a number of trade practices to be enforced by a civil quasi-judicial tribunal (Parts I and III). The proposed tribunal would have been empowered to conduct public hearings on a much less formal basis and with less demanding rules of evidence than occur in criminal proceedings. All of the proposals involving the civil tribunal were founded on the assumption that it was possible to enact civil legislation that would be held by the courts to be within the constitutional powers of the federal government.[9]

The proposed civil tribunal (Competitive Practices Tribunal) would have been composed of seven members appointed for ten-year terms and selected as to bring to their work a mixture of relevant expertise in economics, business and law. The tribunal would conduct hearings, adjudicate and impose remedies. It would, in addition, have undertaken economic studies and issued periodic reports.

While the tribunal would conduct itself in accordance with the principles of "natural justice," its proceedings would be less formal than those now followed in Canadian courts. As envisioned by the Economic Council:

> The prevailing atmosphere [in hearings] would ideally be one of a collective search for understanding of business practice and its economic effects, and for the progressively clearer discernment of the nature of the public interest in particular cases. In line with this objective, the tribunal might wish to give witnesses considerable freedom in their presentation of evidence.[10]

Within the framework of the new legislation the tribunal was envisioned as a court of record which would bring its judgement to bear in an examination of anti-competitive practices. The Competitive Practices Tribunal would perform a broad range of functions (see Figure 7-1), each of which may be examined briefly:

Corporate Mergers (S.32-35)

The tribunal would examine and register corporate mergers where combined assets or annual revenues of the merging companies exceed $5 million or one of the firms was foreign-owned. This review was to determine whether such mergers were on balance in the public interest and, in cases where they might be judged not in the public interest, the tribunal was empowered to impose or recommend appropriate remedies. The tribunal could also give advance approval to proposed mergers. Once advance approval was given, the tribunal could not later recommend action against the merger.

Generally speaking, a merger would have been permissible if an improvement in efficiency unaccompanied by any adverse effect on competition was foreseen. Where an adverse competitive effect was expected, the tribunal could still approve the merger if a substantial portion of the benefits from resulting improvements in efficiency might be expected to accrue to the community in the form of better products or lower prices.

One weakness of this merger section was that neither the bill nor the accompanying 130-page *Explanatory Notes* ever defined what constituted a "substantial portion" of the benefits or how the tribunal was to weigh product improvement. This is particularly significant since at one point in the *Explanatory Notes,* though not in the bill itself, the government states that a merger would be permitted "if substantial benefits will accrue to the community through increased efficiency, better products *or* lower prices." (emphasis added).

The *Interim Report* of the Economic Council, which was written by economists, adopted the sole criterion of economic efficiency apparently assuming that lower costs would invariably be passed on to the consumer in the form of lower prices. In fact, economic efficiency is accepted as the *only* proper goal of combines policy.[11] The legal or political advisors to the government apparently recognized the naivete of this view and, consequently, the bill instructed the tribunal to insure that substantial benefits would be passed on to consumers in a reasonable period of time. However, given the existing structure of the Canadian economy, it may have been impossible for the tribunal to accomplish that goal without engaging in direct price regulation, which was not specifically included in its terms of reference. Application of this section also required determination and allocation of actual cost savings from mergers involving large multiproduct companies. Since such cost allocation decisions are retrospective, extremely complex and highly subjective,[12] the tribunal, unless competently staffed in depth, would have found itself hopelessly overpowered by an army of accountants, lawyers and economists representing affected corporations.

The government did provide some guidelines for the tribunal for evaluating mergers; indeed, it provided an outline for an abbreviated industry study. The following excerpt from S.34 of the bill clearly reveals those elements which the government felt were of significant importance [S.34(4)]:

> In determining whether or not a merger has resulted, is resulting or is likely to result in significantly less competition than would have existed or would have been likely to exist under any of the conditions referred to in paragraphs (1) (a) and (b), the tribunal shall take into consideration the extent to which any of the following factors are present:
>
> (a) the number of independent firms in the relevant market or industry before the merger or proposed merger, and the number of such firms after the merger or that would exist after the merger if it were effected, as the case may be, their respective sizes and their respective actual and potential shares of the relevant market or industry,
>
> (b) the history of previous mergers on the part of any party to the merger, and whether there is a trend toward or away from concentration in the relevant market or industry,
>
> (c) whether or not the merger is likely to make entry into the relevant market or industry by existing or new firms more difficult or to make more difficult the expansion of an existing firm in the relevant market or industry,

(d) the history of coercive, collusive or predatory action or other anti-competitive behaviour on the part of any party to the merger,

(e) the evidence of intent, by or through the merger, to reduce competition or dominate the relevant market or industry,

(f) the amount and intensity of domestic and import competition in the relevant market or industry and the level of any relevant duties of customs or other like factors, and

(g) the likelihood that the merger will result in the foreclosure of sales opportunities or sources of supply in the relevant market or industry,

and any other factors that the tribunal considers to be relevant.

In determining whether a merger has resulted, is resulting or is likely to result in a significant improvement of efficiency over that which any of the parties to the merger could have achieved by commencing or continuing to carry on business independently or in any other manner that would have led to less restriction of competition than resulted or would be likely to result from the merger, the tribunal shall take into consideration the following factors:

(a) the economics of the particular market or industry, including the minimum efficient size of plants and firms therein,

(b) the size of each of the parties involved in the merger and of any resultant firm, relative to the minimum efficient size of firms in the particular market or industry,

(c) any likelihood that the merger will bring about economies of scale.

(d) any likelihood that the merger will facilitate the meeting of import competition,

(e) any likelihood that the merger will facilitate entry into or expansion of export trade, and

(f) any likely effect of the merger on research and development, and any other factors that the tribunal considers to be relevant.

The tribunal would register all mergers involving a foreign owned company where the acquiring company was controlled outside Canada. This provision was to provide policy makers with a continuing record of the nature and extent of foreign ownership in the Canadian economy. It is, however, difficult to envision how this provision could have protected Canadian subsidiaries from being affected by American foreign and anti-trust policy. For example, few subsidiaries of American corporations are likely to propose mergers if the U. S. government is expected to oppose the mergers.

It is unlikely that the proposed act would have prevented the takeover of a Canadian firm by a foreign company not already estab-lished in Canada. Only a very broad interpretation of monopolization would have permitted the bill to have any effect on foreign takeovers. It is possible to reason that if a large integrated multinational cor-poration with substantial economic power merged with a dominant Canadian firm, the net effect would be a diminution of competition in Canada. The proposed bill did permit the tribunal to prohibit a merger involving an international corporation if the effect of the merger was to entrench the firm's monopoly position, to entrench an international cartel or to restrict future Canadian exports. The whole question, however, is academic since there are very few dominant firms in the Canadian economy which are not already foreign owned.[13]

Export, Specialization and Franchise Agreements (S.27-30)

The tribunal could examine certain types of proposed intercompany agreements respecting exports, specialization of production and franchises to determine whether the agreements were on balance in the public interest. If judged to be in the public interest, the tribunal would place the agreements in a public register and designate them as "registered" export, specialization or franchise agreements. Normally all export and franchise agreements would be approved. The primary test in the cases of export and specialization agreements was to be whether a substantial part of the benefits from increased efficiency would be passed on to the public in the form of lower prices or improved products. These agreements would also be permitted where they were necessary to meet import competition. Specialization agreements would be valid for five years unless challenged for competitive abuses, while export agreements was designed to permit the development of export sales. Specialization agreements were envisioned as permitting longer production runs, fewer change overs, lower inventory levels and larger, more specialized and, consequently, more efficient Canadian industrial plants.

The attraction of the specialization agreements, which, for example, would permit one tire manufacturer to produce the tires of one particular type for the entire industry while another company produced a different type, was that they were expected to result in lower unit costs without causing any visible increase in industrial concentration. Again, the council and government's implicit assumption was that the lower costs would, even when accompanied by high industrial concentration and increased interdependence, result in substantial benefits being received by the public without detailed regulation or reduced tariffs.

The principle problem with the legalization of both specialization and export agreements is the opportunity and temptation these arrangements provide for participants to engage in illegal activities. At the very least, both bring otherwise competing management together and promote a sense of commonality and mutual interdependence. In both instances, discussion of some aspects of individual company costs and long-term corporate objectives arise. The temptation and opportunity for consideration of domestic market planning will be of concern to the economist interested in promoting competitive markets domestically.

Restrictive Trade Practices

The tribunal was to be empowered to examine the employment of certain trade practices to determine whether their employment was on balance in the public interest, and in cases where they were judged to be not in the public interest, impose or recommend appropriate remedies including orders to cease and desist. Generally speaking these practices were to be prohibited, although, under special circumstances they could be permitted.

Price Discrimination (S.37 and 38)

Price discrimination between competing customers in the sale of like quantities and qualities of products was to be prohibited under normal circumstances. Discrimination was to be permitted where justified by differences in *delivery costs*, where reasonably necessary to assist in entry to a new market, where no significant competitive advantage was involved, where a general reduction in prices was expected to occur, and where necessary to meet import competition.

The tribunal would have faced the difficult tasks of defining like quantities and qualities and of determing what constituted a significant competitive advantage. Cost differences associated with volume purchases were prohibited under this section without regard to competitive impact. It was surprising that some test of economic significance and competitive effect was not introduced in this section given the frequently expressed criticism of American legislation in this area.

Price discrimination was previously prohibited under S.33A of the Combines Investigation Act. However, by the end of 1971 there had been only one decided case which the Crown lost.[14] The revisions provided in the proposed S.37 and S.38 would have made price discrimination by a dominant firm extremely difficult to justify.

Promotional Allowances (S.37 and 39)

Promotional allowances would be viewed as a special form of price discrimination and consequently face the same test for justification.

Tied Sales (S.40)

A tied sale occurs when a customer is required to buy other products from a supplier as a condition of obtaining supplies of a specifically desired product. Tying arrangements would only be permitted where required by technological relationships between products or when they were an essential part of a franchise agreement or other arrangement.

The tribunal would be required to decide whether it was imperative technologically that an IBM computer use punch cards manufactured by IBM. It would also be required to determine what constitutes an "essential part" of a franchise agreement or other arrangements. The system permits a producer with market power in one sector of the economy to use that power to foreclose compeititon in others.

Directed Sales (S.40)

Directed selling is a distribution system in which each distributor is assigned a geographically defined market. If he sells outside that market, he will face the denial of future supplies. Under the proposed bill directed selling was not to be permitted for major established companies. The system prevents competition among distributors.

Exclusive Dealing (S.40)

Where exclusive dealing is practiced, a customer is required to sell only those products received from or designated by the supplier. The system can limit the number of retail outlets in a given market.

Reciprocal Buying (S.40)

Reciprocal buying involves an agreement by companies to obtain a substantial part of their buying requirements from each other. It has the potential — rarely demonstrated — to foreclose markets. No offence was created under the proposed act when reciprocal buying was necessary to implement a specialization agreement.

Delivered Pricing (S. 42)

Delivered pricing is a practice which involves a supplier refusing to permit a customer from taking delivery at the most economical sales point of the supplier and then requiring the customer to accept delivery at another point of sale at a delivered price which includes a real or arbitrary transportation cost. The system can be utilized to insure that all producers, irrespective of their plant location, quote identical delivered prices to any given customer.

ENTRENCHMENT OF MONOPOLY POWER

When one or more firms acting alone or in concert were completely or substantially in control of a market or accounted for all or substantially all of a commodity or service in a market and had engaged in restrictive practices, the tribunal was empowered to prohibit the companies from further entrenching themselves under S.37(g) and S.48(1)(b). The tribunal could "establish conditions which will permit new entrants into a particular market and restore a higher level of competition."[15] While this section was potentially a forceful weapon for attacking abuses of market power, several operational problems would have been encountered. For instance, the precise means by which the tribunal could create proper conditions in any given situation were not detailed in the legislation, and the power to establish proper conditions was expressed in extremely vague terms. A key question left unanswered was the procedure which the tribunal would follow if an entrenched monopoly was faced with new foreign import competition in a limited geographic market. Such entrenched monopolists might use price discrimination in the competitive region — a legal activity — which, however, results in maintaining its entrenched position — an illegal activity!

SUPPLEMENTARY PROVISIONS

The proposed bill also adopted a number of supplementary provisions which were recommended in the *Interim Report*.

Bank Act Revisions (S.101 and 102.1)

The Bank Act would be amended to prohibit price fixing and other anti-competitive practices in banking activities which are not directly regulated by government. These activities included joint determination of checking service charges and collusive agreements not to compete for established business customers. An interesting question was immediately raised as to what would be the reaction of the major chartered banks if the tribunal ordered them not to charge the same price for checking services. In short, if the tribunal had no control over structure in this industry, any effort to control conduct might have been doomed to frustration.

Collective Bargaining Agreements (S.89)

Collective bargaining agreements remained exempt.

The Insurance Industry (S.90)

Price-setting agreements between general insurance companies would be prohibited. Publicly regulated functions of the insurance companies would not have been affected. The practice of the majority of general insurance companies in Canada of following rates as recommended by the insurance association would probably have been terminated. One solution for the insurance companies would have been to request rate regulation by provincial government insurance boards. The effect of this would be to eliminate all price competition in most lines of insurance.

Investment Dealers (S.91)

Collective agreements by investment dealers in underwriting security and bond issues were exempted.

Regulated Industries (S. 92 and 93)

Regulated activities of regulated firms were exempted.

Professional Groups (S.16 and 92)

The activities of professional associations, except where included under direct provincial regulation, would fall under the proposed legislation. The Economic Council and the federal government were both apparently convinced that not all of the price-setting and licensing activities of professional groups were in the public interest. However, these groups could protect themselves by requesting the establishing of provincial regulations.

Professional and Amateur Sports (S.19)

Professional and amateur sports agreements which imposed "unreasonable" conditions for participation or limit "unduly" the opportunity of a player to negotiate with and play for the team of his choice were to be prohibited. However, the courts were required to take account of certain special circumstances sometimes encountered in sports. The courts were instructed to consider the possibility that when a sport is organized internationally that otherwise restrictive conditions might be reasonable for that purpose. The courts were also required to recognize the desirability of maintaining a reasonable balance among competing teams. Thus, for some inexplicable reason the government adopted the position of the Economic Council that professional sports should be subject to the Combines Act. It then proceeded to introduce two loopholes which made virtually certain that a sport which was organized in the United States and Canada (hockey, baseball, soccer), or which could present the only argument that had ever been seriously offered for the reserve clauses common in sports contracts — that of maintaining team balance — would be exempt from the law.

Administration

Under the proposed bill, the new tribunal could undertake specific as well as general inquiries. Specific inquiries might be undertaken following the request to the tribunal by a person materially affected by a restrictive practice or upon the petition by six Canadian citizens to the commissioner — the chief administration and enforcement official. The commissioner could also initiate specific inquiries where he believed a violation had or was likely to occur. General inquiries could be initiated only at the direct request of the Minister of Consumer and Corporate Affairs. Criminal Code offences would be prosecuted directly in the courts by the Attorney General of Canada, who could personally initiate criminal complaints.

Remedies provided for in the proposed legislation included:

Orders of Prohibition (S.59 and 78)

Orders of prohibition could be issued to enjoin an offending party by the tribunal and by the federal court.

Dissolution and Divestiture (S.54)

Dissolution and divestiture including the power to order the termination of interlocking directorates was permitted.

Patent Rights (S.51)

Modification or removal of patent and other rights would be possible.

Private Actions for Damages (S.55)

Double damages could be obtained by parties injured by restrictive practices. These could be obtained by court order at the time of conviction of the offending party or the damaged party might request damages in civil litigation. The bill instructed the courts to accept as evidence the findings of the court which convicted the offending party in the government's case. If the latter provision was not included, each civil action would require a complete retrial of the offending party. This provision represented a major departure from previous legislation.

Fines and Imprisonment (S.73, 74 and 75)

Prison terms to two years and fines up to $1 million might be imposed for conviction on a first offence and up to $2 million on a conviction for a second offence by the court. Officers of corporations would be personally liable for the decisions made by subordinates regardless of whether they were aware of the acts committed when their corporate responsibilities clearly assign them supervisory roles. An acceptable defence would be for the accused manager to prove that the acts were clearly contrary to his enunciated policies and that they occurred in the absence of his knowledge. This provision was designed to avoid the type of situation which developed in the electrical price-fixing conspiracy case in the United States in the 1950s when senior management denied any knowledge of the activities of subordinates. It would also impose an incentive for internal policing by management. Convictions might have been extremely difficult to obtain under this section, since management could issue a large number of notices to employees admonishing against restrictive practices and still provide implicit or verbal support for "understandings." It should be noted that the existing law did not specify limits for fines or prison terms.

GENERAL EVALUATION

Overall, the proposed combines legislation represented a marked improvement over the existing legislation in spite of the many gaps and ambiguities which remained in it. The government was compelled early to respond to the objection of business spokesmen that the law would place excessive arbitrary powers in the hands of the tribunal (see Chapter 8). These apprehensions may be directly attributed to the failure of the government to provide the tribunal with adequate operational guidelines and the inability of the firms involved to appeal tribunal rulings to the courts on other than points of law. The government also might have attempted to define more narrowly what constituted "substantial benefits" from increased efficiencies. This later point was a particularly serious problem since there is no way under the proposed bill that the tribunal could reconsider a decision once made. This meant that if the benefits from increased efficiency were initially passed on to the public and later reallocated to profits, the tribunal would be powerless to object.

Any evaluation of the proposals of the government, or indeed, the Economic Council's *Interim Report*, upon which they were based, must immediately raise the question: Whose interest is the economic system designed to serve? While a case might be made for the interests of particular groups, the government wholly, and the Economic Council to a lesser extent, accepted the proposition that a combines policy must be primarily designed to serve the public interest which is equated with the consumer's interest.[16] Thus the government went beyond the Economic Council's exclusive concern with static and dynamic efficiency and, in the proposed legislation, designed a framework in which the consumer's interest became paramount.

The new legislation did little to reduce concentrations of economic power which currently existed in the economy. However, the bill did reflect the belief of the government that the prevention of concentration of economic power should be within the scope of combines administration. In the government's view:

Concentrations of power, which can serve to restrict opportunity and individual freedom, are not acceptable in today's social and political environment and a major objective of competition policy must be to insure that such concentrations of power are now allowed to develop.[17]

In its section on monopolization the new legislation also attempted to come to grips with economic power in the form of dominant firms. In each of these respects the government deviated from the recommendatioe Economic Council which suggested power concentration should not be a concern of combines policy and vitually failed to deal meaningfully with the dominant firm phenomenon. This difference in scope of the bill versus the *Interim Report* was well reflected in the government's insistence throughout that, while economic efficiency was a primary goal of combines enforcement, it should remain a goal only so long as the public was assured of receiving a substantial portion of its benefits in the form of lower prices or improved products. The council's report seemed to ignore the fact that the liberation of market forces, which competition policy seeks to achieve, serves no social end if it results in the concentration of economic power which may be accompanied by monopoly profits and/or inefficiency.

In setting practial working rules for an effective competition policy in the 1970s, both the government and council failed to come to grips with the more subtle forms of price control. The absence of an effective treatment of conscious parallelism, price leadership and any effective means of policing conduct of trade associations reflected, in large measure, not the failure of the council but the failure of economics as a "science" to provide an operational theory of oligopoly. Presumably the tribunal would find solutions to these problems. However, economics has not provided operationally meaningful guidelines for competition policy.

If the bill had been passed, little of a definitive nature could be predicted with regard to details. In general, however, it seems most likely that consumers, lawyers, economists and private enterprise, as a system, would all have been winners. Consumers would have received lower prices, and lawyers and economists more consulting fees. In the long run, an *effectively competitive* market system is probably the best defence the private sector can have against direct regulation and public ownership.

NOTES:

[1]"Bill C-256: An Act To Promote Competition, to provide for the general regulation of trade and commerce, to promote honest and fair dealing, to establish a Competitive Practices Tribunal and the Office of the Commissioner, to repeal the Combines Investigation Act and to make consequential amendments to the Bank Act." First Reading: June 29, 1971.

[2]Economic Council of Canada, *Interim Report on Competition Policy*, Ottawa, Queen's Printer, 1969.

[3]Department of Consumer and Corporate Affairs, *The Competition Act — Explanatory Notes*, Ottawa, mimeo, 1971, p. 21.

[4]*Explanatory Notes, op.cit.*, p. 73.

[5]Combines Investigation Act, S.38, S.38(5).

[6]Department of Consumer and Corporate Affairs, *Report of the Director of Investigation and Research — Combines Investigation Act for the Year Ended March 31, 1970*, Ottawa, Information Canada, 1970, pp. 68-69.

[7]Department of Consumer and Corporate Affairs, Bureau of Competition Policy, unpublished register of prosecutions and convictions.

[8]*Ibid.*

[9]There are a variety of opinions on the constitutionality of the Competition Act and its successor, the Stage I amendments to the Combines Act. See S. G. M. Grange, Q.C., *The Constitutionality of Federal Intervention in the Marketplace — The Competition Case*, Montreal, C.D. Howe Research Institute, 1976; Peter W. Hogg and Warren Grover, "The Constitutionality of the Competition Bill," *Canadian Business Law Journal*, Vol. 1, No. 2, April 1976, pp. 198-228; Robert S. Reid, "The New Role of the Restrictive Trade Practices Commission: A Constitutional and Administrative Viewpoint," in W. T. Stanbury (ed.), *Papers on the 1975 Amendments to the Combines Investigation Act*, Vancouver, Faculty of Commerce and Business Administration, University of British Columbia, 1976, pp. 157-186.

[10]*Interim Report, op.cit.*, p. 110.

[11]*Ibid.*, pp. 9, 19.

[12]For a particularly lucid discussion of some of the problems involved see L. A. Skeoch and B. C. McDonald, *Dynamic Change and Accountability in a Canadian Market Economy*, Ottawa, Ministry of Supply and Services Canada, 1976, pp. 260-275.

[13]Herb Gray, *Foreign Direct Investment in Canada*, Ottawa, Information Canada, 1972.

[14]*Regina v. Carnation Co. Ltd.*, (1968) 67 O.L.R. (2d) 215 (1969) 68 W.W.R. 97.

[15]*Explanatory Notes, op.cit.*, p. 73.

[16]The Government did not consider any distinction between the short-term and long-term interests of consumers.

[17]*Explanatory Notes, op.cit.*, p. 9.

Chapter 8

Business and Academic Responses to the Competition Act: June 1971 - June 1973

The Minister of Consumer and Corporate Affairs, Mr. Basford, introduced Bill C-256, the Competition Act, in the House of Comons on June 29, 1971. By several orders of magnitude, this proposal represented the most significant pro-competition, pro-consumer legislation in Canadian history.

The *Explanatory Notes* accompanying the bill incorrectly stated that the proposed legislation "does not represent a major departure from established Canadian competition policy."[1] In the *Notes,* competition policy was defined as "maintaining healthy competition so that all consumers may have freedom of choice of product and quality at the lowest possible price in respect of their requirements, be they goods or services."[2]

INITIAL EDITORIAL REACTION

The *Explanatory Notes* were much too modest. As K. Wayne McCracken, a Toronto lawyer, stated, "The bill represents a marked and, in many respects, a radical revamping of competition law in Canada."[3] The Kingston *Whig Standard* recognized the non-incremental nature of the proposed legislation when it stated, "The government has bitten off a very big and tough mouthful. Will it be able to chew it satisfactorily - and then digest it?"[4] The same point was made by the Winnipeg *Free Press,* which thought that Mr. Basford "may be too modest" in saying that the act "does not represent a major departure from established Candian competition policy."[5] Harlow Unger, correspondent of the London *Sunday Times,* described the Competition Act as "the most sweeping anti-trust legislation in North American history" and "probably the toughest set of business regulations anywhere in the free world."[6] The initial editorial reaction was mixed and not actively hostile to the bill. Perhaps the newspaper editors and columnists were waiting for business' reaction before taking a stronger position.

One week after its introduction, the *Financial Times* welcomed Bill C-256. "The old combines act was, in name and in fact, negative and punitive. The Competition Act, in name and intent, is much more positive. It introduces new economic criteria in place of deadly and unworkable legal sanctions."[7] A Victoria *Times* editorial discussed some of the criticisms of the bill, but concluded "nevertheless it represents a strong effort to help the public without imposing restrictions on business that seriously cripples it. . . ."[8] The Montreal *Star* described Mr. Basford as "a loud advocate for what he considers the consumer interest. . . ." It did, however, think that the tabling of the bill "may . . . produce a rational debate on a subject which only too often is clouded by both prejudice and ignorance."[9] This was to be a vain hope. As Professor William Neilson remarked, "The simple point is that the realities of our lobbying process will never allow us to see the issues responsibly discussed and canvassed."[10] He pointed out that hundreds of individual law firms could deploy a greater number of persons to argue the bill than the entire federal government!

Harold Buchwald, chairman of the Canadian Consumer Council, was to write later, "Almost from the introduction of [Bill C-256] the atmosphere [was] overladen with hostility and invective in the attacks on the bill and its underlying principles. And these assaults have not been limited to the expression of intellectual differences. They have been punctuated by emotionalism and vituperation."[11]

Some editorial support for the bill was evident. Under the headline "We need a new, tougher consumer law," the Peterborough *Examiner* summarized its position.

> The new legislation covers a large territory and extends to many fields. This means that the debate over it will probably be extensive and heated. But if it leads to new laws protecting the public in general and Canadian businesses in particular, it's worth every minute spent on it.[12]

An Ottawa *Le Droit* editorial, reprinted in a number of newspapers, supported the legislation.

> All considered, the bill on competition, when passed, will do more for the Canadian consumer than all other existing laws, which is the most important.[13]

Support for the bill could also be found in some of the trade periodicals. *Canadian Petroleum* saw the bill as outranking the Canada Corporations Act and the income tax reform legislation in its importance — "it will alter the very pattern of virtually every activity of the free enterprise system," the magazine said. The editorial recognized that there would be opposition to the bill but felt it was a "highly praiseworthy legislative effort."[14] The *Automotive Retailer* of Vancouver supported the legislation.

> The Competition Act as tabled represents a major step forward in the evolution of a workable and equitable competition policy

consistent with the modern needs of the market economy. At the
same time, the government's commitment is to the central policy
objective of producing an efficient and competitive economy fully
responsive to the needs and desires of all citizens.[15]

The Medicine Hat *News* raised a point that was seldom discussed in
the subsequent debate — "the Canadian authorities must ask themselves
how they shall enforce the new law . . . better than the old combines
law. It is a vital point. Without effective enforcement, the law will be of
little value."[16] The same issue was raised by the St. John's *Evening
Telegram*, "Needless to say, laws are not much good without enforcement.
Passing legislation that is then shoved into pigeonholes is merely giving
lip-service to popular outcries. The Department of Corporate Affairs
must show, by demonstration, that its law has teeth."[17] The Winnipeg
Free Press recognized the gap between the intentions and effectiveness of
the legislation.

> Consumer groups should beware, however, of judging the proposed
> act solely on the basis of the objectives sought, which may appear
> generally admirable. What is required is an effective law; one that
> will stand up in the courts and preserve competition not through
> friendly chats in the office of a commissioner but through mean-
> ingful deterrents to such interests as may be tempted to evade
> or violate the law.[18]

Recognizing the scope and complexity of the legislation, shortly
after it was introduced the department organized a series of four
seminars for the press in Montreal, Toronto, Vancouver and Winnipeg
at which senior civil servants, including the deputy minister and the
Director of Investigation and Research, explained the legislation. This
was questioned by the Calgary *Herald*.

> The proposed legislation constitutes one of the most sweeping
> reforms of business practice in the history of this country. Perhaps
> the departmental officials seek to head off criticism as they ply the
> curiosity of the media from province to province, but at least they are
> demonstrating an awareness of the fact the concern exists.[19]

The *Financial Times* referred to these meetings as part of a "road
show" and the civil servants as "Mr. Basford's barkers." The editorial
asked, "where does explanation end and propaganda begin? Does
explanation promote criticism or smother it?" The editors concluded
that "it smells too much like a propaganda campaign to ensure that the
Competition Act is presented in the form the government wants."[20]

The Toronto *Globe and Mail* stated: "There is too much in the
proposed Competition At that is ambiguous, undefined or misconceived."
However, the editors praised the government for its "flexibility about
amending proposed legislation" and cited the white paper on taxation as
an example. Like many other papers, the *Globe and Mail* advanced the

view, "It is plain that the Combines Investigation Act should be replaced. Few could be found to argue against that." But, like most editorial opinion, the paper was critical of the legislation on the matter of the tribunal — "it provides for largely autocratic and undefined rule by a tribunal insulated from Government and public alike. The Competitive Practices Tribunal would be lawmaker, policeman and judge."[21]

The Montreal *Gazette* also expressed concern about the scope of the tribunal: "Very few working Canadians wil escape the consequences of its all-pervasive influence, whether on the factory floor, in the executive suite, in the professions or self-employed," the paper wrote. The editors indicated that the Competition Act "could actively distort the character of Canada's economy and dangerously inhibit its growth." They concluded that "this is not a risk which should be comtemplated under any circumstances."[22] The Toronto *Telegram* did not want to "extend the Big Brother concept to the degree indicated by the Competition Act." The editors queried whether there was a middle-ground. "Surely there is a sensible middle-ground between 19th-century laissez-faire capitalism on the one hand and strict state control of all significant business decisions on the other."[23]

Columnist Maurice Western described the Competition Act as a "supplement to the welfare state which might perhaps be described as the schoolmarm state."[24]

We noted that very shortly after Bill C-256 was introduced the *Financial Times* had welcomed it as introducing "new economic criteria in place of deadly and unworkable legal sanctions." A little over two months later it described what it had praised as "A badly-botched bill." It argued that "It is a dangerous bill. Under the pretext of relaxing the criminal law, it establishes a civil tribunal with power to police, regulate and veto many, if not most, of the day-to-day business practices of Canadians. Under the pretext of judging business behaviour by its economic effects, it tries to impose a detailed pattern based on a highly theoretical view of the unlimited virtue of competition."[25]

EARLY BUSINESS REACTION

James W. Younger, Q.C., secretary and general counsel for the Steel Company of Canada, in September 1971, charged that Bill C-256 "betrays a frightening ideological approach to individual rights. . . . it would force a restructuring of the whole marketing and planning areas of our commercial life with unsettling and stultifying results."[26] Mr. Younger went on to argue that "the dislocation to business from implementing the legislation is likely to be serious. Business enterprise would be frustrated by the constant threat of bureaucratic review of its planning and marketing strategies." In addition, "the cost to the consumer may well exceed the benefits" and "the cost of compliance with such legislation in terms of executive and professional time and of enterpreneurial decisions delayed and actions not taken is incalculable." Finally he argued that "the legislation involves a serious encroachment by the Federal Government on the jurisdiction of the provinces over property and civil rights."[27]

Speaking at the same conference at which Mr. Younger spoke, Douglas I. W. Bruce, vice-president and secretary of Westinghouse Canada Limited effectively summarized the views of those who felt the Bill C-256 was the product of ivory tower academics:

> I have little faith that the aspirations of men can be achieved by the contemplation of economic models. It is apparent that the drafting of this Bill was much influenced by the alarming, and apparently growing, tendency of the Government of Canada to rely on persons (usually academics), whom it chooses to call "experts," in establishing policy. It is only after the plaster is set that those who will have to live with the consequences are invited in to look for the "cracks."[28]

Yet, Dr. A. J. R. Smith, then chairman of the Economic Council of Canada, argued that "the basic philosophy underlying the bill as a whole, as well as many of the provisions in it . . . follow . . . closely the Economic Council's general approach." He went on to say, "The concepts that we eventually adopted emerged from a good deal of discussion among a broad cross-section of people from different parts of the country."[29]

Mr. Younger also raised the issue of the removal of the word "unduly" in respect of price fixing and simlar conspiracies. He argued,

> What businessmen have said is not, let's get rid of the concept of undueness; they have said, let's retain the concept of undueness and in addition to the structural criteria which have been used in the past, introduce the possibility of a defence based on performance. . . . if we show that our prices . . . have not been unreasonably high or our returns have not been unreasonable, and so on, then we shouldn't be convicted.[30]

To this point Professor Milton Moore replied, "But that is not the relevant test. The relevant test has to be what the performance would have been if the industry had been competitive."[31]

Lawyer Gordon Blair, who had represented a number of large corporations in combines cases, raised an issue which was to be part of business' complaints with respect to the Competition Act, namely, that the act was excessively concerned with price competition and low prices for consumers. He said, "it is this picking on that aspect of lowest price that concerns me, because there is no point in having lowest price to consumers if the consumers are unemployed and unable to buy."[32] H. J.

Hemens, Q.C., vice-president, secretary and general counsel of DuPont of Canada echoed this theme. He noted that while the Department of Consumer and Corporate Affairs was seeking "the popularization of its proposed Competition Act . . . in what must be conceded to be at least a lateral attack on freedom of contract and therefore on free entrprise," Manpower and Immigration's advertisements were stating, "Jobs don't grow on trees. They grow from the initiative and enterprise of the private sector. . . ."[33]

After having argued that Bill C-256 amounted to an all-out assault on freedom of commerce or freedom of contract in commercial matters,[34] Mr. Hemens endorsed "a reasonable competition policy," saying,

> My experience with fairly large-sized business is that I know of no really large-sized business that is not in favour of a competition policy. The only difference is that they are in favour of a reasonable competition policy.[35]

By this he meant that competition policy must serve larger national economic objectives, specifically "the attainment of a vigorous and sustained rate of long-term economic growth . . . which is largely dependent on [the] achievement of optimum productivity."[36] He repeatedly rejected what he described as "competition for the sake of competition."[37] Hemens concluded by stating that "the country's competition policy should . . . be directed toward encouraging freedom of commerce and freedom to contract to the point where it is clearly demonstrable that an action or a series of actions contravenes the public interest."[38] In this argument it is taken as self-evident that freedom of contract is a superordinate objective (or value), that the burden of proof is on those who would constrain this freedom and that this burden can be discharged only if it is "clearly demonstrable" that unconstrained freedom of contract is not in the public interest.

Unlike the overwhelming majority of businessmen and lawyer, Gordon Blair supported the move to civil procedures with adjudicatory power lodged in a specialized tribunal:

> . . . this type of complicated economic determination is beyond the capacity of a traditional court, for the reason that courts are bound by rigid rules of procedure and the principle of *stare decisis.* They are also bound by the limited experience of the judiciary. I do not find it surprising to have this type of decision-making confined to an administrative type of tribunal which within certain fixed guidelines is able to exercise considerable discretion.[39]

The more common business view of the tribunal was voiced by J. W. Younger of the Steel Company of Canada who saw it as "centralizing . . . decision-making power in the hands of a group of technocrats bound only by the vaguest rules."[40] Mr. Younger indicated that the "highest priority in our society must be given . . . to the rule of law." By this he meant a free and responsible society in which the role of the state is narrowly circumscribed, where most relationships are determined by freedom of contract enforced by private rather than public law and where the courts stand as impartial arbiters between individuals and between the state and subject."[41] Like Mr. Hemens, Younger found the extended list of prohibited trade practices objectionable because of his ideological commitment to "the principle that everything ought to be permitted unless it is clearly wrong and its corollary that acts, prohibited by legislation, ought to be clearly defined."[42] Mr. Younger only occasionally descended into specifics but on one point, at least, he did so. "At the very least," he argued, the concept of "undueness" ought to be restored in defining illegal restaints in trade. "In addition," he continued, "the concept of the relevant market . . . should be liberalized to take into account the dynamic nature of competition, and a defence based on performance should be permitted."[43] This modest mouthful would have the effect of almost entirely negating the conspiracy provisions of the Combines Act (S. 32). Mr. Younger, by this proposal, would not simply have us return to *status quo ante*, he would have us return to the anti-combines law of 1889, which, as we have seen, was completely ineffectual.

G. L. Draeske, speaking for the Council of Forest Industries of British Columbia, in a long letter to the minister in October stated that the objectives set out in the Economic Council's *Interim Report* were contradictory. One was "intended to benefit the Canadian *economy*" and the other was "intended to benefit Canadian *consumers*, and it is the latter policy which appears in Bill C-256."[44] Mr. Draeske was particularly offended by the anti-merger provisions of the bill, (supporting as he does the "rationalization" of the Canadian economy to facilitate competition in export markets), the constraints on price discrimination, the elimination of the requirement of "undueness" and the establishment of a number of *per se* offences which would not require *mens rea* or guilty intent.

K. Wayne McCracken pointed out that the conspiracy section of the Competition Act, which removed the requirement of "undueness," "may make unlawful many agreements in their entirety and may prohibit certain standard clauses in various categories of agreements."[45] He cited the following examples: shopping centre leases, rights of first refusal, agencies and distributorships, employment agreements, financing convenants and joint ventures. McCracken argued that the "public's interest in free competition" will be best protected by provisions which would outlaw "agreements that lessen competition to a material extent"[46] rather than making them illegal *per se*. He was referring to the sections on price discrimination. These were described by the chief administrative officer of the Grocery Products Manufacturers of Canada as being "up on cloud nine."[47]

The attacks on the bill continued. Gerard Filion, president of the Canadian Manufacturers' Association, who was later to come under indictment in the Hamilton dredging scandal,[48] criticized Bill C-256 because for some offences the onus of proof shifted from the Crown to the defendant, because it undermined the businessman's freedom of contract, because the tests to be used by the tribunal were "too narrow, particularly in their emphasis on cost reductions and the passing of such savings to the consumer" and finally because of the "lodging of virtually uncontrolled discretion over important business decisions with a group of fallible government appointees."[49]

H. P. Bell-Irving, president of the Canadian Real Estate Association, charged that Bill C-256 "would destroy the real estate business as it is now known." Bell-Irving admitted, however, that "the Multiple Listing Service is . . . a monopolistic tool but it can be used to maintain standards within our industry."[50]

Peter V. V. Betts, Q.C., viewed the act as a "vendetta against prosperity" and counselled politicians not to "lash out against business for its effect on the grandstand," but for "moderation in all things."[51] Mr. Betts was also concerned about the "whim(s) of a politically controlled Tribunal,"[52] describing it later in his article as an "economic czar."[53] He concluded with the following: "Hail Caesar, those about to die salute you!"[54]

Bruce Johnson, president of the Institute of Canadian Advertising, complained, "If they [the courts] interpret the Act literally, advertising creativity will be terrifically stifled."[55]

THE ACADEMICS' VIEWS OF THE COMPETITION ACT

Academics were broadly supportive of the proposed legislation, but some were critical of both the draftsmanship and the central thrust of it.

One strong and vocal supporter of the legislation thought it did not go far enough in protecting and enhancing the consumer interest. Professor Milton Moore remarked in September 1971, "The Bill [C-256] is a much more modest document than what I advocate."[56] He was commissioned by the Economic Council to do a study of Canadian competition policy during its work on its *Interim Report on Competition Policy* published in mid-1969. The council would not publish his work. As Moore observed in 1971, "I had my day in court with the individuals who were working with the Economic Council with reference to the council's report on competition. I think it would be fair to say that in most respects I failed to persuade them."[57] Moore's study was published in December 1970 by McGill-Queen's Press. Entitled, *How Much Price Competition? The*

Prerequisites of an Effective Canadian Competition Policy, Moore's study assumed that the objectives of competition policy is to increase real income per capita by increasing productivity and to reduce avoidable wastes of production and distribution.[58] Policy actions were to be judged by two criteria: the rule of consumers' sovereignty[59] and the rule of fair competition among companies.[60] The former specified that the consumer is entitled to be provided with goods and services of his choice at the lowest attainable cost, to be offered as much or as little service with a commodity as he wishes to buy and to be accurately informed. The latter held that no party in the economic process is to have a privileged position, each person is free to engage in the business of his choice subject to the efficient operation of the price system and that competitive advantages should rest solely upon superior efficiency. Moore's view represented a clear and open challenge to conventional views and particularly those of businessmen. He argued, for example, that there is no ground on which an individual can rest a claim to any natural economic rights or privileges; all economic rights are conferred on the individual by the community — including the right to income earned in the economy. He defined the conflict of interest between producers and consumers and advocated that policy makers should put the interests of citizens as consumers ahead of those of citizens as producers as it is a necessary condition for increasing efficiency and thereby increasing real income per caita.[61] Moore denied the traditional "rights" of companies to refuse to sell, i.e., choose their own retail and wholesale customers, to use conventional pricing practices such as basing-point schemes, the "right" to engage in systematic price discrimination and the right to engage in mergers solely for private gains.[62]

Returning to Moore's remarks at the conference on Bill C-256 in September 1971, in trying to find some common ground at the outset, he asserted,

> Economists have never suggested that the pursuit of self-interest, including the pursuit of profits, free of any constraint and with no holds barred, serves the public interest. It has always been understood that the pursuit of profit must be constrained to create a mutuality of interests.[63]

He then reviewed a number of facets of the bill. Moore endorsed the *per se* ban on price agreements proposed in C-256, "because a seemingly innocuous price agreement may degenerate into something worse, such as a division of markets and, more important, because a ban on price agreements is a necessary condition of an effective competition policy. . . . Of course, price competition is not itself an end, but rather a means to the elimination of waste and the production of goods at least cost."[64] Moore argued that a case-by-case approach in which the defendants could plead no public detriment "would eventually lead us back to where we are now" because "consistency and natural justice would dictate that some criteria be evolved for determining public detriment. He then asks, "What criteria are possible?" and continues, "Either one accepts the reasoning that leads to the conclusion that, in the generality of cases, the competitive free enterprise is the most efficient of all practicable systems or one does not."[65]

Moore's position on the merger provisions is more complex. He recognizes that while increased profits is a significant motive of merging enterprises, "effecting economies in production is rarely realized or intended. . . . There can be no presumption that mergers increase efficiency. On the contrary, the objectives are increased market power, the increase or protection of market shares, conglomerate size and diversification and sometimes capital gains for those who manage the merger or engineer the takeover."[66] Since Moore does not believe that the degree of competition in a market depends critically upon the number of competitors, he appears to have reached the position of seeing neither compelling reasons for allowing mergers nor compelling reasons for preventing them. In fact, his recommendation is that certain types of mergers be attacked. Although the basis of his concern has little to do with economic efficiency, Moore apparently wishes to restrict takeovers by foreign firms. Second, Moore wishes to confine the lack of price competition to the manufacturing level and argues that "all forward integration into distribution and marketing should receive particularly searching scrutiny."[67] Third, he sees public detriment if "an aggressive competitive company is taken over by a company with the opposite characteristics."[68] Fourth, "there is detriment when an efficient company is taken over by an inefficient one."[69]

David L. McQueen, then chairman of the Department of Economics at York University, was a strong supporter of the Competition Act. This is hardly surprising, since he is believed to have been the principal author of the Economic Council's *Interim Report*. As we have noted, most of the key proposals of the council were incorporated in Bill C-256. He advocated a "meaningful competition policy in Canada . . . [because] it will save us a lot of unnecessary, heavy-handed and inefficient direct government regulation and government ownership of industry."[70] Directing his remarks to the problem of mergers, McQueen observed,

At the present time [September, 1971], Canada has no merger law to speak of . . . *de facto*, Canada has virtually no merger law.[71]

While many mergers may be harmless or even helpful to the public, McQueen noted that "some may involve real dangers of monopolization, especially in our relatively small economy. They can amount to essentially irreversible changes in the structure of industry, having some of the same general effects as illegal price fixing. . . ."[72] As he saw it "if . . . a small proportion of bad mergers could be headed off in their incipiency, there would be more market freedom for everybody."[73]

The nub of the administration and enforcement of merger policy was defined by McQueen to be the fact that "you cannot have, at one and the same time, perfect certainty and perfect sensitivity to the economics of individual cases."[74] A specialized tribunal seemed the best alternative for "it seemed to us that only a mixed expert tribunal, including members with appropriately varied backgrounds in law, economics and business, could provide the knowledgeable weighing of economic evidence and the difficult balancing of judgments that merger cases would make necessary."[75]

McQueen rejected the argument that appeal to the higher courts from the tribunal's decisions should be allowed on substantive grounds (e.g., findings of fact, findings of law or with respect to penalties or remedies). If this were done, "the higher court would be where the real action took place. The Tribunal's role would be reduced to that of second-guessing the higher court and holding up production by interposing a delaying stage."[76]

With respect to the charge that the tribunal will become an all-embracing vehicle for government control, McQueen urged that businessmen "not let imagination run riot. A seven-man Tribunal of this sort will not and cannot run the whole of Canadian business."[77] In fact, it will tend to "discourage tendencies toward generalized wage/price controls and the bureacratic governmental overseing of a much wider range of business decision making."[78]

University of British Columbia economist Dale F. Orr supported Bill C-256 but "reluctantly [came] to the conclusion that the impact of [the] Act on the level of competition in the economy will likely be fairly insignificant."[79] Orr gave two major reasons. First, the Canadian economy is already highly concentrated and in such industries oligopolistic coordination, which keeps prices high, cannot be attacked by the legislation.[80] Second, Orr estimated that about 47 percent of economic activity is largely exempted from combines policy when one recognizes provincial jurisdiction, and the so-called regulated industries.[81] Orr saw the solution as beyond the scope of the Competition Act.

> If the government really was serious about the objectives stated in the Act, specifically increased competition and efficiency, it would reduce tariffs and quotas, reduce the monopoly power of government-operated or regulated firms, and revise the regulatory process. It would encourage provincial governments to abandon such monopolistic and inefficient operations as agricultural marketing boards which restrict output. . . .[82]

Professor L. A. Skeoch of Queen's University, who had once been a senior official in the Combines Branch, was not an enthusiastic supporter of the Competition Act. With the exception of one short article,[83] Skeoch's views were made known at a conference on Bill C-256 he organized in January 1972[84] and by his wide-ranging personal contacts in academia, business, politics and the bureaucracy.

Skeoch's criticism of Bill C-256 centred on the proposition that "the legislation is too much concerned with short-run considerations and adopts a segmented approach which misses the point that it is the 'wholeness' of the situation that is significant even in the short run."[85] Skeoch continued, "it is the failure to incorporate dynamic considerations that most concerns me." He stated what was to become the theme of his report on proposed Stage II legislation in 1976[86] when he said,

> the central focus of policy relating to industrial organization should be to promote dynamic change and growth through encouraging flexibility and adaptability in the economy. Such a policy must emphasize not the efficient allocation of existing resources among alternative uses in terms of keeping down costs and profits, but the encouragement of new methods of production and distribution, the development of new institutions for liberating and expanding the growth opportunities in the economy.[87]

Skeoch's approach to civil procedures and the role of the tribunal was to find much support among businessmen. He stated that "the concept of a tribunal . . . has much to recommend it . . . [but] I would consider it more useful to have the Tribunal serve for a limited period of time as a negotiating agency with powers to investigate and attempt to reach agreement with the firms . . . involved in changes that would make the merger, price discrimination, or whatever, more acceptable as a vehicle for growth or change."[88] If an agreement could not be concluded, Skeoch saw the tribunal making a report to the government recommending a variety of remedial measures: tariff changes, changes in patents, even the breadth of action to coordinate industrial organization policy with other elements of economic policy."[89]

For one as close to combines policy as Dr. Skeoch has been over many years, this is a remarkable statement. Since 1952 the Restrictive Trade Practices Commission, following the intiative of the Director of Investigation and Research, has evaluated the competitive situation of many industries and literally hundreds of firms. Between 1953 and 1972 it published seventy-one reports. In about one-fifth of these it recommended to the government of the day remedies of the sort outlined by Skeoch. Almost without exception such recommendations were ignored. Another Ottawa reality militates against Skeoch's approach. In the interdepartmental bargaining over the many facets of economic policy among the Departments of Finance, Industry, Trade and Commerce, External Affairs and Consumer and Corporate Affairs, the advocates of a strong competition policy are seldom able to sustain their position. Producer interests almost always dominate consumer interests both in the bureaucracy and in political decision making by elected officials. Skeoch's proposal would guarantee the continuation of this historical pattern.

At the January 1972 conference on Bill C-256 organized by Skeoch, a number of other academics gave papers. One was H. E. English of Carleton University who reviewed the nature of specialization and export agreements and the proposed policy towards them.[90] He found "the criteria governing the tribunal's decision . . . general satisfactory, but they do signal certain problems and beg questions about the possibility of more objective conditions."[91] The tribunal was instructed to approve specialization agreements if they did not lessen competition significantly and, in the case of export agreements, if they did not "affect competition . . .adversely." As English remarked, these criteria "provide a very wide scope for the tribunal."[92] He offered "a more objective criterion", namely, that "any agreement would be registered where relevant tariffs or other barriers to competition were removed over the period of the agreement."[93] Why was this not done? English postulated that "the failure to include such a provision in the law arises from the familiar jurisdictional problem in government,"[94] i.e., tariffs are primarily the responsibility of the Department of Finance. English concluded that the registration of specialization and export agreements "should be handled . . . with some care lest they lead to a further degree or a different form of departure from the condition of dynamic efficiency in Canada."[95]

H. W. Arthurs of Osgoode Hall Law School at York University examined the Competition Act as it related to the professions.[96] He began his paper by indicating he was "broadly in favour of the proposed Competition Act, the philosophy it expounds and the mechanisms it advances to implement that philosophy."[97] However, Arthurs was "basically skeptical that the bill does very much to secure the public interest in relation to professional services."[98] By the latter he meant that "professional services of a high calibre are delivered to the public at a price everyone can afford and through procedures which make them fully and easily accessible."[99]

Arthurs noted that price-fixing by professional bodies is prohibited by C-256, but that "the bill does provide protection for professional fee tariffs established and implemented in accordance with S. 92 of the Bill."[100] After reviewing the exemption provisions, he concluded that what is proposed "is probably of benefit to both the public and the profession, but likely of only marginal importance. So far as many lay people are concerned they cannot afford any fee at all, no matter how it is fixed. . . ."[101] Beyond this point, Arthurs observed that "S. 92 provides no immunity for monopolistic conduct by the professions," yet "it is virtually certain that the Bill is not intended to dismantle the whole structure of professional government."[102]

Arthurs then described four approaches for reconciling the public interest with the continued existence of professional monopoly. These related to "substantive structural or institutional reforms,"[103] which have a much greater potential for benefiting the public than competition policy embodied in Bill C-256, he said.

Professor G. L. Reuber of the University of Western Ontario took the classic internationalist economic position in his criticism of the bill.[104] Essentially he advocated virtually unrestricted competition in the market for capital assets, i.e., a less restrictive policy toward mergers than was advocated in the Competition Act. He expressed concern that S. 35 of the bill, "taken at face value . . . arms the tribunal with very sweeping powers. . . .[it] could well rule out virtually all foreign mergers."[105] Reuber argued that "it seems likely that firms acquired by foreign firms frequently may be expected to expand very rapidly after their acquisition . . . [and in doing so] will tend to depress domestic prices and expand sales."[106] Reuber believed that the merger provisions of C-256 "will create considerable uncertainty [and] could serve as a major deterrent to foreign takeovers."[107] He saw the bill as having a paradoxical feature — if it "brings about a significant increase in competition it is likely *ipso facto* to promote both foreign and domestic merger activity . . . because a significant increase in competition is likely to be associated with an increase in bankruptcies as well as a weakening of the financial viability of many, especially smaller, firms."[108]

By "stifling foreign investment [e.g., foreign mergers] . . . [Canada] may not only reduce the wealth of the country but current income flows and employment as well."[109] This would occur, said Reuber, because the reduction in foreign competition for domestic assets will reduce their value both to their owners and the country as a whole. Reuber's concern to see few inhibitions placed on foreign investment in Canada was based, in part, on the perceived benefits of such investment: "In the past foreign competition in markets for goods, services and assets has played a key role in maintaining and promoting competitive market conditions in this country. As an effective force in the promotion of this objective, foreign competition has been more important than direct legislation."[110] Although this proposition is correct, the problem lies more in the ineffectiveness of competition legislation in Canada, then in the efficacy of foreign competition.

Professor W. M. H. Grover of Osgoode Hall Law School wrote a paper examining the legal and operational aspects of Bill C-256.[111] He began by levelling two criticisms at S. 16 of the act which specify the practices made illegal *per se*. First, he argued there should be a *de minimus* exception. Second, he asserted the net cast by the section may be too broad. "There is an overreaching here which masks the basic worth of the section generally."[112]

The bulk of Mr. Grover's paper was devoted to an examination of seven criticisms of the Competitive Practices Tribunal.[113]

1. It will be difficult to get properly qualified persons to sit on the tribunal in light of the terms and conditions specified.
2. "The standards the tribunal is asked to apply are so imprecise as to defy rational economic analogies."
3. "The standards are wrong anyway; what we want is dynamic long run gains not short run efficiency."
4. The function of the tribunal ought to be negotiate not adjudicate.
5. The tribunal should not have the power to initiate proceedings [per S. 27 (4)] when it is empowered to review the matter.
6. "The procedural safeguards are inadequate. . . ."
7. "The tribunal has too much power. In particular, the supplementary remedies of patent revocation, *ex parte* injunctions and forbidding Canadian subsidiaries to obey their parents' orders are too wide."

Grover found some merit with respect to (1), (2), (5) and (7). He was less persuaded by the others, particularly if some improvements were made in the redrafting.

Grover pointed out that, with respect to mergers, the tribunal may be bypassed if the commissioner negotiates an acceptable solution with the firms involved on an informal basis. "This leads to no guidelines to help future business decisions."[114] He defended the price discrimination provisions in the bill, noting that wide-ranging defences could be considered by the tribunal.[115] Finally, Grover recognized the uncertainty as to the constitutionality of Bill C-256. He suggested the provinces ask for a reference to the Supreme Court before long.[116]

THE DEBATE CONTINUES

By far the most controversial issue in C-256 was the proposed Competitive Practices Tribunal. Excluding the list of offences made illegal per se, the tribunal was to utilize civil procedures to evaluate a wide range of business practices including mergers, rationalization, specialization and export agreements, resale price maintenance and price discrimination. The Toronto *Globe and Mail* stated, "uncertainty is a cancer to business" and "arbitrary rule breeds contempt for authority." The editorial went on to define the defects in tf tribunal: no right of appeal on the merits of the case, the ten-year term of the tribunal members and the uncertainty surrounding the guidance rules of the tribunal.[117] The Regina *Leader-Post* stated a common theme. The legislation "puts far too much power in the hands of what could be an autocratic tribunal."[118] The Truro *Daily News* quoted Gerard Filion, president of the Canadian Manufacturers Association, who criticized the tribunal:

> The principles implicit in this approach contradict the traditions of our domestic society. As the bill now stands, the tests according to which the tribunal must be satisfied are too narrow so that the power of business decision effectively rests with the tribunal.[119]

An editorial in *Broadcaster* by J. W. Younger, entitled "Competition Act — 1971 or 1984?" stressed that "what Big Brother really wants is to scrutinize and control business decisions. The name of the game is not efficiency or consumerism, but power." Mr. Younger continued:

> Almost every arrangement between competing businessmen is now outlawed whether or not it has an undue effect on competition. Normal and harmless business practices like price leadership, meeting spot competition by reducing prices, choosing your own customers and quantity discounts based on savings in production costs will either be illegal in themselves or may be prohibited. Almost every merger is subject to investigation and liable to prohibition.[120]

An editorial in *Jobber News* held the apocalyptic view that Bill C-256 and the proposed federal labour legislation "if enacted in their present form, could well spell the death knell of private enterprise as it is known in this country." The editors continued, "It is the duty of every trade association to interpret the bills and provide members with the ammunition, so that intelligent and positive suggestions can be made to parliamentarians."[121] The Winnipeg *Tribune* described the bill as "an excessively restrictive and punitive piece of legislation. . . . In effect, the Basford bill will give a small group of government apointees and the horde of bureaucrats which, undoubtedly, will build up around the tribunal, autocratic powers of coercion over business." The *Tribune* concluded that C-256 demonstrated "an excessive zeal by Ottawa to control and intimidate business" and that it might be unconstitutional.[122] In the Sudbury *Star*, Mr. Basford was described as a "czar" in an editorial, the tone of which can be determined from its title, "Super-Bureaucrats Would Rule Market."[123]

The attack on the tribunal came from other sources as well. The Toronto *Star* took the following view:

> It is bad bill that should be dropped. The proposed legislation confers almost limitless discretionary power on a seven-man tribunal, whose members are to have ten-year tenure, and are not to be directly answerable to Parliament. The powers of this civil tribunal appear so

large that the legislation as it now stands could easily be challenged on its constitutionality, and voided by the Supreme Court. Let no one imagine that the seven tribunes need limit their scrutiny to big corporations. On the contrary, it is specifically proposed to cover not only manufacturing, but all services including professional sport. The tribunal will examine lawyers' fees, brokers' commission, insurance salesmen's canvassing techniques, banks' charges, barbers' rates, shopkeepers' practices, even perhaps newsboys' sales pitches.[124]

The harsh criticism of C-256 by business prompted the president of the Consumers' Association of Canada (Maryon Brechin) to write a letter to a number of newspapers stating the CAC was "deeply disturbed by the attacks mounted against Bill C-256." She described the bill as "most progressive legislation." Apparently trying to reassure the critics, she asserted, "The bill does not represent a fundamental departure from established competition policy. Many of its provisions are merely extensions of present prohibitions, more clearly defined." She noted also "The present Combines Act has scarcely been spectacularly successful in guarding the consumer against concentrated ownership in Canada."[125]

A theme that was to be repeated for the next several years was that the government officials had drafted the bill in isolation and were trying to achieve a theoretical ideal with the Competition Act. John Meyer, writing in the Ottawa *Journal*, said that Bill C-256 "showed a pronounced bias which could only have resulted from legislating in isolation. . . . The realities of business activity were largely ignored in favour of theory." Mr. Meyer said that the Chamber of Commerce hoped that this weakness could be overcome by having combines and Department of Justice officials "engage in continuous and direct discussions with a representative group of businessmen in the course of rewriting the bill."[126]

Five months after the Competition Act had been introduced, the *Financial Post* felt able to state, "Not since the early days of the great tax debate has a single government proposal aroused the ire of the business community to the extent the Competition Act has." In the same article it was noted that "the Cabinet ministers are actively opposed to it."[127] In an editorial reprinted in at least four other eastern papers, the Hamilton *Spectator*, as early as January 12, 1972, mooted the demise of Mr. Basford as Minister of Consumer or Corporate Affairs.

> The Competition Act is so consumer-oriented in its philosophy that should it by any miracle happen to be drastically amended in the interests of fairness, Consumer Affairs Minister Ron Basford will have nothing but false pride to encourage him to remain on in the Cabinet.

The *Spectator* recognized that support for the bill in the Cabinet was not wholehearted: "Fortunately, there are a few men in Cabinet who think so little of the act that they wouldn't use it to wrap garbage." Mr. Basford was described as "either Canada's answer to Lord Olivier in the acting field or . . . a dangerous fanatic." The tone of the editorial was maintained with such statements as, "The punishments, incidentally, for breaking some of the laws proposed by the Competition Act would make a Siberian salt mine seem like a Garden of Eden."[128]

A CHANGE OF MINISTERS

A major Cabinet shuffle in late January 1972 resulted in the appointment of Mr. Robert Andras, formerly the Minister of State for Urban Affairs, as Minister of Consumer and Corporate Affairs. Mr. Basford took over Mr. Andras's job at urban affairs. At the same time the Minister of Finance, Mr. Benson, moved to defence; the Minister of Justice, Mr. Turner, took over finance; the Minister of Labour, Mr. Mackasey, became Minister of Manpower and Immigration; and Mr. Lang moved from manpower to become Minister of Justice.

The Sudbury *Star* recognized the nature of these changes in the Cabinet in an editorial entitled, "Trudeau's Cabinet Shuffle Clearly Election-Oriented." The Basford-Andras shift was described as follows:

> For Ron Basford, the consumer and corporate affairs portfolio had provided a personal political bandwagon. He rode it into a knock-down-drag-out fight with the business community over his ill-conceived new Competition Act. . . . The act as it stood contained a mish-mash of highly restrictive regulations and poorly defined powers which would do nothing to enhance the position of Canadian firms competing for markets at home and abroad against the industrial giants of the United States, Europe and Asia. Now Mr. Basford moves to urban affairs, up until now a backwater appointment. He has been demoted, exchanging jobs with Robert Andras, a man with a smoother, conciliatory approach, who just, incidentally, happens also to be co-chairman of the Liberal campaign committee. Mr. Trudeau had obviously given a good deal of thought to his appointment.[129]

The Prince George *Citizen* noted, "there is political expediency in the cabinet shuffle.   .   .   ." It suggested that "Robert Andras is probably a good choice to take over consumer affairs, but unless he is prepared to make concessions to repair the damage caused by his predecessor, he too will have a hot time of it piloting the Competition Act, as it now stands, through the House."[130] The connection between Mr. Andras's appointment to replace Mr. Basford and Mr. Andras's other role as a Liberal Party co-chairman of the Liberal Party's 1972 election campaign was noted by the Moncton *Times*.

> Some stories have it that the proposed Competition Act had so alienated Canada's business community that the Liberal bagman [sic]

were finding the traditional 60-40 ratio of contribution to government and Opposition being split 50-50. Political realities may have dictated this shift.[131]

Shortly after leaving the Department of Consumer and Corporate Affairs, Mr. Basford spoke of the attitudes of business toward the new legislation: "My principal disappointment and regret, I suppose, is the hostility — the almost viciousness — that some seem to feel towards the consumer point of view."[132]

WHO WAS MAKING THE NOISE?

As of January 18, 1972 the Department of Consumer and Corporate Affairs had received 217 briefs or proposals for amendments in response to the Competition Act.[133] From a list of briefs provided by the department, we have categorized the major submissions in Table 8-1. While the minister reportedly received some 300 submissions on Bill C-256,[134] the 197 reported in Table 8-1 represent the most substantial briefs. It indicates that 77 percent of the briefs came from individual business firms, joint briefs from several firms or from business or trade associations. Only 2 of the 197 briefs came from consumer organizations. Individual lawyers or law firms on their own behalf submitted ten briefs, compared with only six from academics. Because services, including professional services, were to come under the legislation, briefs were received from twelve professional associations, four of which were comprised of engineers.

Almost without exception, the submissions, dominated by those from producer groups, were sharply critical of Bill C-256 and sought to weaken or eliminate the legislation. Graeme Hughes, manager of the Legislation Department of the Canadian Manufacturers' Association, stated that the briefs contained "roughly the same message — withdraw the bill, then amend it radically."[135]

Harold Buchwald, chairman of the Canadian Consumer Council, addressing the twenty-fifth anniversary meeting of the Consumers' Association of Canada in June 1972, said that the effectiveness of the business lobbying over the Competition Act pointed out the need for an effective consumer lobby "in what is basically an adversary process." He pointed out that industry was able to conduct a tax-deductible campaign assisted by "highly qualified lawyers, accountants [and] economists and was "able to utilize the public platforms and harness the news media to mount a sustained attack." He continued, "Consumer interest groups simply were not able to afford comparable expertise."[136] One group which might have been expected to support the legislation did little to defend it publicly. As Professor William Neilson observed,

TABLE 8-1

Submissions to the Department of Consumer and Corporate Affairs re. the Competition Act, c. 1971-73

Category	Authorized Release to Public	Release Not Authorized in Whole Or in Part	Total
Individual business firms	69	14	83
Joint brief by several firms	2[1]	0	2
Business and trade associations	73	3	76
Governments/Regulatory Agency	3[5]	1[4]	4
Professional associations	12[6]	0	12
Consumer organizations	2[2]	0	2
Professional sports organizations	1	0	1
Lawyers (on own behalf)	5	5	10
Academics	6	0	6[3]
Individuals	0	1	1
	173	24	197

[1] Includes the "Stelco group" brief, i.e., Abitibi Paper, Algoma Steel, Canada Packers, Cominco, Dofasco, T. Eaton Co., John Labatt Ltd., MacMillan-Bloedel, Moore Corporation, Noranda, Power Corporation, Simpsons Ltd. and the Steel Company of Canada.

[2] Consumers Association of Canada and Saskatchewan Home Economics Association.

[3] Four economists and two lawyers.

[4] Canadian Transport Commission.

[5] Provinces of Manitoba, Newfoundland and Ontario.

[6] Engineers (4), lawyers (2), dentists, chartered accountants, quantity surveyors, T.V. and radio artists optometrists, architects.

SOURCE: Categorized by the author from a list of briefs supplied by the Department of Consumer and Corporate Affairs, Bureau of Competition Policy, Ottawa.

Organized labour, for its part, preserved its dubious record for legislative comment (except where its own narrowly defined interests are directly in danger) by refraining from offering its views on the Bill until December 6th. Not to be outdone by the sight of a chummy Cabinet-business leaders' meeting privately convened late in November, the Canadian Labour Congress managed to obtain a similar closed meeting with the Cabinet where they indicated their support for the proposed Competition Act. C.L.C. president, Donald MacDonald is reported as having said that "the C.L.C. had intended all along to support the Bill but had planned to wait for discussion by a parliamentary committee after Second Reading." Quite a feat of public responsibility considering the six months of intensive public discussion (read as business attack) on the Bill.[137]

THE RETREAT BEGINS

The message from business and producer interest groups found in their briefs and which was reflected by the daily newspapers and the trade press (see Figure 4-1 in Chapter 4) was getting through to both the new minister and his appointed officials.

At a seminar for corporation lawyers in Ottawa on March 17, 1972 Mr. Andras said that the federal government planned "substantial changes" in the Competition Act before it would be reintroduced in the House of Commons. He said, "The recommendations in the briefs have led us to accept that there must be substantial changes in the act." At the same seminar D. H. W. Henry, then Director of Investigation and Research, indicated the main areas in which the government was considering changes: in the powers of the tribunal, sections dealing with mergers, quantity discounts, the list of per se offences, resale price maintenance and the extension of the act to cover services.[138]

An Edmonton *Journal* editorial took the view that "it wasn't so much the intent but the content of the new Competition Act which incensed the Canadian business community." The editors argued that "some of the acrimony between the federal government and the business community would have been avoided had Ottawa prepared the initial legislative proposal in concert with the private sector — producers and consumers alike."[139] By the end of March, the *Financial Post* perceived a "new amiability" between the government and business. The editorial went on.

> To gauge the remarkable distance Ottawa has come in switching from the stifling rules it originally wanted to impose, note this from a very senior departmental spokesman: "What we need to kow is whether the broad policy changes we re making are going to meet in general the major problems of industry. Once we are satisfied those needs have been met, then we will proceed with drafting the legislation."[140]

The Ottawa *Journal* hailed Mr. Andras's statesman-like approach and stated that his "agreement to revise the bill is no sellout to big business. Reasonable changes can be made in this act without destroying its purpose of developing a more equitable and competitive economy in Canada."[141] The Toronto *Globe and Mail* also congratulated the government's decision to bring in a new bill. "Robert Andras has rightly discerned that the flaws so patently obvious to businessmen and consumers alike make keeping Mr. Basford's belated promsie of mere modifications an exercise too ridiculous to be feasible. Accordingly, we are to get a new bill."[142] The Montreal *Gazette* echoed the same theme, describing the original bill as a "legally illiterate and grossly uninformed a piece of legislation as ever there was" and concluded that "the new competition bill can't help but be an improvement on the old."[143]

How did the government propose to change the Competition Act in March 1972? As the Director of Investigation and Research, Mr. Henry, modestly stated, "a number of points that have caused difficulty or concern can be identified." He went on to indicate, "the main areas where there would appear to be considerable room for improvement and possible alternatives. . . ."[144] They were as follows:

1. With respect to S.16, which listed ten per se offences, "the net is cast too wide." Mr. Henry indicated, "the main alternative is to relate the prohibition to the effect that the agreement has on competition," e.g., by returning to the "undueness" test, by adopting a stronger standard such as that of "materially" lessening competition or by exempting *de minimus* agreements.[145]
1. With respect to S17, monopolizing, the offence was too broadly defined. Mr. Henry noted, "the intention is to confine the criminal offence to cases where a firm seeks to stifle competition by predatory behaviour."[146]
3. S.18, price maintenance, would have to be modified to deal with actions which affect prices, but which are not anti-competitive and to more appropriately deal with the practices of suggested resale prices and preticketing by suppliers.[147]
4. Mr. Henry did not think a persuasive case has been made for the elimination of the Competitive Practices Tribunal and a reversion to either the criminal or civil courts. He asserted that "much of these criticisms [sic] are the result of misunderstanding of how the tribunal's powers will be used, uncertainty as to its composition and method of operating, and confusion over the detailed criteria it will apply." He then listed "the more important proposals for improvement that must be considered and carefully weighed":[148]

    • Indicate more clearly the stature of the Tribunal by requiring the chairman to be a judge of the Federal Court.
    • Define more clearly the positive role of the Tribunal in facilitating rationalization and specialization, development of scale economies to meet international competition, the pre-

servation of the competitive market as a mechanism to stimulate growth and innovation.

- Clarify and simplify the details of the provisions relating to mergers, restrictive practices, refusal to deal and delivered pricing.
- Set out more comprehensively the rights of parties to judicial review of the tribunal's decisions, the right to a full hearing, the protection of confidentiality of certain information and other safeguards of the individual's rights.
- Make it clear that the tribunal does not intervene on its own initiative in business conduct, that it has no investigatory powers, that it deals only with situations brought before it as a court does and that it is not concerned with most day-to-day business decisions.

5. With respect to mergers, ". . . reasonably simple drafting changes can make it clear that most mergers will not be challenged." In addition, Mr. Henry was willing to eliminate the registration and notification requirements or have them made to the commissioner rather than the tribunal. He realized that the legislation in regard to foreign mergers would have to be harmonized with foreign investment policy machinery. Mr. Henry made it clear the department was considering either eliminating the criteria relating to competition or efficiency, and including a failing firm provision. Alternatively, if the efficiency criterion was retained, the new bill would not require that the benefits be passed on to consumers, but would enlarge the scope of those benefiting to include industrial and commercial buyers.[149]

6. The price discrimination provisions had been attacked for their possible restriction on quantity discounts and on a firm's ability to meet spot competition. Mr. Henry indicated that one alternative was to return to the existing criminal provisions, but he was considering a civil provision permitting quantity discounts which could be challenged as the abuse of market power or on the basis that such discounts are likely to materially lessen competition. In both cases the requirement that a practice of discriminating would have to be shown.[150]

7. Mr. Henry indicated a number of changes could be made with respect to procedural issues in Bill C-256. In particular he conceded that the reverse onus provision was objectionable, but contented that changing S.16 to incorporate a competition test would obviate the need to eliminate the reverse onus element. Less onerous liability should attach to officers and directors of corporations convicted of offences. Consideration should be given to *expressly* providing for the right to call witnesses, present argument, cross-examine the Crown's witnesses, be represented by counsel and obtain written reasons for tribunal decisions.[151]

8. Because the Combines Act has not been applied to them, many regulated service industries were uncertain as to how the Competition Act would be applied. Mr. Henry indicated that until discussions were held with the provinces it was premature to specify what modifications might be made.[152]

THE GOVERNMENT'S PROPOSED AMENDMENTS STILL INSUFFICIENT

Despite Mr. Andras's statements, some businessmen were not reassured and continued to complain. Robert Scrivener, president of Bell Canada, objected to the whole intent of the bill. "It's futile to argue about such things in parts, when it's wrong in principle. To approach a national industrial strategy in the name of the consumer shows a confused concern."[153] Mr. Schrivener wanted the focus of policy to be the ability of Canadian firms to compete "with international giants." These arguments were echoed by H. J. Hemens, vice-president and general counsel of DuPont of Canada, who also stressed the employment variable. Regarding mergers, he suggested that there could be no broad social savings from the preventing mergers since the rejection of a merger might result in unemployment. "If we increase jobs, then we have achieved what is economically good for Canada,"[154] he argued.

Michael Barkway, editor of the *Financial Times*, was doubtful, after a careful reading of Mr. Andras's and Mr. Henry's March 17 papers, whether the announced the changes "go nearly far enough." He concluded that "there is no hint that [the department] is prepared to reconsider the fundamental approach to competition policy which most of the critics have called fundamentally wrong."[155] Editorially, the *Financial Times* was "sceptical" about what Mr. Henry had described as "relatively simple drafting changes" after "the horrible example of Bill C-256."[156]

J. Peter Gordon, president of the Steel Company of Canada, in an interview in *Canadian Business*, continued to be unimpressed with the Competition Act.

> What I think the Competition Act should do is define specific types of economic conduct which are not permissible, and include, in this context, the concept of "undueness" — a concept which was already in the previous act, but which was dropped in Bill C-256. There's the competitive Practices Tribunal which would have incredibly broad powers, and whose rulings would not be subject to appeal. It's the philosophy which underlies such a tribunal which I think is so wrong. Surely, in any free society — if it is truly to be a free society — everything should be permitted unless it can be shown to be clearly detrimental to society.[157]

The executive vice-president of the Canadian Real Estate Association was of the view that Mr. Andras's decision to make substantial changes in the original proposals and bring forth a new bill "was not the result of business pressure," but of "business common sense expressed through the medium of some three hundred submissions that pointed out the effect and impact the bill would have on normal business practice." The problem with the original legislation was that the bill was drafted by bureaucrats "up in the ivory towers of the Consumer and Corporate Affairs Department," who were "operating in [a] type of Ottawa vacuum."[158]

Some of the business critics were less condemnatory of the amendments the government proposed. As Graeme Hughes put it, "the proposed amendments amount to substantial alteration to the Bill and go a long way to meet industry's objections. Nevertheless, the Department has retained the general framework of Bill C-256."[159] The CMA indicated there were still two matters of fundamental principal requiring further amendment. "The first relates to the competition test. . . . The association prefers 'undue' as a competition test, but if 'material' is to be adopted it should be defined in the act to mean that there would be no material restraint in competition so long as *effective* competition remained."[160] While requiring that the government define "material," Mr. Hughes did not think it necessary to define "effective competition." Second, the CMA wanted to see the ordinary courts of law and not the proposed Competitive Practices Tribunal decide whether any activity offends the civil or criminal provisions of the act. "The tribunal should function separately as a body that could exempt commercial conduct which might otherwise be subject to a civil prohibition."[161]

In an article in the *Financial Post*, W. A. Macdonald, a member of the Toronto law firm of McMillan Binch, undertook to advise Mr. Andras about the priorities of legislation.

> The legislation relating to competition is not one of the high priority issues facing Canada at the present time. It would be major error to waste public policy energy on a low priority area, and to create uncertainty and poor relations with the private sector, where only the most marginal gains, at best, are likely to ensue. The minister should insist on starting from where we are. It may well be that some specific items in the consumer protection field could be dealt with immediately on a broadly acceptable basis. . . . The minister should be a hard-to-get-at skeptic, unimpressed with general economic theory and only impressed when his officials could produce hard evidence of damage to the Canadian economy or serious unfairness to consumers or competitors.[162]

While responding to the criticisms business interest groups levied against Bill C-256, the minister also sought to reassure the consumer constituency. Before the Consumers' Association of Canada, Mr. Andras spoke of the revisions of the Competition Act, but he stated, "it is not my purpose in life to disembowel the competition bill." Columnist Maurice Western argued that this amounted to "a rather emphatic statement suggesting that the government has not been much moved by more serious criticisms of the bill."[163]

Business continued to press for more favourable amendments. But even this process was questioned and it was suggested that an entirely new bill be drafted. Writing in the July 1972 issue of *Canadian Business,* Claudy Kyles stated: "It is by no means irrelevant to question the fundamental wisdom of the original Bill, and many of the inadequate amendments proposed in recent months. Should, in fact, the Competition Bill in its present form be scrapped altogether, and let Robert Andras make a fresh start?"[164]

A GENERAL ELECTION AND ANOTHER NEW MINISTER

A federal general election was held on October 30, 1972. The Liberals retained power, but became a minority government with 109 seats to the Conservatives' 107. The prime minister's reaction was philosophical — "Whether or not it is clear to you, no doubt the universe is unfolding as it should."[165]

The voice of business had to be heeded. Apparently business' dislike of the Competition Act "was reflected in much-reduced corporate contributions to Liberal campaign funds."[166] In the Throne speech only one paragraph was devoted to the ill-fated Competition Act, indicating that the bill would be revised. The speech also promised that "the new policy will be in harmony with industrial policies in general and foreign investment policy in particular."

On November 27, 1972, Mr. Andras became Minister of Manpower and Immigration (which includes responsibility for unemployment insurance) and Mr. Herb Gray became Minister of Consumer and Corporate Affairs, having been Minister of National Revenue. In his previous post Mr. Gray had been responsible for the 523-page report *Foreign Direct Investment in Canada,* published in May 1972.[167] Shortly after his appointment, *Marketing* magazine described Mr. Gray as "a hard slogger" and his style as "unspectacular and methodical." They went on to say "he's not the kind of man . . . who will unduly antagonize those Canadians who are affected by consumer and corporate laws."[168] In the context of minority government and its demonstrated contentiousness, the competition legislation was low on the government's list of priorities. In any event, Mr. Gray made it clear that the department would not proceed until he had reviewed the outcome of the consultation with business and made up his own mind as to what to recommend to the Cabinet.[169]

Between the election and March 1973, the number of newspaper stories and editorials dealing with competition policy plummeted as the government busied itself with redrafting the legislation. During this period inflation and, in particular, the rise in food prices, received a large volume of newspaper coverage. In March the hearings of the House of

Commons Special Committee on Trends in Food Prices received widespread media attention. The Minister of Consumer and Corporate Affairs, accompanied by senior officials, testified twice before the committee. On april 27, 1973 the minister announced the establishment of the Food Prices Review Board to prepare quarterly reviews of trends in food prices and to make special inquiries into the causes of particular increases in food prices. Two days later Mr. Gray named Mrs. Beryl Plumptre, a former president of the Consumers' Association of Canada, as the full-time chairman of the board.

Then for the time being at least, competition policy had apparently been moved to the back burner. The *Financial Post* editorialized that "it was Prime Minister Trudeau's desire to cool off the overheated and strained relations Basford had created with businessmen that dictated his replacements — first cool Bob Andras, and then quiet herb Gray."[170] Another article in the *Financial Post* of March 10, 1973, pointed out that Bill C-256

> . . . aroused widespread antipathy in corporate circles — a disenchantment that was reflected in much-reduced corporate contributions to Liberal campaign funds. With another costly election possible almost any time, the wise course from the government viewpoint would be to sit on the competition policy as long as possible.[171]

An important, but little-noted, event affecting competition policy occurred early in February when D. H. W. Henry, the Director of Investigation and Research since September 1960, resigned to accept an appointment to the Supreme Court of Ontario. It was frequently suggested that Mr. Henry was the principal architect of the Competition Act. It was also suggested he would be the first chairman of the controversial Competitive Practices Tribunal after Bill C-256 became law. The *Financial Times* quoted an unnamed government official, "You can't lose a very experienced and very able man like David Henry without slowing things down." An advisor to business said, "I don't know where they're going to find anybody equally good. . . . He'd support whatever policy his minister endorsed. At the same time, he'd understand the industry point of view."[172] Mr. Henry's deputy director, J. J. Quinlan, became the acting director. On March 1, 1973, after less than one year in the post, Gordon F. Osbaldeston, the Deputy Minister of Consumer and Corporate Affairs moved to the Treasury Board. He was succeeded by Michael Pitfield, who had been senior deputy secretary to the Cabinet and deputy clerk to the Privy Council. Not only did the Department of Consumer Affairs experience a high turnover of ministers, it also had to live with a high rate of turnover of its deputy minister. Between mid-1971 and mid-1975 the department had four different deputies — excluding those appointed as acting deputy minister. Of particular importance was the loss of J. F. Grandy in September 1971. Until March 1, 1972, when G. R. Osbaldeston assumed the job, the department operated for five months with only an acting administrative head. Because of his strong reputation within the bureaucracy, and his closeness to the creation of Bill C-256, Grandy's transfer could not have come at a less opportune time. Under heavy fire from business interests, finding little support from other constituencies, the Competition Act needed a strong sponsor to defend it within the interdepartmental bureaucracy. With Grandy gone, by the late fall of 1971 Bill C-256 lost what little support it had within the federal mandarinate.

There were some practical political reasons, in addition to the time-consuming task of redrafting, for not pushing the revised bill into Parliament at an early date. This was the delicate balance of the Liberal's minority government. It was generally conceded that the new legislation would have to wait until the Liberals were able to win a clear majority in another general election. An article in *Canadian Printer and Publisher* said,

> Gray would have to work some kind of minor miracle if he is to come up with an acceptable bill this year. The Conservatives are unalterably opposed to the original bill as being too restrictive, and the NDP, which holds the balance of power in the House of minorities, attacks it for not going far enough.[173]

At about the same time the Province of Ontario, through a position paper by the Provincial Secretary for Justice entered the discussions by challenging the federal government's "misplaced" emphasis on "the fostering of domestic competition as a national objective."[174] Instead, Ontario favoured the "rationalization" of industry through mergers and consolidations to enhance the export capability of Canadian business. In addition, the provincial government was determined jealously to guard its constitutional prerogatives in the area of consumer protection.

While the official announcement was not made until July 18, 1973, it was apparent early in May that the government would proceed incrementally with the revised Competition Act. Mr. Gray was quoted in an interview as saying, "Originally I was working on the total package, but we now think that it will be more appropriate to bring it forward in stages."[175] One reason for doing so given by Mr. Gray was that the first stage could be presented to Parliament more quickly. The incremental approach had been pushed by a number of senior business leaders at a conference at Montebello, Quebec on November 9-11, 1972. The conference was attended by seventy-three business executives, lawyers, academics and civil servants. The chairman of the steering committee stated that it departed from the usual pattern of debate on competition policy in two respects:[176]

- we emphasized the importance of considering competition policy in relation to our general objectives for Canada; rather than as a problem that can be solved in isolation. . . .

- we considered competition policy in different industrial sectors — rather than following the usual course of discussing competition policy in general.

In regard to the latter point, the conference dealt only with semi-processed and processed goods and manufactured industrial products — circumstances in which "sophisticated sellers deal with sophisticted buyers. The general public is not directly involved."[177]

The conference produced a fifteen-page summary of conclusions (together with a similar number of modifying or dissenting footnotes) and a list of twelve recommendations to the minister. The recommendations also produced an equal number of similar footnotes.

The recommendations were as follows:[178]

1. The proposed new legislation should not be proceeded with. It does not promote the real interest of the consumer. It will hinder businessmen and government in the efforts they must make to rationalize our economy and make it competitive.

2. Instead of wiping out the present act and introducing a completely new bill, attention should be concentrated on improving the regulations now in force where they can be demonstrated to be unsatisfactory.

3. In any legislative moves, we must take into account fundamental changes in Canada's economic position since the drafting of the new statute was embarked upon.

4. Competition policy should be considered in the context of a national strategy, and not in isolation. It is a means to an end and not an end in itself.

5. In the essential task of consultation, criticism must be encouraged (and attended to) on the basic principles of proposed amendments — and not just on details of lesser importance. The suggested changes so far proposed by department officials, as a result of briefs submitted and hearings held, are not far-reaching enough to meet the many basic criticisms that have been made.

6. In judging the effectiveness of any regulation, the general impact on the economy is the important criterion, and not simply the problems it imposes on those administering the legislation.

7. The concept of "undueness" should be retained. The proposed move to per se offences is undesirable and would seriously impair the effectiveness of the act.

8. The choice between setting up an administrative tribunal and continuing to work through the regular courts, is a contentious one, and needs careful consideration. We do believe an administrative tribunal could be useful, but that it should not have as wide powers as contemplated in Bill C-256. Its main function should be to exempt mergers that are desirable on economic grounds from restrictions under the legislation. And it should not be expected to review every merger that comes along. To this end, the proposed requirement that all mergers be registered should be dropped.

9. The enormous importance of Canada's export trade should be recognized, and the clear necessity for cooperative arrangements between Canadian corporations in developing export markets should receive greater encouragement than would appear possible under Bill C-256.

10. Specialization agreements are essential to our developing economy. These too should be facilitated by eliminating the present qualifications and limitations in the proposed legislation.

11. While healthy competition is clearly an essential element in every free enterprise economy, it does not follow that more competition is always better than less; and our regulations should be drafted with this in mind.

12. The proposed penalties in Bill C-256 are far too drastic, and bear no relation to the amounts the courts have, up to the present, imposed in their discretion.

While some of the dissenting footnotes were even *less* conciliatory than the recommendations, a number of them were interesting for they revealed that, while the vast majority of businessmen and their trade associations wanted to scrap Bill C-256, a number supported it on some points at least.Purdy Crawford and J. T. Kennish dissented sharply with Recommendation 7. They stated, "The argument that the 'undueness' test should be retained is a complete denial of the need for reform."[179] They were prepared to support the suggested test of "significantly lessening competition." A. M. Hurley and W. P. McKeown disagreed with Recommendation 12. They wished to retain severe penalties for price-fixing violations.[180]

In contrast to these few leaning against the wind, most of the "dissenters" thought the recommendations did not go far enough. C. W. Brazier, a Vancouver lawyer, and E. Jacques Courtois rejected the whole idea of a civil tribunal. A similar position was taken by W. M. Winterton.[181] W. R. Clerehue voiced the Canadian businessman's preference for government-assisted combines when he said, "where imports represent a significant or significantly increasing share of the market, encouragement and sanction should be fostered for possible combinations or cooperative arrangements among domestic manufacturers and not be considered violations under competition legislation."[182] In other words, if import competition is beginning to be effective (probably after hurdling a high Canadian tariff), let the domestic manufacturers combine and engage in price fixing.

In a little less than two years after the Competition Act had been introduced, the concerted pressure of producer interests, almost entirely uncontested except by the energy and will of a handful of civil servants in the Department of Consumer and Corporate Affairs, had been able to turn back or at least modify significantly the nature of the reform of competition policy.

The retreat of the government was readily apparent. In June 1973, the *Financial Times* quotes a departmental official as follows:

> Nobody [in government] will be looking for perfection any more. There's a greater tendency to say, "that's pretty good. That's as far as we're prepared to go. There's no point in upsetting everybody.[183]

For civil servants closely associated with Bill C-256, the retreat was painful. A business critic describes Roy Davidson's, Deputy Director of Investigation and Research, reaction. "He was kind of bitter about the whole thing. 'Probably,' admits Mr. Davidson. 'I react rather vigorously. . . . When I don't agree with something I say so. But the bitterness doesn't last.'"[184]

NOTES

[1]Department of Consumer Affairs, *The Competition Act, Explanatory Notes*, Ottawa, 1971, mimeo, p. 1.

[2]*Ibid.*, p. 8.

[3]K. Wayne McCracken, "'Conspiracy' and the Competition Act: Certain Questions," *University of Toronto Law Journal*, Vol. 22, 1972, p. 60.

[4]July 2, 1971.

[5]July 17, 1971.

[6]Cited in *Leader-Post* (Regina), July 12, 1971, p. 30.

[6]July 5, 1971, p. 8.

[8]July 9, 1971.

[9]July 6, 1971.

[10]William Neilson, "The Competition Act and the Public," *Canadian Forum*, January-February, 1972, p. 2.

[11]Canadian Consumer Council, *Annual Report, 1971*, Ottawa, Queen's Printer, 1972, p. 10.

[12]July 2, 1971.

[13]As reprinted in the *Gleaner*, (Fredericton), Sept. 13, 1971.

[14]Toronto, August, 1971.

[15]Vancouver, August, 1971.

[16]July 3, 1971.

[17]July 1, 1971.

[18]July 17, 1971.

[19]July 28, 1971.

[20]July 26, 1971.

[21]August 2, 1971.

[22]August 6, 1971.

[23]August 9, 1971.

[24]*Sun*, (Vancouver), July 6, 1971, p. 4.

[25]September 6, 1971.

[26]James W. Younger "A Critique of the Competition Act in the Light of the Rule of Law," *Canada's Competition Policy*, Ottawa, the Conference Board in Canada, 1972, p. 74.

[27]*Ibid.*, pp. 76, 77. The costs of compliance argument was strongly echoed by Peter V. V. Betts in his article, "Hail Caesar," in the *Business Quarterly*, Winter 1971, p. 14. Additional critiques of the bill by lawyers and economists can be found in L. A. Skeoch (ed.), *Canadian Competition Policy*, Kingston, Industrial Relations Centre, Queen's University, 1972.

[28]Douglas I. W. Bruce, "Rationalization and Foreign Ownership," in *Canada's Competition Policy*, Ottawa, the Conference Board in Canada, 1972, p. 36.

[29]A. J. R. Smith, in *Canada's Competition Policy*, p. 39.

[30]Younger, *op.cit.*, pp. 31, 32.

[31]Milton Moore, in *Canada's Competition Policy*, p. 32.

[32]D. Gordon Blair, "Procedure," in *Canada's Competition Policy*, p. 42.

[33]H. J. Hemens, "Freedom of Commerce," in *Canada's Competition Policy*, p. 51.

[34]*Ibid.*, pp. 49-51.

[35]*Ibid.*, p. 64.

[36]*Ibid.*, p. 52.

[37]*Ibid.*, p. 53.

[38]*Ibid.*

[39]Blair, *op.cit.*, p. 68.

[40]Younger, *op.cit.*, p. 78.

[41]*Ibid.*, p. 80.

[42]*Ibid.*, p. 81.

[43]*Ibid.*

[44]October 28, 1971.

[45]McCracken, *op.cit.*, p. 61.

[46]*Ibid.*, p. 66.

[47]*Globe and Mail*, (Toronto), October 6, 1971, p. B4.

[48]*Time* (Canadian edition) March 24, 1975, p. 9.

[49]*Globe and Mail* (Toronto) October 21, 1971, p. B12.

[50]*Ibid.*, October 22, 1971, p. B3.

[51]Peter V. V. Betts, "Hail Caesar," *Business Quarterly*, Winter 1971, p. 15.

[52]*Ibid.*, p. 16.

[53]*Ibid.*, p. 18.

[54]*Ibid.*, p. 19.

[55]*Globe and Mail* (Toronto) Sept. 25, 1971, p. B3.

[56]Moore, *op.cit.*, p. 86.

[57]*Ibid.*, p. 86.

[58]Milton Moore, *How Much Price Competition? The Prerequisites of an Effective Canadian Competition Policy*, Montreal, McGill-Queen's Press, 1970, p. 127.

[59]*Ibid.*, pp. 68-75.

[60]*Ibid.*, p. 127.

[61]*Ibid.*, p. 130-131.

[62]*Ibid.*, pp. 131-134.

[63]Milton Moore, "Mergers and Price Agreements," in *Canada's Competition Policy*, pp. 21-22.

[64]*Ibid.*, p. 22.

[65]*Ibid.*, p. 24.

[66]*Ibid.*, p. 25

[67]*Ibid.*, p. 26.

[68]*Ibid.*

[69]*Ibid.*

[70]David L. McQueen, "Tribunals and Takeovers in Canada,"
in *Canada's Competition Policy*, p. 55.

[71]*Ibid.*, pp. 56-57.

[72]*Ibid.*, p. 57.

[73]*Ibid.*

[74]*Ibid.*, p. 58.

[75]*Ibid.*, p. 60.

[76]*Ibid.*, p. 61.

[77]*Ibid.*, p. 63.

[78]*Ibid.*

[79]Dale Orr, "What the Competition Act Doesn't Do," unpublished paper presented at the Faculty of Commerce and Business Administration, University of British Columbia, Continuing Education Seminar, November 19, 1971, p. 5.

[80]*Ibid.*, p. 6.

[81]*Ibid.*, p. 7.

[82]D. Orr, "The Competition Act and Its Application to the Service Sector," *B.C. Studies*, No. 13, Spring 1972.

[83]L. A. Skeoch, "Basic Economic and Policy Considerations," in L. A. Skeoch (ed.), *Canadian Competition Policy*, Kingston, Industrial Relations Centre, Queen's University, 1972, pp. 3-9.

[84]See note 83 for the conference proceedings.

[85]Skeoch, *op.cit.*, p. 9.

[86]L. A. Skeoch with B. C. McDonald in consultation with M. Belanger, R. M. Bromstein, W. O. Twaits, *Dynamic Change and Accountability in a Canadian Market Economy*, Ottawa, Supply and Services Canada, 1976.

[87]Skeoch, *op.cit.*, p. 8.

[88]*Ibid.*, p. 9.

[89]*Ibid.*

[90]H. E. English, "Specialization and Export Agreements: Their Potentials and Limitations," in L. A. Skeoch (ed.), *Canadian Competition Policy*, pp. 28-34.

[91]*Ibid.*, p. 33

[92]*Ibid.*

93Ibid.

94Ibid., p. 34

95Ibid.

96H. W. Arthurs, "The Professions and Competition Policy," in L. A. Skeoch (ed.), Canada's Competition Policy, pp. 50-56.

97Ibid., p. 50.

98Ibid.

99Ibid.

100Ibid., p. 51.

101Ibid., p. 52.

102Ibid., p. 54.

103Ibid., p. 54-56.

104G. L. Reuber, "Foreign Ownership and Competition Policy," in L. A. Skeoch (ed.), Canadian Competition Policy, pp. 57-65.

105Ibid., p. 58.

106Ibid., pp. 58-59.

107Ibid., p. 59.

108Ibid., p. 60.

109Ibid., p. 62.

110Ibid., p. 64.

111W. M. H. Gover, "Bill C-256: Legal and Operational Aspects," in L. A. Skeoch (ed.), Canadian Competition Policy, pp. 76-80.

112Ibid., p. 77.

113Ibid., pp. 77-78.

114Ibid., p. 78.

115Ibid., p. 79.

116Ibid., p. 80.

117October 4, 1971. One of the best discussions of the tribunal was contained in B. C. McDonald's paper, "The Central Legal Issues Raised By The Government Proposals,"in L. A. Skeoch (ed.), Canadian Competition Policy, pp. 10-17.

118November 3, 1971.

119November 25, 1971.

120Broadcaster, Toronto, November, 1971.

121Toronto, December, 1971. This view was shared by Mr. J. T. Jackson, executive vice-president of the Canadian Real Estate Association, who described C-256 as the "most dangerous and ominious piece of legislation ever presented" (Press [Timmins], December 10, 1971). The Globe and Mail [(Toronto) November 21, 1971] said, "Had the Competition Act been passed in its present formit would have had a ruinous effect upon the Canadian business community."

122October 30, 1971. The Herald [(Calgary) November 24, 1971] argued in an editorial that before a great effort was expended in moving the draft bill through the consultative process and the parliamentary committees, that its constitutionality be determined by a reference to the Supreme Court of Canada.

123October 27, 1971.

124As reprinted in the Tribune (Winnipeg), December 16, 1971. See also Norman P. Goldman, "Canadian Competition Law and Unfair Trade Practices," Boston College Industrial and Commercial Law Review, Vol. 13, No. 6, June 1972, p. 1329. Unfortunately, however, it would seem that the proposed act attempts to introduce a set of business ethics which is in direct contradiction with the concepts of a normally ethical businessman. Furthermore, the framing of the proposed legislation in concise but general language is of little use to a businessman who seeks to know whether a particular situation would be classified as having a "significant" restraint on competition. It would seem that even though the concept of "undueness" has been removed from the act, the alternative phraseology in using the term "significant" does not create more precision and certainty in the legislative language. Furthermore, the formation of a tribunal of seven individuals who would then be in a position to shape national policy in areas of great economic importance appears to be an excessive grant of power. In accordance with the proposed legislation, this quasi-judicial body wil be able to determine whether, and to what extent, Canadian companies may grow larger by merger, may attain more efficient production or distribution by a cooperative effort, or engage in certain trade practices of questionable benefit to the public interest. As a result, it would appear that by establishing a tribunal with such powers, many of the day-to-day business practices in Canada would be regulated by a detailed code of business ethics based on a highly theoretical view of competition policy. No doubt, there is a need for a tribunal which is better qualified to judge economic realities than the criminal courts. However, this need must be balanced against the questionable wisdom of creating a quasi-judicial body whose pwoers might greatly curtail business initiative."

[125]Maryon Brechin, Letter to the Editor, *Herald* (Calgary), December 18, 1971.

[126]*Journal* (Ottawa) December 20, 1971. Such consultation was highly functional, for Mr. Meyer noted, "Business has as great a stake in preparing the legislation as Mr. Basford." He also assured us that, "there need not be the conflicts of interest which are so readily presumed by sponsors of such legislation."

[127]December 11, 1971.

[128]The *Spectator* (Hamilton) was a strong and consistent opponent of C-256. On January 7, 1972 it stated: "In our opinion, the Competition Act, even if it is amended, has such a strong anti-business bias that it would have to be completely rewritten and have an entirely different philosophy in order for it not to place so much of Canada's commercial life in jeopardy. Practically every citizen will suffer unnecessarily if Mr. Basford has his way." A similar view as expressed by the *Observer* [(Sarnia) January 14, 1971)] which described the act as "overcure," a term analogous to overkill in nuclear terminology. The editorial cites the analysis by lawyer Len Weldon which "demonstrated that the act doesn't threaten just special interest groups, or big business or 'them' — whoever they are — but just about everyone."

[129]January 31, 1972.

[130]February 1, 1972.

[131]February 1, 1972.

[132]*Sun* (Vancouver), March 20, 1972.

[133]Memorandum prepared by or for Mr. G. C. Gascoigne, "Bill C-256 — The Competition Act," Department of Consumer and Corporate Affairs, January 1972, p. 2.

[134]D. H. W. Henry, memorandum, "Notes for Officials in Seminars on Competitive Policy," Department of Consumer and Corporate Affairs, March 9, 1972, p. 1.

[135]Graeme Hughes, "It's Still The Competition Act!" *Industrial Canada*, May 1972, p. 27.

[136]*Star-Phoenix*, (Regina) June 8, 1972. The views of Mr. Buchwald were also discussed in the *Financial Post*, November 6, 1971, p. 33.

[137]Neilson, *op.cit.*, p. 3.

[138]*Star* (Toronto), March 18, 1972. In March and April a series of seminars by departmental officials on the amendments to Bill C-256 were confined to the legal advisors of business, labour and consumer groups.

[139]March 24, 1972.

[140]March 24, 1972. The *Financial Post* had earlier expressed concern over the confrontation between the government and business. On January 29, 1972 the *Post* stated that ". . . the

present row [over Bill C-256] is widening the gap dangerously between business and government." The desire for conciliation was also voiced by the *Journal* [(Ottawa) February 1, 1971]. The crucial issue between business and the government was the tribunal and its extensive powers. "For all the shouting, government and business seem not far apart on changes required in the Competition Act. If the new Consumer Affairs Minister, Robert Andras, will meet reasonable requests for changes, in the form of the tribunal and other phases, the bill can be revised without destroying its purpose of developing a more equitable and competitive economy in Canada."

[141]April 4, 1972. The *Canadian Grocer*, (March 1972) stated that Mr. Andras "does not have the immediate inflammatory flamboyancy of his predecessor" and went on to describe him as "a man of quiet resolution" having "the entrepreneurial wisdom of a successful salesman." The article pointed out that the new minister had joined Ford of Canada in 1946 and was marketing director when he left in 1958 "to set up the first of four auto sales firms at the Lakehead."

[142]April 5, 1972.

[143]April 7, 1972, p. 6.

[144]Henry, *op.cit.*, p. 2.

[145]*Ibid.*, pp. 2-3.

[146]*Ibid.*, p. 3.

[147]*Ibid.*

[148]*Ibid.*, p. 4.

[149]*Ibid.*, p. 5.

[150]*Ibid.*, p. 6.

[151]*Ibid.*, pp. 6-7.

[152]*Ibid.*, p. 7.

[153]Cited in Claudy Kyles, "Should the Competition Bill be Scrapped?" *Canadian Business*, July 1972, p. 22.

[154]*Ibid.*, p. 22.

[155]April 10, 1972.

[156]April 10, 1972.

[157]March, 1972.

[158]*Globe and Mail* (Toronto), April 25, 1972.

[159]Hughes, *op.cit.*, p. 27.

[160]*Ibid.*, p. 30.

[161]*Ibid.*

[162]June 17, 1972.

[163]*Free Press* (Winnipeg), June 9, 1972, p. 17.

[164]Claudy Kyles, "Should the Competition Bill be Scrapped?" *Canadian Business*, July 1972, p. 24.

[165]*Journal* (Ottawa), October 31, 1972.

[166]Stephen Duncan, *Financial Post*, March 10, 1973.

[167]Before the official publication, the December 1971 edition of the *Canadian Forum* offered its readers "an abbreviated but authentic version of the Gray report on foreign ownership. . . . edited down to about one-quarter of its original size." The journal obtained all but the last two chapters of the memorandum to the Cabinet entitled "Domestic Control of the National Economic Environment: The Problems of Foreign Ownership and Control." The concern over foreign takeovers of Canadian firms and the level of foreign investment in Canada resulted in the Foreign Investment Review Act. It is interesting to note that the principal author of *Foreign Direct Investment in Canada*, Joel Bell, was also a special advisor to Mr. Basford on the preparation of the Competition Act.

[168]December 4, 1972, p. 1.

[169]*Financial Times,* December 19, 1972, p. 12.

[170]March 17, 1973.

[171]March 10, 1973.

[172]June 18, 1973, p. 6.

[173]Maurice Cutler and Douglas Brown, "New Consumer Affairs Minister Unlikely to Antagonize Businessmen," *Canadian Printer and Publisher,* March 1973, p. 18.

[174]*Financial Post,* March 10, 1973, p. 5. In March 1972 the Province of Manitoba had agreed not to challenge the constitutionality of the proposed legislation [*Globe and Mail* (Toronto) March 13, 1972]. At the Queen's Conference in January of 1972, H. I. MacDonald, Deputy Treasurer and Deputy Minister of Economics in the Ontario Department of Treasury and Economics invited his audience to "read between the lines [to] get the message without compromising [his] bureaucratic neutrality" in his paper which was sharply critical of Bill C-256. See H. I. MacDonald, "Competition Policy and Provincial Economic Development," in L. A. Skeoch (ed.), *Canadian Competition Policy,* pp. 18-27.

[175]Ian Urquhart, "The Competition Act, Contested Bill Is Back — In Bits," *Star* (Toronto), May 5, 1973, p. 27. Apparently in response to the publication by Statistics Canada in May 1973 of figures measuring the concentration in Canadian manufacturing industries in 1968, the Toronto *Star* called for the government to bring in *all* of its amended Competition Act quickly. The editorial pointed out that "Canada has no legislation either to encourage beneficial consolidation of some firms, or effectively to prevent mergers that simply create harmful monopoly" (June 1, 1973, p. 6).

[176]*Competition Policy in the Context of A Canadian Industrial Strategy,* summarizing discussion of the Seventh McGill Government — Industry Conference, Montreal, Faculty of Management, 1973, p. vii.

[177]*Ibid.,* p. vii.

[178]*Ibid.,* pp. 16-19.

[179]*Ibid.,* p. 17, footnote 17.

[180]*Ibid.,* p. 19, footnote 21.

[181]*Ibid.,* p. 18, fotnote 18.

[182]*Ibid.,* p. 19, footnote, 19.

[183]*Financial Times,* June 19, 1973.

[184]*Ibid.*

Chapter 9

Stage I: The Competition Act Becomes a Series of Amendments to the Combines Investigation Act

On July 18, 1973 the Minister of Consumer and Corporate Affairs, Mr. Gray, announced in the House of Commons that "instead of bringing forward legislation concerning competition policy in a single complex bill, the government has decided to implement the policy in stages."[1] On November 6, 1973 Stage I of Canada's proposed new competition policy was introduced in the House of Commons as Bill C-227, an act to amend the Combines Investigation Act. With C-227 another round of controversy began. It elicited a substantial volume of editorial comment and a variety of responses by columnists. Maurice Western summed it up nicely when he said that the "grand design [was] shelved for the sake of the possible." He continued,

> Experience, an even better teacher than the Economic Council, has persuaded the government that heaven is not reached in a single bound and the ministers have prudently decided, in the "first stage," to seek the politically attainable.[2]

As Mr. Western pointed out, "the government has reverted to the traditional approach. It is trying to repair the deficiencies of the old act and to add new protections intended to meet the changed needs of our time." The original bill (C-256) was described as "a full and politically glamorous response to the radical recommendations of the Economic Council." Mr. Western argued that "two years have been largely wasted in furious controversy with nothing accomplished." On the contrary, the virtually one-sided "debate" which ensued from Bill C-256 was productive in showing the very limited support that exists in Canada for an effective competition policy. The intense, narrowly focused interest of business easily defeated the broader and diffuse interests of consumers.[3] The limits of reform were clearly established — and they were only marginally (in terms of their real impact on market power) beyond our current provisions; provisions which have been greatly weakend or rendered virtually inoperative by restrictive judicial interpretations.[4]

THE CONTENTS OF STAGE I

The Stage I amendments incorporated a number of the changes in public policy embodied in the Competition Act some 28 months earlier. They also reflected, in part, the views of the business interests who had been extremely critical of Bill C-256. Finally, by design, the Stage I amendments did not incorporate a number of important issues in Canadian competition policy which were to be held over for Stage II.

The main elements of the Stage I legislation dealt with the following:[5]

1. The inclusion of a commercial services, including those of professionals, under the provisions of the Combines Investigation Act.
2. The establishment of civil procedures under which a number of "reviewable matters" could be brought before the Restrictive Trade Practices Commission by the Director of Investigation and Research. These included five trade practices (refusal to deal, consignment selling, exclusive dealing, tied selling and market restriction) and foreign laws and directives (see Figure 9-1). The RTPC was to be given the power to issue injunctive orders.
3. The establishment of the right of private parties to pursue single damage actions for (a) losses as a result of criminal offences under the act, and (b) losses as a result of a failure of a firm to comply with an order of the RTPC (see Figure 9-1).
4. A potentially significant expansion of the provisions relating to resale price maintenance (renamed price maintenance).
5. A major expansion and revision of the sections dealing with misleading advertising and a variety of deceptive trade practices.
6. Authority for the Director to intervene, either at his initiative or at the request of the regulatory agency, in the hearings of federal regulatory agencies in respect of the maintenance of competition.
7. Amendments to S.32, the principal section dealing with conspiracies, which saw the retention of the word "unduly," but eliminated the "virtual monopoly" test which had grown up in some of the decided cases. Bid rigging was prohibited per se and conspiracies involving professional sports were brought under the act.
8. Maximum penalties (fines and imprisonment) were increased for a number of offences, and new remedies were provided, i.e., interim injunctions, ones dealing with intellectual and industrial property.

The significance of the provisions will be discussed in the remainder of this chapter and in Chapter 10. A more comprehensive summary of the Stage I amendments as proposed in November 1973 is given in Appendix B.

It might be argued that most of the important issues were to be left to the Stage II amendments. These include:[6]

FIGURE 9-1

FIGURE 1

Competition Policy: Proposed Administration and Enforcement in the Stage I Amendments

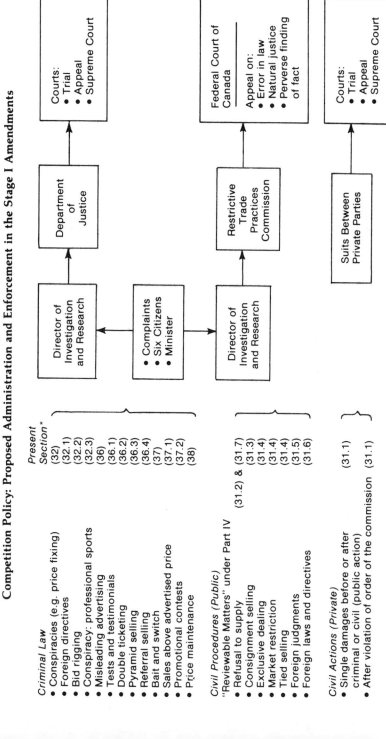

- Mergers
- Monopoly/monopolization/dominant firm problem
- Price discrimination (including advertising allowances)
- Loss leader selling
- Pricing practices, i.e., basing-point pricing, delivered pricing, etc.
- Consumer class actions
- Rationalization, specialization and export agreements
- Specialized tribunal to adjudicate cases brought under civil procedures
- Interlocking directorates

The advantages of the incremental approach were substantial. By framing the new competition policy as a series of amendments to a long existing statute (in largely its present form since 1923), the government reassured businessmen that it is building on the known body of the statute and the established judicial decisions. By retaining the word "unduly," the new amendments had a familiar ring, not to mention the high threshold for criminal liability. By turning over to the Restrictive Trade Practices Commission only a very small part of the role proposed for the Competitive Practices Uribunal (the name itself had negative connotations for business) the government substituted a known quantity for the fear of the unknown. The RTPC is known to be ineffectual. Even the Director of Investigation and Research has all but ignored it in recent years by sending his summary of evidence from his investigations directly to the Department of Justice for prosecution under S.15 of the act. In casting the reforms as amendments rather than as an entirely new act, the *process* was more familiar to business and, thus, more comforting. Substantively, the amendments were not too threatening either. By introducing the legislation in stages, Mr. Gray avoided imposing a major discontinuity on businessmen:

> It will be much easier for businessmen to learn to live under the new system when they are given time to adjust to one interrelated set of regulations before they have to grapple with new laws affecting mergers, amalgamations and other such matters that affect the efficiency and general structure of the economy.[7]

The Medicine Hat *News* saw the new bill (C-227) as "protecting small business from domination by big suppliers who use their economic power to control distribution and pricing." In addition, it thought that the misleading advertising provisions would "allow consumers to shop with greater confidence."[8]

John Bulloch, president of the Canadian Federation of Independent Business described the new bill as "moderate and responsible." He went on to say, "It's very important to small business that they can claim damages and costs from restrictive trade practices. Big business wanted this struck from the bill, but I'm pleased that Herb Gray has kept it in. The bill is a cautious first step in increasing the enforcement powers of the Crown in monopoly situations."[9]

The Victoria *Times* was critical of the new bill, stating that "there is no doubt that the new amendments are a pale shadow of the original Competitions [sic] Act."[10]

The Windsor *Star*, in Mr. Gray's own constituency, saw the bill as being "in the grand tradition of Liberal procrastination over controversial legislation." It said it was like the foreign takeover legislation for it left "gaps large enough to drive a herd of elephants through." Specifically, the *Star* stated, "This bill leaves far too much to be defined by the courts and by federal agencies." The editorial was also critical of the fact that the most important part of the reforms, that dealing with mergers, was to be included in the succeeding phase of the legislation: "That part of the legislation is being delayed, no doubt, because Ottawa wants the clearance of the business community first, and wants a reaction to the wishy-washy first half, now before the House of Commons." The *Star* concluded that the Liberal government's approach to the competition legislation was "the cowardly way out."[11]

A similar view was expressed by the Peterborough *Examiner*, which stated that Bill C-227 "may please some consumers with its limited provisions, but it will have little significant effect on the total market place." It concluded that "the government's new bill is just legislating against shady practices that should have been outlawed long ago." Like the Windsor *Star*, the *Examiner* said the true test of the government's will in the area of competition policy would have to wait until the second stage of amendments:

> The revised bill shows it is willing to move against racketeers and cheats. Only the second part of the bill will reveal whether the government will as courageously take on the combined strength of the business community.[12]

The London *Evening Free Press* thought the new bill contained "some striking improvements" in the area of consumer protection, and "one conspicuous retreat." The editorial praised the broadened misleading advertising/deceptive practices sections but was critical of the fact that, unlike the original Bill c-256, the amendments made "no attempt to bar manufacturers' use of the suggested retail price device to fix prices." Over one-half the editorial was devoted to a discussion of the powers of the tribunal as set out in the original Competition Act.[13]

The St. John's *Evening Telegram* proposed a behavioural test of the effectiveness of the Stage I amendments.

> A useful gauge of the effectiveness of the bill will be the amount of fuss made by the businessmen's association. If they set up a powerful

> lobby against the bill then the average consumer can guess that there
> must be a lot of protection in it for him.[14]

The editors noted that with the original bill there was a "lack of organized support for it from consumer groups and the labour movement." They suggested that if such groups find the new bill has been "seriously weakened . . . they should put pressure on the federal politicians to have any missing teeth put back in the bill."[15]

Having concluded that Bill C-227 was an "emasculated version" of Basford's original bill, columnist Charles Lynch viewed the situation at that time as follows: "Consumer Affairs Minister Herb Gray treads more softly into the field of competition policy than did his predecessor, Ron Basford, who got his shiny block knocked off. . . . Gray plays his music through a muted horn." He noted that Gray continues to invite "the views and recommendations of all interested parties" in attempting to come up with a"model statute."[16] In the same vein, Clair Balfour of the Ottawa *Citizen* noted: "Gone is the missionary zeal for sweeping reform that produced the draft competition Bill C-256 in June in 1971."[17] One might say that the climate of November 1973 was cool and grey in contrast to the sunshine and optimism of June 1971.

A fair number of positive views were expressed. The Kingston *Whig Standard* saw the bill "as putting some muscle behind the Combines Investigation Act" and as one that "should be welcomed by all consumers." It praised the sections on tests and testimonials and the general impression test proposed for misleading advertising. On the other hand, it recognized that "the onus for prosecution has still been left primarily on the shoulders of the consuming public" and was critical of the fact that no plan "has been established to aid consumers directly in their own legal battles with misleading advertisers." The editorial concluded that "without some convenient means of prosecuting offenders, all the comprehensiveness of the proposed bill is rendered next to useless."[18]

W. A. Wilson, writing in the Montreal *Star*, described C-227 as "a modest bill" and thought it deserved "modest praise." As he pointed out, the big and most contentious issues had been left for another day. He pinpointed very clearly the unresolved trade-off between the number of firms (competitive environment) and efficiency in terms of fewer, larger units (economies of scale).

> . . . we have never decided as a matter of agreed policy whether we
> should aim for the economies of scale, hoping that that will make us
> competition in the world and keep prices down at home, or whether
> we should encourage the existence of smaller, less efficient units and
> hope that competition between them will in some way provide
> adequate advantages.[19]

In terms of what was *not* eliminated from Stage I, Wilson correctly observed that the severity of the approach toward misleading advertising was the same in Bill C-227 as it was in Bill C-256. Wilson provides a good explanation: "Misleading advertising is closely related to fraud and it is, therefore, extremely difficult to defend, even by men who do not really want to stop exaggerating the merits of their products or inventing fictional values for them."[20] More cynically, one could suggest that a tough line on misleading advertising could be maintained because most of those with real market power in the Canadian economy would not be affected by such legislation. For example, the *Financial Post* called for stronger federal and provincial legislation against pyramid selling. It asked, "is catching the pusher of a pyramid scheme on a charge of misleading advertising good enough?"[21] We would argue that this is a "safe" target, as compared to a tough anti-merger law which would definitely cause a strong negative reaction in the business community.

Vincent Egan, business and consumer affairs analyst for the Thomson News Service, supported the new legislation and urged that Parliament pass the legislation quickly "for the sake of the Canadian consumer." Mr. Egan proved to be much too sanguine when he said, "Surely no party in parliament will be able to find much fault with the Gray proposals." Egan saw the new bill as "vastly superior to the top-to-bottom competition bill introduced in 1971 . . ." which "seemed to have been the product of firebreathing consumer activities and theoretical economists who envisaged a Utopia of perfect competition." The only disquieting note in Mr. Egan's column was the problem of enforcement which, if left up to consumers, he thought would not be effective.[22]

The *Financial Times,* which had strongly opposed Bill C-256, argued that, "Anyone who has been misled into regarding the new amendments to the Combines Act as a paper tiger should take a second look." The editors said that, "considerable chunks" of the 1971 bill were adopted in the Stage I legislation. They viewed the amendments as a being "presented, blatantly and officially, as a response to the wave of consumer complaints about inflation."[23] Apparently, the *Financial Times* would have the government be highly responsive to the complaints of business, but not to those of consumers — a not surprising inconsistency. The Toronto *Star* suggested that it "is not an unduly cynical view" to depict the bill as be "a shiny sham hurried forward to make it appear that the government is at least doing something about rising prices." Along with a number of other papers, the *Star* indicated that Canada would "not have a real competition policy . . . until we get a bill which deals with monopolies in light of national industrial strategy."[24]

BILL C-227 BECOMES BILL C-7

At the Christmas recess Bill C-227 was still before Parliament. On March 11, 1974 Mr. Gray reintroduced the Stage I amendments unchanged as Bill C-7. On April 1, after six days of debate, the bill passed Second Reading and was then referred to the House Standing Committee on Finance, Trade and Economic Affairs. The committee originally set May 15 as the deadline for written submissions. This deadline was later extended.

The reintroduction of the bill touched off another round of critical comment. Toronto lawyer W. A. Macdonald described the bill as a "slimmed down and cleaned up" version of Bill C-256, but noted that "it could still turn out to be a political sleeper with enough dynamite to cause the minority Liberal government as much trouble as the original 'horror'." While Gray's approach was viewed as "a vast improvement over Basford's . . . the guts of the old Ottawa syndrome remains. Their reflection in the power of the tribunal and the strong move into provincial jurisdiction have a continuing potential for major harm to the economy, responsibility in government, the conduct of our international economic relations and the balance of our constitutional arrangements."[25]

Although the tribunal was not to be found in the Stage I amendments, a number of writers saw evils similar to those ascribed to the tribunal in the new duties assigned to the RTPC. John Meyer was concerned about the commission's discretion to interpret the criteria of "adequate competition" and its "authority to implement its judgment." He argued that "the commission should be required to submit its judgments to the test of an impartial referee." By this he meant the courts. He wanted the "watchdog over competition . . . kept under reasonable restraint."[26]

The Toronto *Star* objected to the new role given the RTPC in that "it would make its own law as it goes from case to case." It wanted Parliament to give the commission guidelines as to what it meant by "adequate competition" to avoid having to wait for "10 years of experience" of decided cases to obtain a working definition. The editorial concluded that "Parliament has an obligation to spell out what the law means rather than delegate that right to an appointed body."[27]

Michael Barkway of the *Financial Times* devoted an entire column to his concern about the undefined powers of the RTPC over such established practices as refusal to deal, exclusive dealing (including he argued patented or copyrighted items and franchises), tied sales and market restrictions. "The central complaint [is] that no one knows, because the bill does not define, what the Restrictive Trade Practices Commission might do with its proposed powers."[28]

The editorial position of the *Financial Times* was that M.P.s had "very little understanding of the scope" of Bill C-7 or "any awareness of the sweeping discretionary powers which they are asked to give to the Restrictive Trade Practices Commission. . . . The bugbear of Mr. Gray's bill is 'an adequate degree of competition'."[29]

Canadian businessmen strongly rejected the original approach which would have set out quite a long list of criteria to be used by the tribunals in arriving at its decisions and also provided a list of per se offences in favour of a "less restrictive approach." Paradoxically, when only broad terms are proposed for the RTPC so that it can utilize a case-by-case approach, these are also rejected as being "undefined" and endowing the commission with too much discretionary power. What businessmen reject for the RTPC they apparently endorse for the courts. They are no doubt aware that the courts have adopted narrowly defined (implicit) criteria in combines matters and have enforcee a high standard of proof in these criminal offences.

In an article in the Toronto *Globe and Mail*, W. A. Macdonald continued to attack the bill and in particular the powers of RTPC.

> For the first time in Canadian peacetime history there is to be a centralized, not-accountable-to-anyone bureaucracy with virtually unfettered surveillance power over a central segment of the national economy. The segment that gets goods and services to market. If Parliament accepts this radical approach, it will almost certainly be only the first step in a major expansion of tribunal power to cover such important aspects of industrial policy as mergers, pricing, export ventures and specialization arrangements.[30]

In reply, Professor D. McQueen of York University and Professor J. Ziegel of the University of Toronto described Macdonald's article as "tale-spinning and the vigorous waving of bogeymen before the business community . . . too imaginative to be credible in the Canada of 1974." They argued that the efforts of big business to "scuttle Bill C-7" were "misguided" and that business "would do well to ponder whether a reasonable competition policy is a greater evil than the much closer intervention public opinion is bound to demand sooner or later if the present bill is emasculated beyond recognition."[31]

In any event, Mr. Macdonald's statement that the RTPC would not be accountable to anyone was factually incorrect. The commission was made subject to the Federal Court Act, S.28 of which provides for the review of decisions of federal boards, commissions and tribunals on a number of grounds: (i) failure to observe principles of natural justice or action beyond jurisdiction or failure to exercise jurisdiction; (ii) errors in law in reaching decisions; and (iii) basing decisions on errors in fact made perversely or capriciously or without regarding material before them.

McQueen and Ziegel pointed out two additional significant

misstatements in Macdonald's argument regarding refusal to deal and exclusive dealing.[32]

The fears of Mr. Macdonald seemed to be somewhat exaggerated. For example, J. W. Rowley, also a Toronto lawyer, pointed out in an accompanying article that "where a price-fixing agreement is alleged — and such an agreement is clearly detrimental to consumers — it must be proved beyond a reasonable doubt that competition has been unduly lessened before a conviction can be found." This is precisely the test which has been in existence in the Combines Act for many years. The fact that Bill C-7 eliminated the "virtual monopoly" doctrine in conspiracy cases simply writes out of future judicial decisions a doctrine given exaggerated prominence by its adoption in two key *merger* cases decided in 1960, *Canadian Breweries* and *B.C. Sugar*.[33]

Conservative M.P. for Peel-Dufferin-Simcoe, Ellwood Madill, was critical of the bill for both going too far and not far enough. He called it the "government interference bill." In this vein he was critical of the sections concerning the RTPC, "giving it almost unlimited powers and no corresponding responsibility." He continued, "It becomes investigator, judge, jury and prosecutor all rolled into one." On the other hand, he noted that "supervision of competition among bankers has been left to the Inspector General of Banks who has only a staff of two. What a farce if the government is really serious about promoting competition!" Procedurally, Mr. Madill said that Conservative members were "concerned that the persons, associations, business and consumer interests which will be affected by the bill be given sufficient opportunity to express their opinions. The Liberal government should not be allowed to railroad this bill through the committee and Third Reading in the face of so much opposition." He urged "complacent Canadians" not to leave the bill to the experts but to write and join with others to make their voices heard.[34]

Mr. Madill's article is fascinating because exactly one day earlier in the Fredericton *Gleaner*, the Conservative M.P. for York-Sunbury published an article *identical* to that of Mr. Madill except for the headline. Similarly, on the same day as Mr. Madill published his article, the Conservative M.P. for Grenville-Carleton published the same article (under the title "Walter Baker Comments on Competition Policy") in the Winchester *Press*. The question that arises is whether the Conservative M.P.s were indulging in plagiarism (if so, who was copying whom?), or whether none of the M.P.s wrote the article but simply adopted as their own the words of a third party — perhaps the research staff of the Conservative caucus? The mystery remains.

Certainly one group which made its voice heard was the so-called "Stelco Group." It was formed in 1971 when the chairman of the Steel Company of Canada organized a number of business executives to write the prime minister about the proposed Canada Labour Code. In early 1974 there were thirteen firms in the group. The brief presented to Herb Gray in April 1974 was the third since the beginning of 1972. A. J. MacIntosh, a senior partner in Blake, Cassels and Graydon, a Toronto law firm, apparently monitored legislative developments and drafted the group's briefs. Excluding one member (T. Eaton Co. Ltd.), the *Financial Times* put the group's combined revenues at $7.8 billion and their assets at $7.5 billion in 1973.[35] The group supplemented their briefs by visits to Ottawa for face-to-face discussions with the minister and, more particularly, with the senior civil servants in charge of rewriting the original Competition Act.On April 4, 1974, less than a month after the Stage I amendments were reintroduced, the Toronto *Star* stated that "a massive business lobby is building up against the government's new competition bill." The article suggested that the efforts of the lobbyists were directed towards the Progressive Conservatives, "who are seen as the last hope for stopping the bill or at least substantially amending it before it becomes law."

On the issue of getting the bill changed, W. A. Macdonald concluded that "the politics of the minority government will determine that — and what business and the public, including the press, have to say between now and the committee report will determine the outcome.[36]

Among the lobbyists cited by name in the *Star* article were J. W. Younger of Stelco, G. G. E. Steele of the Grocery Products Manufacturers' of Canada[37] and W. A. Macdonald. The florid rhetoric continued unabated. Mr. Younger was quoted as saying, "As we look into the unkempt cemetery of Canadian industrial policy, it seems to me that the last ghost is pointing a bony finger at a gravestone bearing the legend 'Canadian Business Freedom and the Rule of Law, R.I.P.'"[38] By now the rules of the business-government competition policy game were well-defined. An aide in Herb Gray's office is quoted as saying, "We expected a business lobby against it. It would not be a very good competition bill if it wasn't attacked by business."[39]

THE SENATE GETS STARTED ON COMMITTEE HEARINGS

Recognizing the importance of the legislation to business, Senator Salter A. Hayden, chairman of the Standing Senate Committee on Banking, Trade and Commerce, on March 27, 1974 moved that his committee "be authorized to examine and report any bill relating to competition in Canadthe combines Investigation Act, in advance of the said bill coming before the Senate, or on any matter relating thereto . . . ." In his argument for getting his committee underway, nineteen months before the bill passed the House of Comons, the Senator cited Mr. Gray's reference to the "sheer extensiveness" and "complexity" of the bill.[40] The

Senator also indicated that he viewed himself as taking up the minister's invitation to business and others to seek clarification of the proposals and to indicate their views on Stage I. It is believed that Mr. Gray himself favoured early examination of the Stage I amendments by the Senate committee because he would be able to deal with the concerns of both the House and Senate committees at the same time. In this way he hoped to move the bill more rapidly through the legislative process.

Speaking on Senator Hayden's motion, Senator Jacques Flynn described the procedure as "rather unorthodox," but good "in the sense that it is half way between our legislative responsibilities and the responsibility we have assumed over the years in the field of investigation." He continued, "We are not really dealing with the bill, we are dealing with the problem and we are trying to find out whether the proposed bill really meets the situation."[41] He thought that this was just the sort of bill "of which the Senate is eminently qualified to study the substance." Senator Flynn quoted a *Financial Times* editorial which stated that "the House of Commons faces Bill C-7 with very little understanding of its scope." The editorial was particularly concerned with "the sweeping discretionary powers" of the RTPC. Senator Flynn saw the Senate committee as "being in a position to hear witnesses and obtain briefs from people who are really qualified to comment on and really concerned with the substance of the legislation."[42] Senator Paul Martin echoed Senator Flynn, "The committee . . . is particularly qualified to deal with matters of this kind because of the great experience of its members, and the experience of so many other senators as well."[43] Senator Hayden's motion was agreed to and the committee's first day of hearings was May 1, when a large delegation from the Canadian Manufacturers' Association appeared. At the second day of hearings, officials of the Canadian Chamber of commerce and the Canadian Real Estate Association gave testimony. In both cases they plunged directly into the detailed wording of the Stage I proposals. Senator Flynn's desire to deal with the problem and not with the bill was nowhere in evidence.

Henry Aubin of the Montreal *Gazette* said that the reason that the Senate was "taking the unusual step of viewing the legislation in advance of the House was so that the complaints made by the witnesses at its hearings may have more impact on the Department of Consumer and Corporate Affairs . . . when it redrafts the bill."[44] As to the "great experience" of the committee, Mr. Aubin indicated that of its 22 members 12 were officers or directors of 114 companies according to the *Financial Post's Directory of Directors.*[45] Senator Hayden raised the average. He was a director or officer in thirteen firms, not to mention being a member of one of Canada's largest law firms, McCarthy and McCarthy.

CONFLICT OF INTEREST IN THE SENATE?

Senator Hayden in 1975 had been chairman of the Standing Senate Committee on Banking, Trade and Finance for a quarter of a century and member of the Senate for thirty-five years. He was also, for many years, a vice-president and a director of Atlantic Sugar Refineries Co. Ltd. and its later owner, Jannock Corporation.[46]

In November 1958 and February 1959 Hayden appeared as counsel with two other members of his Toronto law firm for Acadia-Atlantic Sugar Refineries and its associated companies in hearings on the Director of Investigation and Research's Statement of Evidence before the Restrictive Trade Practices Commission.[47] The RTPC concluded "that the practices engaged in by the three eastern refiners . . . have limited competition in the eastern sugar refining industry to the detriment of the public."[48] In March 1962 the three companies were charged with conspiring to prevent or lessen competition unduly in the production, manufacture, purchase, barter sale, transportation or supply of refined sugar in eastern Canada. All three pleaded guilty and were convicted on January 15, 1963. On March 18, 1963 they were each fined $25,000 and made subject to an order prohibiting the continuation or repetition of the offence. Atlantic appealed the terms of the Prohibition Order. A final decision by the Quebec Court of Appeal upholding the Crown, was not rendered until July 21, 1967. Although the indictment covered only the period 1950 to 1953, the agreement by the three refiners "extended over a considerable number of years."[49]

Senator Hayden's efforts on behalf of Atlantic Sugar while he was both chairman of the senate committee, which reviews combines legislation, and an officer and director of the sugar refiner, apparently continued. In 1963 the Senator's help was solicited by the president of Atlantic at the time a new entrant to the industry was about to appear on the scene. Justice Kenneth MacKay, in his judgment in recent eastern sugar case stated:

> . . . Paton's efforts to have the Cartier project "nipped in the bud" as
> he asked Atlantic's politically influential vice-president, Senator
> Salter Hayden, to do (Exhibit p-2, 8-14), were in the long run
> unsuccessful. . . .[50]

Senator Hayden's multiple connections seemed evident in the choice of the counsel for the Senate Standing Committee which reviewed Bill-C-2. Rober J. Cowling, the committee's counsel, was a law partner of Yves Fortier who, in turn, is a member of Jannock Corporation Ltd.'s board of directors and the counsel for Atlantic (part of Jannock) in the big sugar case tried during 1974 and 1975. When asked about Cowling's appointment, Hayden pointed out that as chairman of the committee he doesn't vote, "the committee makes the decisions." Mr. Cowling was "highly recommended." Hayden told the *Globe and Mail* reporter, "Even if I recalled who recommended him, I don't think it's any of your business to know."[51]

When asked whether his interests were closer to Jannock or to the Canadian public when his committee was studying the combines legislation, Senator Hayden thought the question was "hypothetical" and "stupid." "Are you suggesting that I couldn't be honest?" he asked. He retreated to the "experience" argument as a number of his colleagues had done. "If I bring the experience I've acquired to the benefit of the Senate, I think that's a good thing."[52]

Another facet of the conflict of interest issue came out when two of Senator Hayden's colleagues rose to do him honour after he announced his retirement from what was referred to as "a very brilliant and highly successful legal career during which he served Canada and his fellow Canadians for some fifty-three consecutive years."[53] In the same speech, Senator Desruisseaux indicated that Senator Hayden had spent forty years in the Senate [sic] for twenty-five of which he was chairman of the Standing Committee on Banking, Trade and Commerce. The unitiated may wonder how the Senator kept his law practice and his Senate duties separate. Senator David Croll thought he did not.

> This guy Hayden makes a career out of practicing law as chairman of the committee. That's what he did and that's what I've always objected to. But there are too damn many around him who are also interested.
> I've no interest in Hayden one way or the other, but this is a wrong thing for him to do. No lawyer should be chairman of a committee if he's in the practice of law.
> He's got a terrific advantage and he could lure clients. The temptation is too great. He's in a different position and he shouldn't be using it. If he were a doctor or an engineer, I couldn't care less, but as a lawyer he deals with clients — tax clients — and has something to offer.[54]

Whether he was "practicing law" in the Senate or not, Senator Hayden's great skills as a committee chairman have long been recognized. He cultivated other senators', M.P.s' and even Cabinet ministers' reliance on him for advice on pieces of complex legislation affecting business. He was a master of detail who "did his homework" and his interpersonal skills were great. The following comment by Senator Walker is illuminating.

> Day after day we get these long-winded witnesses in the Banking, Trade and Commerce committee and he would just say, "Leave it to me." He would, without offending them, or hurting them, or even without their knowing about it, cut them down to size. They would even go away rejoicing that they had such a good hearing. That is a talent that very few of us can match.[55]

Senator Hayden's multiple connections to business, their legal representatives and legislative power are not unique in the Canadian Senate.

In 1973, the 91 members of the 102-seat body held 220 corporate directorships as recorded in the *Parliamentary Guide* and two financial directories.[56] However, these directorships were (and are) highly concentrated in relatively few hands. The 22 members of the Senate Banking, Trade and Commerce committee held 165 of the 220 directorships. Only 8 senators held 130 directorships and one (Louis-Philippe Gelinas) held 24. Others with many directorships indicated: John Aird (14), Paul Desruisseux (18), Harry Hays (11), Alan MacNaughton (20), Jacques Flynn (9), Louis-Philippe Beaubien (16), Salter Hayden (18).[57]

"Senator Gelinas argues that it is important to his role as a legislator to hold directorships, to enable him to be 'appraised of what's going on in the economy'." Senator Government Leader Paul Martin noted, "There's no obligation, no law which says a man can't be a director of a company."[58] True, the question is whether legislators should also be company directors. While, as Senator Flynn has noted, the committee only votes once a year, it serves as a prestigious and sympathetic forum for business interests on important legislation. Stanley Knowles, NDP House Leader in the Commons, makes the point when he stated, "It's the whole social attitude of people who are directors of corporations. Their basic concern is for success and profitability of business. They just don't have the viewpoint of ordinary Canadians."[59]

Another perspective on the Senate and conflict of interest is offered by Banking, Trade and Commece committee clerk F. A. Jackson. He says that in his eight years with the Senate banking committee he had

> often been surprised at how objective these guys are. Senators, he says, very often "bend over backwards to be fair."
>
> A lot of people who aren't on the scene think a senator is going to take care of the bank of whatever, but this is rarely the case. Mind you, they may be smart about it and keep teeing up the bank's lawyers on inside information, what to watch out for and what's coming up.
>
> Mr. Jackson says such exchanges of information are not visible, even to him, but "after all, it's human nature."[60]

As the decennial revisions of the Bank Act move toward consideration by the Senate Standing Committee on Banking, Trade and Commerce we are reminded that eight of the committee's more senior members hold one or more directorships in financial institutions.[61] Four are directors of chartered banks. Finance Minister Donald Macdonald said, "I don't know if there's anything we can do about asking the senators to stand down when this legislation is going through the Senate. But I would hope — expect — they would be discreet in the way they approach legislation."[62] Later, five senators announced they would not sit or vote on the committee while the Bank Act is being discussed.[63] However, Alan MacNaughton, the deputy chairman of the committee, was reported to have "said he had no intention of stepping down despite the fact he is an international advisor to the Swiss Bank Corporation. He told the Senate he intended to make 'the best possible use of his time'"[64] in his official position.

In the fall of 1976 efforts were made by members of the Senate to remove Senator Salter Hayden from his chairmanship of the Senate Banking, Trade and Commerce committee. The eighty-year-old senator and his allies were able to defeat the opposition and ensure that he would shepherd through the amendments to the Bank Act.[65] Geoffrey Stevens of the *Globe and Mail*, writing about the banking committee's treatment of Bill C-58, the magazine and broadcasting legislation in mid-1976, described the power of Hayden and his committee.

> Its recommendations tend to be regarded as Holy Writ by the Senate as a whole. Senator Hayden, 80, who is the dean of the Senate, is probably the most influential single member of the Upper House; he carries more clout than Senator Ray Perrault, the Government Leader.[66]

Returning to the issue of conflict of interest among senators with respect to the Stage I amendments, we find that Senator Godfrey commented on this issue on October 22, 1975 in the debate on the amendments. He stated: "Before I was appointed to the Senate [late in 1973], I was active in the preparation of briefs, on behalf of clients of my firm, addressed to the minister concerned." Senator Godfrey felt he should make a "public declaration" of what he considered to be his conflict of interest. He stated he would not participate in the debate, in any votes or in the discussions in committee.[67] On the next day that debate resumed on the amendments. Seantor Jacques Flynn noted Senator Godfrey's speech and said, ". . . I would suggest that he should not want to impose on others his criteria as to what constitutes conflict of interest."[68] He pointed out that "it would be very difficult for the Senate to operate," if senators, having taken an interest in a piece of legislation on behalf of clients, felt they could not give an opinion on it in the Senate. He asked, "If all the expertise we have in the Senate could not be put to use of what use then would the Senate be?"[69]

The following day Senator Godfrey, on a question of privilege, stated that he believed that his remarks on conflict of interest had been "misunderstood." He reviewed the definitions and proposals set out in the Green Paper, *Members of Parliament and Conflict of Interest*, which was then being considered by the Standing Senate Committee on Legal and Constitutional Affairs. He then stated his own position:

> . . . in my judgement it would be highly improper for any member of Parliament, be he in the Commons or the Senate, to accept a fee, professionaly or otherwise to either personally make direct representation to a minister, or for his personal assistance with the preparation of a brief to a minister, with respect to legislation then before Parliament.[70]

He then put in the usual courtesy caveat. "Knowing the members of this house as I do, it would be inconceivable to me that any member would do so," he said.[71]

It is a trenchant comment on Canadian political life that it was one of the recommendations of the Green Paper that the following be incorporated into the Standing Orders of the House and the Rules of the Senate in 1975:

> A Member [Senator] shall not advocate any matter or cause related to his personal, private or professional interests among Members or Senators, or among public servants, or before any Government boards or tribunals, for a fee or reward, direct or indirect.[72]

The Green Paper on conflict of interest was presented to Parliament in July 1973. Two years later the Commons Standing Committee on Privileges and Elections presented its report on the Green Paper to the House.[73] One year after that the Standing Senate Committee on Legal and Constitutional Affairs presented its report to the Senate.[74] Almost four years after the Green Paper was made public, Canada still has no legislation dealing with conflict of interest as it relates to members of Parliament and senators.[75]

ANOTHER ELECTION, ANOTHER MINISTER OF CONSUMER AND CORPORATE AFFAIRS

On April 1, 1974 the House of Commons referred Bill C-7 (the Stage I amendments to the Combines Investigation Act) to the House Standing Committee on Finance, Trade and Economic Affairs. The committee began its hearings on April 24 when the minister, Mr. Gray, appeared to introduce the bill accompanied by his senior officials. Mr. Gray continued his testimony on April 25, 30 and on May 3.

On May 8, 1974 the minority Liberal government was defeated on a want of confidence motion. Parliament was dissolved the next day. Also on May 8 J. J. Quinlan, the Acting Director of Investigation and Research since February 1973 was appointed chairman of the RTPC. Mr. R. J. Bertrand was appointed the Director of Investigation and Research.

In the ensuing general election of July 8 the Liberals were returned with 141 seats to the Conservatives' 95 and so had a sizeable majority to work with. Exactly one month later, Andre Ouellet, the Postmaster General, was appointed as Minister of Consumer and Corporate Affairs while his predecessor, Herb Gray, was dropped from the Cabinet.

In what appears to be a prophetic article less than one week before the government fell, *The 4th Estate* of Halifax pointed out that the hunting record of big business in regard to proposed competition legislation was pretty good. "The heads of two Consumer and Corporate Affairs ministers are already stuffed and mounted in the private lounges of Bay and St. James Street. . . . We hear that [Mr. Gray's] measurements are being taken and a space being already readied on the walls of business clubs."[76] In an article in the Windsor *Star*, also published one week before Parliament was dissolved, it was argued that Mr. Gray was "being cruelly exploited by the government," for it had "taken much of his work over the last four years and treated it with near contempt." The article cited the foreign investment review process, the Competition Act and the anti-profiteering bill.[77] Although Herb Gray had defended the anti-profiteering legislation as "designed essentially to prevent business firms from exploiting current inflationary conditions to unduly enhance profits by engaging in specific price gouging and profiteering practices,"[78] he was "all but abandoned in his efforts to defend it. The day Gray opened debate, the Liberal front benches were empty."[79] The bill died on the order paper after Second Reading when Parliament was dissolved early in May. Mr. Gray's exit was described in the Montreal *Gazette* as a "fast slide down Ottawa's razor blade."[80] Mr. Gray himself, was at a total loss to understand where he went wrong, although the newspapers most commonly attributed his exit to his very low profile and his lack of ability as a "communicator." In 1972 Ron Basford was transferred out of consumer and corporate affairs for what appeared to be the opposite reasons. He communicated the consumer point of view too well and he maintained too high a profile.

The *Financial Times* viewed the appointment of Mr. Ouellet "as puzzling as the dismissal of Mr. Gray." Mr. Ouellet was described as "amiable, young and presumably a person for whom the prime minister has great hopes." But, the article noted, "he is virtually unknown to the business community."[81] At the time of his appointment, Mr. Ouellet was thirty-five, the youngest member of the Cabinet. Maurice Cutler, in *Marketing*, gave what now (in light of his 1976 citation for contempt of court) must be an ironic description of the new minister: "A smooth, cool operator, he is unlikely to shoot from the hip."[82] The *Financial Post* called consumer and corporate affairs "a tough portfolio" and noted that the new minister would have his hands full learning about the department's legislation either recently passed, before Parliament or in the proposal stage. Apparently referring to Mr. Gray's alleged deficiencies, the *Post* stated:

> No one knows about Andre Ouellet's ability as a communicator of government policy. But the cards are surely stacked against him. It's

difficult, on the corporate side, to make witty, entertaining speeches on specialization agreements or trademark law.[83]

In September, Mr. Ouellet began "communicating" by publicly criticizing the Minister of Agriculture, Eugene Whelan, for his attacks on the Food Prices Review Board. Ouellet is quoted as saying, "If I had to criticize the prime minister on this, I would have done it too. Consumers were being unfairly treated and, whether it had meant criticizing a minister, the prime minister, or the queen, it had to be said."[84]

In reference to another proposed piece of legislation, Mr. Ouellet said in late September that the "government is committed to an anti-profiteering bill." His interviewer noted that "his emphasis is on the word 'an' and he broadly hints that major changes will be made in the badly drafted legislation."[85] Two weeks earlier, the *Financial Post* had advised its readers, "Don't be too surprised if the government's controversial anti-profiteering bill just quietly fades away. Although Prime Minister Trudeau promised during the recent election campaign that the bill would be reintroduced during the new session, there seems to be little enthusiasm among senior Cabinet officials for its return. . . . With the government's new independence from the NDP, much of the political motivation for the bill has disappeared. . . . The anti-profiteering bill always was regarded as a bit of Liberal strategy to maintain NDP support in the last precarious minority Parliament."[86]

STAGE I BECOMES BILL C-2

On October 2, 1974 Mr. Ouellet introduced Bill C-2 into the House of Commons and it was given First Reading. The bill was identical to its predecessors, C-7 and C-227. It was given Second Reading on October 22 and was sent to the House Standing Committee on Finance, Trade and Economic Affairs on October 28.

The reintroduction of the Stage I amendments elicited a smaller volume of editorial and columnist comment than had been the case in March. The Toronto *Star* restated its opposition to the vague wording of the act which "gives the commission [RTPC] virtual power to write the law as it goes along."[87] Paul Hellyer, a former Liberal Cabinet minister, but a newspaper columnist at the time, attacked the misleading advertising sections of the bill. He argued that Mr. Ouellet and Mr. Gray "might be a bit more cautious [in their claims for the bill] if the section on misleading advertising applied equally to politicians as with businessmen." He stated that "the government's repeated pledge that the bill will be of significant benefit in controlling inflation is . . . highly misleading." Mr. Hellyer was also critical of the exceptions to the bill and he cited the case of professions subject to provincial legislation and banks subject to the authorization of the Minister of Finance.[88]

With respect to both the competition and anti-profiteering bills, the *Financial Times* gave the following advice:

> Rather than opposing the government's intent, the business community should concentrate on giving Mr. Ouellet as good advice as possible so that the laws, when they do reach the statute books, will be as workable and sensible as possible.[89]

By late October business was gearing up to present its case yet again. The Canadian Manufacturers' Association had indicated it wanted a meeting with Mr. Ouellet within thirty days. A similar request came from the Canadian Chamber of Commerce. The Canadian Bar Association indicated it would probably ask to make an oral submission at the committee stage to follow up its earlier written submission. Activity now focused on getting amendments during the hearings before the House Committee. The best way to ensure the passage of such amendments was to persuade the minister to include them in *his* list of amendments to be presented to the committee. Mr. Ouellet's amendments, thirty in number, were presented to the House of Committee on December 3, 1974.

Before his amendments were presented, Mr. Ouellet's views started to be expressed in his speeches. In his first major address to businessmen in Montreal in October 1974, the minister indicated that he saw Canadian consumers as his main constituency and that the interests of the consumer could be best served if the market functioned effectively and equitably. Mr. Ouellet recognized the dual role of his department and indicated he would take an evenhanded approach.

> As much as I intend to work for a fair deal for consumers, I have no intention of achieving this in ways I consider unfair to producer or business interests. In the long run a fair market place means fair for all and I intend to adopt an evenhanded approach to my ministerial responsibilities. I don't intend to present myself as the enemy of businessmen or business interests. I say this because I honestly don't believe that our goals are really all that incompatible.[90]

The Senate committee resumed its hearings on October 30, 1974 and continued through November and December. Both the House and the Senate committees worked on the bill after the Christmas recess in February and March. On March 18, 1975 the Senate committee's interim report was presented. A further two days of hearings were held in April (16th and 23rd) and another one in June, with the second interim report given on June 26. The minister appeared before the House committee to speak to his amendments. He and his senior officials, who also testified, gave their evidence April 8, 10, 16, 22, 24, 29 and May 2, 8, 12, 20, 22, 27, 29, 30 and on June 2 and 3.

TABLE 9-1

Briefs and Testimony Before the House and Senate Committees Considering the Stage 1 Amendments to the Combines Investigation Act, 1974-75

Category of Brief or Testimony	Senate Committee		House Committee	
	Brief	Testimony	Brief	Testimony
Individual firms	8[1]	3[1]	22	2
Business and trade organization	26	16	45	11
Provincial government	1	0	0	0
Professional organization	2	2	5	0
Consumer organization	1	1	2	2
Professional Sports organization	1	2	0	0
Amateur sports organization	2	5	1	1
Other	0	0	7[2]	0
TOTAL	41	29[3]	82	16[4]

[1]Includes the joint brief and appearance on behalf of Stelco and twelve other large firms, counted as a single brief and appearance.

[2]Includes C. D. Howe Research Institute, an association of cooperatives, National Farmers Union, Professor D. N. Thompson and three law firms or individual lawyers.

[3]Only five of the twenty-nine did not also present a formal brief.

[4]All sixteen also presented a formal brief.

SOURCE:

Tabulation by the author from Tables 9-2, 9-3, 9-4.

REPRESENTATIONS TO THE HOUSE AND SENATE COMMITTEES

By late March 1975 the House Standing Committee on Finance, Trade and Economic Affairs had received written submissions from seventy-seven organizations, primarily business or business-oriented. As the Toronto *Globe and Mail* put it, "almost without exception, the briefs have been hostile. The members studying the bill in committee and the members of Parliament generally are feeling the heat." The chairman of the committee is quoted as saying, "Some of the members of the committee have been hit pretty hard by the associations."[91]

Altogether, the House committee received eighty-two briefs, sixty-seven of which were from individual firms or trade organizations. Representatives of sixteen firms, business and consumer organizations appeared before the House committee to present their brief and to give testimony on it. Thirteen of these were from producer groups (see Table 9-1). The Senate Committee on Banking, Trade and Commerce received forty-one briefs and heard testimony from twenty-nine representatives of firms, trade organizations, professional associations, a consumer organization and both professional and amateur sports organizations. Thirty-four of the forty-one briefs and nineteen of the twenty-nine representatives giving testimony were from individual business firms or trade associations (see Table 9-1). The consumer point of view was represented by the brief and appearances before both committees by the Consumers' Association of Canada and by Action Bell Canada, which presented a two-page brief and testified before the House committee.

Table 9-2 lists the names of the individuals or organizations who presented a brief to and/or testified before the Standing Senate Committee on Banking, Trade and Commerce. Table 9-3 lists the names of the sixteen organizations, representatives of which appeared before the House committee. It also indicates whether or not that organization *also* presented a brief and/or appeared before the Senate committee.

Seven organizations, six of which were business entities, both presented a brief and appeared before the Senate committee. Three other organizations, all trade associations, also presented a brief, but did not appear before the Senate committee.

Table 9-4 lists the names of the individuals and organizations who presented briefs to the House of Commons Standing Committee on Finance, Trade and Economic Affairs but who were not invited to appear before it. The same table indicates that twenty of these sixty-six organizations also sent a brief to the Senate committee. Nineteen of the twenty were business firms or trade associations. Nine of the twenty were also invited to appear and give testimony before the Senate committee — eight were trade associations and/or individual business firms. Between the Senate and House committees it is hard to think of a

TABLE 9-2

Briefs and Testimony Before the Standing Senate Committee on Banking, Trade and Commerce Re. Stage I, 1974, 1975

	Brief	Testimony
1. Association of Canadian Advertisers	yes	yes
2. Allied Beauty Association	yes	yes
3. Canadian Institute of Chartered Accountants	yes	yes
4. National Automotive Trades Association of Canada	yes	yes
5. Blake, Cassels and Graydon (for the Stelco groups of thirteen firms)	yes	yes
6. The Board of Trade of Metropolitan Toronto	yes	no
7. The Canadian Chamber of Commerce	yes	yes
8. Coca-Cola Limited	yes	yes
9. The Canadian Bar Association	yes	no
10. Canadian Construction Association	yes	no
11. Consumers' Association of Canada	yes	yes
12. Canadian Amateur Hockey Association	yes	yes
13. Canadian Lacrosse Association	yes	yes
14. Dominion Dairies Limited	yes	yes
15. Dominion Foundries and Steel, Limited	yes	no
16. The Federation of Automobile Dealers Associations of Canada	yes	no
17. National Hockey League Players' Association	yes	yes
18. Canadian Federation of Insurance Agents and Brokers Associations	yes	yes
19. The Institute of Canadian Advertising	yes	yes
20. Imperial Oil Limited	yes	no
21. Insurance Bureau of Canada	yes	no
22. International Harvester Company	yes	no
23. The Investment Dealers' Association of Canada	yes	yes
24. Canadian Manufacturers' Association	yes	yes
25. Ontario Road Builders' Association	yes	no
26. Patent and Trademark Institute of Canada	yes	yes
27. The Canadian Petroleum Association	yes	yes
28. The Canadian Real Estate Association	yes	yes
29. Sun Oil Company Limited	yes	no
30. Canadian Trucking Association	yes	yes
31. Union Oil Company of Canada Limited	yes	no
32. Grocery Products Manufacturers' of Canada	yes	no
33. The Toronto Stock Exchange	yes	no
34. Canadian Institute of Plumbing and Heating	yes	no
35. Honourable Robert Welch, Ontario Provincial Secretary for Justice	yes	no
36. Canadian Lumbermen's Association	yes	no
37. Ontario Lumber Manufacturers' Association	yes	no
38. International Air Transport Association	yes	yes
39. Air Transport Association of Canada	no	yes
40. Winnipeg Commodity Exchange	yes	yes
41. National Association of Tobacco and Confectionary Distributors	yes	yes
42. Association of Canadian Franchisors and Independent Grocers' Alliance	yes	yes
43. Sports Federation of Canada	no	yes
44. Canadian Federation of Provincial School Athletics Association[1]	no	yes
45. Canadian Federation of Amateur Aquatics[1]	no	yes
46. Clarence Campbell, President, National Hockey League	no	yes

[1]Part of a larger number of amateur sports organizations within the Sports Federation of Canada. Officials of these two organizations testified before the committee.

SOURCE:

Standing Senate Committee on Banking, Trade and Commerce, Interim Report, *Proceedings,* Issue #33, March 18, 1975 and other issues of the *Proceedings.*

TABLE 9-3

Appearances[1] Before the House of Commons Standing Committee on Finance, Trade and Economic Affairs Re. Stage I, 1974, 1975

Organizations Appearing Before the House Committee	Relationship to the Senate Committee	
	Brief	Appearance
1. Sports Federation of Canada (amateur)	no	no
2. National Association of Tobacco and Confectionary Distributors	yes	no
3. Canadian Real Estate Association	yes	yes
4. Investment Dealers' Association of Canada	yes	no
5. Canadian Manufacturers' Association	yes	yes
6. Canadian Chamber of Commerce	yes	no
7. Canadian Federation of Insurance Agents and Brokers Association	yes	yes
8. Stelco *et al.*[3] (group of thirteen firms)	yes	yes
9. Allied Beauty Association (manufacturers and dealers)	yes	yes
10. Action Bell Canada[2]	no	no
11. Canadian Federation of Independent Business	no	no
12. Association of Canadian Advertisers	yes	yes
13. Consumers' Association of Canada	yes	yes
14. Dominion Stores Limited	no	no
15. Canadian Daily Newspaper Publishers' Association	no	no
16. Retail Council of Canada	no	no

[1]Does not include appearances by the minister and/or his staff. Except as indicated in footnote 2, a formal brief was appended to the committee's *Proceedings*.

[2]Made a statement, but no brief was attached to the *Proceedings;* in fact, a two-page brief was submitted to the committee.

[3]In the Senate committee *Proceedings* this brief was listed under the name of the group's counsel Blake, Cassels and Graydon.

SOURCE: See Table 9-4.

TABLE 9-4

List of Individuals and Organizations Who Submitted Briefs to the House of Commons Standing Committee on Finance, Trade and Economic Affairs Re. Stage I But Were Not Invited To Appear Before the Committee

Individuals and Organizations Submitting a Brief to the House Committee	Relationship to the Senate Committee	
	Brief[1]	Appearance[1]
1. Appraisal Associates of Ottawa Limited		
2. Association of Consulting Engineers of Canada		
3. Automobile Importers of Canada		
4. Bakery Council of Canada		
5. Becker Milk Company Limited		
6. Board of Trade of Metropolitan Toronto	yes	no
7. C. D. Howe Research Institute		
8. The Canadian Association of Broadcasters		
9. Canadian Association of Equipment Distributors		
10. Canadian Construction Association	yes	no
11. Canadian Council of Furniture Manufacturers		
12. The Canadian Council of Professional Engineers		
13. The Canadian Institute of Chartered Accountants	yes	yes
14. Canadian Institute of Plumbing and Heating	yes	no
15. Canadian Machine Tool Distributors Association		

	Relationship to the Senate Committee	
	Brief[1]	Appearance[1]
16. Canadian Petroleum Association	yes	yes
17. The Canadian Steel Service Centre Institute		
18. Canadian Soft Drink Association		
19. Canadian Tire Corporation Limited		
20. Canadian Trucking Association	yes	yes
21. Central Contract Bottlers Association		
22. Coca-Cola Limited	yes	yes
23. Comcheq Services Limited		
24. Consolidated-Bathurst Limited		
25. Dominion Dairies Limited	yes	yes
26. Dominion Foundries and Steel Limited	yes	no
27. Employers' Association of Saskatchewan		
28. La Federation des ACEF du Quebec (Association of Cooperatives)		
29. Federation of Law Societies of Canada		
30. Fisheries Council of Canada		
31. Gray, Ross G.		
32. Grocery Products Manufacturers' of Canada		
33. Hawker, James L. (lawyer, on own behalf)		
34. Heating, Refrigeration and Air Conditioning Institute of Canada		
35. Holiday Magic Limited		
36. Imperial Oil Limited	yes	no
37. Independent Grocers' Alliance	yes	no
38. Institute of Canadian Advertising	yes	yes
39. Insurance Bureau of Canada	yes	no
40. The London Chamber of Commerce		
41. Mack Trucks Canada Limited		
42. McMillan, Binch (William Atwood Macdonald and John William Rowley, lawyers on their own behalf)		
43. National Association of Tobacco and Confectionary Distributors	yes	no
44. The National Automotive Trades Association of Canada	yes	yes
45. National Farmers' Union		
46. Ontario Press Council		
47. Ontario Road Builders' Association	yes	no
48. Oxley, Sinclair and Partners Limited (consultants)		
49. Pacific Trollers Association		
50. J. Pascal Hardware Company Limited		
51. Patent and Trademark Institute of Canada	yes	yes
52. Periodical Distributors of Canada		
53. Reimer Express Lines Limited		
54. Reinforcing Steel Institute of Ontario		
55. Retail Merchants Association of Canada Inc.		
56. Saint John Beverages Limited		
57. Seven-up Canada Limited		
58. Societe des Boissons Gazeuses (Sherbrooke) Inc. (local bottler)		
59. The Society of Ontario Hydro Professional Engineers and Associates		
60. Southern Ontario News Agency		
61. Sun Oil Company Limited	yes	no
62. Thompson, Donald N. (Professor, York University)		
63. 3M Limited		
64. Toilet Goods Manufacturers' Association		
65. Toronto Stock Exchange		
66. Winnipeg Commodity Exchange		

[1]If *no* entry appears, neither a brief was submitted nor an appearance made before the Senate committee.

SOURCE:

House of Commons Standing Committee on Finance, Trade and Economic Affairs *Proceedings*, Issue #43, May 2, 1975, Appendix EE.

major business/trade association which did not make its views known to the government through a brief, face-to-face discussions with the minister and/or his officials or by testimony before one or both of the committees reviewing the legislation.

The stack of briefs and testimony was eighteen inches high. Testimony alone before the House committee covered 1,141 small-print, double column pages — one in English and the other in French. In the Senate committee testimony covered 434 pages — of similarly small print, double columned, but entirely in English. It is hardly surprising that business as an interest group was able not only to make itself heard but also to influence the content of Stage I between the time it was introduced in November 1973 and the time it received Third Reading on October 16, 1975.

Table 9-5 provides a tabulation of the frequency with which specific amendments were dealt with in fifty briefs presented by business firms and trade associations to the House committee. While such a table does not provide information as to the quality of the analysis presented, its length or the intensity with which it was expressed, it does give some idea of the amendments most frequently attacked by producer interests. The amendments dealing with the civil procedures in respect of exclusive dealing, market restriction and tied selling were mentioned in three-fifths of business briefs. One-half the briefs expressed concern over the civil procedures in respect of refusal to deal. Forty percent of the briefs were critical, in whole or in part, of the broadened misleading advertising section and the new price maintenance section. About one-third of the briefs objected to amendments to the conspiracy section which would prevent application of the "virtual monopoly" doctrine by the courts. Almost a similar proportion objected to the amendment permitting private civil actions for both criminal offences under the act and violations of orders of the RTPC under the new civil procedures. One-fifth of the briefs objected to the inclusion of services in the existing price discrimination section. Other sections came in for a smaller number of complaints, but many of the amendments caught the ire of at least a few briefs (see Table 9-5).

BILL C-2, THE LAST LAP: NOVEMBER 1974 TO DECEMBER 1975

During the last year of the four-and-one-half-year struggle to give birth to Canada's new competition policy, the volume of editorial and columnist comment on the legislation diminished sharply.

The attention of the press was focused on different issues such as inflation, especially food prices, and the possibility of wage and price controls despite the victorious Liberals' campaign position against such

TABLE 9-5

Analysis of Fifty Briefs Presented by Business Firms and Trade Associations to the House Committee on Finance, Trade and Economic Affairs: Re the Stage I Amendments to the Combines Investigation Act, 1973-75

Section Number	Issue	Number of Briefs Commenting on Amendment
4	Exemption of collective bargaining activities	5
16	Changes in the structure of the RTPC including its ability to make its own rules of proceedings	4
27	RTPC hearings to be held in public	2
27.1	Director able to intervene in federal regulatory proceedings	2
29	Inclusion of copyrights and registered industrial designs in patent remedy section	4
29.1	Provision for ex parte interim injunctions	4
30	Change in appeal procedure to distinguish between Federal Court — Trial Division and Federal Court of Appeal	1
31.1	Provision for private civil actions	14
31.2	Civil procedures, RPTC, refusal to supply	25
31.3	Civil procedures, RTPC, consignment selling	7
31.4	Civil procedures, RTPC, exclusive dealing, market restriction, tied selling	29
31.5	Civil procedures, RTPC, foreign judgments	3
31.2-31.6 in general	See above.	3
32	Conspiracy — ruling out the "virtual monopoly" doctrine	16
32.2	Bid rigging made illegal per se	13
34	Inclusion of services in existing price discrimination provisions	10
35	Inclusion of services in existing provisions regarding discriminatory advertising allowances	1
36	New misleading advertising section, including general impression test	19
36.1	Representation as to reasonable test and publication of testimonials	2
36.2	Double ticketing	7
36.3	Pyramid selling	1
37	Definition of a bargain price in misleading advertising	6
37.1	Sales above advertised price	4
37.2	Promotional contests	3
37.3	Publishers' defence re S.36 to 37.2	2
38	Broadened price maintenance section	19
45	Definition of "participant" in an offence	1
45.1	Admissability of statistics	1
45.2	Statistics collected by sampling methods	1
45.3	Notice regarding statistics	4
46	Option of Attorney General to proceed by indictment to the Federal Court — Trial Division	5
46.1	Penalties for failure to comply with an order of the RTPC	2
e.g. 36	Issue of strict liability with respect to certain criminal offences	7
n.a.	Constitutionality of the legislation	2

SOURCE:
The author's analysis of briefs.

controls. However, a continuing but smaller flow of stories appeared about C-2 as it wound its way through the House and Senate committees and finally into the House and Senate chambers for final debate and passage. Certainly the bill's crtics continued to vastly outnumber its supporters.

Raymond Faucher, a lawyer associated with the pyramid sales section of the Quebec Department of Justice, criticized the provisions of Stage I in regard to pyramid selling schemes. He said that "since 1968, promoters operating these plans have drained $60 million from Quebec, mostly to the United States." His criticism was that Stage I made such schemes illegal only if misrepresentation occurred as to the amount of profit a person could reasonably expect to receive through the plan. Mr. Faucher supported the amendment which would ban any pyramid scheme not registered with a provincial government.[92] This amendment was incorporated in the bill when it was enacted late in 1975.

Appearing before the Senate Banking and Finance Committee, Clarence Campbell, president of the National Hockey League, predicted that no professional sports league could continue to operate if the Stage I proposals were enacted. He said,

> It is hard to conceive of a single regulation or rule in professional sports that is not basically in direct contravention of the literal text of the Combines Investigation Act.[93]

Mr. Campbell recognized that legislation may be necessary for the protection of the individual player and he pointed out that in the U.S. the anti-trust laws recognized that certain agreements among professional sports organizations were necessary. He argued that "the major portion of all professional sports legislation and regulations consists of the etablishment of rules to ensure balanced competition, not to eliminate it."[94] A week later the director of the Sports Federation of Canada told the Senate committee that "this legislation as it stands may jeopardize the 1976 Olympic Games, in addition to the opportunities for international competition by the national team of any sport."[95] He asked that amateur sports be exempted from the bill because any court order not to conform to the rules and regulations of international boards "could destroy the whole fabrc of amateur sport in Canada."[96] This was done before the bill was enacted.

A. J. MacIntosh, speaking on behalf of the Stelco group, appeared before the same committee to argue again that the RTPC's discretionary power ought to be constrained by guidelines established by Parliament. In particular, the group was concerned with the definition of "adequate competition," in the context of refusal to supply situations. They objected to the RTPC's power to order a firm to supply a customer against its wishes. Mr. MacIntosh said that the effect of such rulings would be to remove the power over market decisions from producers and create "a situation where decisions of great economic impact will be made by people who are either economists or lawyers . . . and I suggest that sometimes they should not be making public policy in this area."[97]

Herb Gray, who apparently had been dropped from the Cabinet because of his low profile, began to make his presence felt as a backbencher. InOctober he started what was to be a running critique of the Liberal government's anti-inflation policy. He stated that the government's reliance on "broad brush" monetary and fiscal policies was inadequate. He argued that the strategy of "increasing the supply of goods and services will do little, if anything, to lower prices if suppliers, because of their economic power, can keep their prices at the same level — or even increase them."[98] Gray advocated the rapid implementation of the anti-profiteering legislation and the new competition policy. He was critical of Andre Ouellet's intention to canvas business opinion again on the issues of mergers, monopoly and specialization agreements which were to be included in Stage II. Gray said it was unnecessary, "After all, the process of review of competition policy has been going on since 1966. I believe that now is the time for decision and action on the bills covering both stages."[99]

At the hearings of the special Commons committee on the Canadian Egg Marketing Agency's (CEMA) destruction of millions of rotten eggs, Gray was described as "coming on like Perry Mason the way he's questioning witnesses and getting into this thing. . . . It's really impresisve."[100] Mr. Gray insisted that his aggressive approach was really not new, pointing out that he had been elected six times in a row in his Windsor constituency.

> I've always been known to be active, almost abrasive, in Cabinet and caucus.
> You've got to remember that when I was in the Cabinet, we were in a minority situation and I felt I had to do what I did to help the government survive. At that time a public dispute between ministers could have caused the fall of the government.
> But I was never afraid to get into areas of political controversy. I was quite daring in many ways.[101]

Perhaps goaded by Mr. Gray, Mr. Ouellet told the committee investigating CEMA that he would like to see federal representation on the agency, but not necessarily representatives with a consumer point of view. Rather than the existing representatives of the ten producer-dominated provincial egg marketing boards, Ouellet suggested that "user representatives," including consumers, business and labour be appointed.[102] The Toronto *Globe and Mail* described Mr. Ouellet as "a doubtful defender" of the consumer interest in the matter. The editorial continued, "unbelievable as it may seem to consumers, Mr. Ouellet thinks that they could be properly represented by somebody from the Department of Agriculture. This would be like asking a flock of chickens to accept the protection of a fox."[103] The editors pointed out that Mr. Ouellet had in September defended Mrs. Plumptre, chairman of the Food Prices Review Board, when Agriculture Minister Eugene Whelan, had referred to her remarks on egg prices as "hogwash." Mr. Ouellet had also said he would urge Cabinet support of the appointment of consumer representatives to CEMA. The *Globe and Mail* suggested that Mr. Ouellet "could learn a little from Mr. Whelan," who "represents farmers out the window and to hell with consumers."[104]

In a speech to the Canadian Advertising Advisory Board, the minister suggested that the sections of Stage I dealing with misleading advertising were not revolutionary but that the "general impression" test was a significant innovation. He stated that he thought the industry would support the broadening of the act. "Through cooperation, education and self-regulation I would like to see less and less misleading advertising," the minister continued. "At the same time, I would like to see more severe penalties for those who do transgress." He said that many of the fines "are far too small in today's context."[105] In the same speech Mr. Ouellet congratulated the industry for avoiding "a slick and superficial public relations and lobbying approach to prove that everyone is perfect in the advertising world."[106] The trade journal, *Marketing,* stated that the minister "seemed to indicate he would prefer a policy of consultation rather than confrontation with the ad industry. . . . But as some observers said, there was a hint of an iron fist in the velvet glove."[107]

By November 1974 the minister had begun to lay the groundwork for Stage II. *Canadian Grocer* stated that "he is assuring extensive discussions with industry on as intensive a liaison as possible between now and the introduction of Part II of the Combines Investigation Act sometime next year." The article went on to say that Stage II "will not be seen until 'extensive talks' create a better opportunity for industry support." Mr. Ouellet is quoted as saying, "I don't want to bulldoze the second phase because it comes to the crunch of business philosophy."[108] No doubt the fate of Mr. Basford was a factor in his statement.

When Mr. Ouellet tabled the government's thirty amendments on December 3, Mr. Gray pointed out that "about 80 percent of the amendments" were ones he had already agreed to make in the spring of 1974. Mr. Gray was "mildly critical" of the exclusion of amateur sports from the orbit of the bill.[109] In introducing these amendments, the minister reportedly "denied the government is backing off significantly . . . but he said 'they should go a long way to satisfying the demands for change that business had made in hundreds of submissions'." The minister was quoted as saying, "I don't think I've backed off in a way that the main thrust of the bill is changed."[110] The Canadian Chamber of Commerce and The Canadian Manufacturers' Association apparently took Mr. Ouellet at his word for they planned careful reviews of the amendments and further written an oral submissions. Senator Salter Hayden, chairman of the Senate committee studying Stage I, described the minister's amendments as "a step in the right direciton," but warned that his committee was still likely to want "quite a number of amendments" of its own.[111]

Speaking before the Senate committee, Professor David McQueen, representing the Consumers' Association of Canada, praised the general thrust of Stage I. But he noted, after reading the corporations' briefs submitted to the committee, "some of them would not leave much of substance in the existing combines act, let alone the proposed one." He urged Hayden's committee to "watch those loopholes" and to pay attention to the "broader considerations of the national interest . . . of millions of individuals in this country who are not corporate persons but just ordinary persons. . . ."[112]

As the year ended, the work of the House and Senate committees was still underway. On the anti-inflation front, Mr. Ouellet had indicated that the anti-profiteering bill, which had been introduced shortly before the July 1974 federal general election, would be extensively revised and reintroduced in the spring of 1975. The original bill was described as "shockingly deficient in concept and draftsmanship" in an editorial in Executive magazine. In the same column, it was argued that the anti-profiteering legislation, the competition legislation and the foreign investment review legislation, all of which would create (or did create) administrative tribunals, "threatens to become the means of ultimately destroying the private sector."[113]

The same writer suggested that the government, in order to speed the passage of Stage I, had publicized the fuss over a Cuban order for $2 million-worth of typewriters that the Department of Industry, Trade and Commerce had forwarded to IBM's Canadian subsidiary.[114] At about the same time the Canadian subsidiary of Litton Business Equipment Ltd. did not fill another Cuban order, this one for desks, because of the U.S. government's objections to "trading with the enemy."[115]

Stage I had been repeatedly trumpeted as of major benefit to consumers and to small businessmen. The minister had stated, "I am . . . convinced that this necessary and long-awaited bill will prove infinitely important not only to all Canadian consumers but even more so to the small Canadian businessman."[116] Not everyone agreed. North Vancouver Conservative M.P. Ron Huntington, himself a small businessman, attacked the bill as being ineffective against big firms and a burden to small firms. He argued that the amendments to the Combines Act "will not stop rising prices" and "will not increase competition . . . or impede the big guy." He said they would "add to the burden of the small entrepreneur." "You're imposing more and more paperwork on the poor bugger's desk. You increase his legal work; and he doesn't have the fancy lawyers, like the big firms. Trivia and regulations are snuffing out the light and fire of Canadian business." A similar view was put forward by Social Credit M.P. C. A. Gauthier. "It has been proved by experience that the big multi-national companies like the huge cartels . . . will always find a way to pay the accountants, economists and lawyers needed to evade the law or to avail themselves of some protection of which the people will be unaware."[117]

The editorial writers continued in their attempts to soften the bill. Noting that 40 percent of the real estate boards in Canada had "scrapped their fixed commission rates in anticipation of passage of amendments to the Competition Act," the *Financial Post* argued that the legislation should be modified to permit a board to suggest a commission rate. Their reasoning was, "If the industry cannot recommend what it considers a reasonable charge, the customer will have no guideline to help him judge whether or not the charge levied by a particular broker is fair."[118] The idea that competition might establish a reasonable charge was beyond the comprehension of the *Post*.

The Toronto *Star* objected to the exemption of agreements aimed at the restriction of advertising or promotion from S.32 of the proposed act. The *Star* argued that the advertising exception violated the spirit of the rest of the act. "If, for some sound business reason an advertiser chooses to cut costs by reducing advertising, he should make that competitive decision individually, not in concert with others." However, the potential economic impact of agreements to cut advertising expenditures was also mentioned: "For many newspapers . . . advertising accounts for about 75 percent of their revenue. . . ." The *Star* concluded its editorial by invoking the cherished argument about "a free press, impervious to special interest pressures. . . ."[119]

The Winnipeg *Free Press*, in an editorial entitled "Approved Price Fixing," noted that "the government which supports the combines branch takes a radically different approach to the air carriers whose practices affect far more people." The *Free Press* pointed out that "far from condemning price fixing, the Canadian Transport Commission . . . actively encourages it."[120]

The push for amendments reflecting the concerns of specific industries also continued. The president of the Investment Dealers' Association of Canada, whose members account for 90 percent of the nation's security dealers, argued that the section dealing with misleading advertising would adversely affect small firms seeking to raise capital unless security dealers were shielded from liability for misleading advertising. Of particular concern was the "general impression conveyed" by the information disseminated by the dealer. The IDA view was that dealers would turn cautious and confine their efforts to information on large, reputable companies, hence small firms would have difficulty attracting funds. The IDA asked to have security dealers exempted from S.36 or, in lieu, to have a "due diligence" defence inserted in the section.[121]

DOWN TO THE WIRE

As the House and Senate committees worked their way through the large stacks of briefs and the thirty amendments proposed by the minister, the parliamentary secretary to the minister waxed sanguine about the progress of the bill. On May 9, 1975 Norman Cafik was reported as saying he thought Third Reading would be given by the end of that month and that Stage I would become law by the end of June.[122] However, on May 20 the "light at the end of the tunnel" seemed dimmer as the minister claimed that Conservative M.P. Sinclair Stevens (York-Simcoe) was "deliberately obstructing the proposed combines amendments" in the House committee. The Vancouver *Sun* reported: "Ouellet said . . . the government intends to have Parliament pass stage one of its controversial business competition policy before the end of June."[123] At that point, the committee had only reached the twelfth of thirty amendments introduced by the minister on December 3, 1974. Two days later the minister and Mr. Stevens clashed again, the latter saying the minister was trying to ramrod the legislation through the committee, Mr. Ouellet accused Mr. Stevens of asking the same question four or five times, thus showing his ignorance about the proposals.[124] It is interesting that Mr. Stevens's efforts to slow the amending process coincided with the government's amendments dealing with the application of orders by the RTPC in respect to exclusive dealing, market restrictions and tied selling. In particular, Mr. Stevens wanted to go beyond the government-proposed "bottlers amendment," which would have exempted local franchises of the national soft drink companies from market restriction orders made by the RTPC. Mr. Stevens wanted a broad amendment that would exempt virtually all franchise operations from RTPC orders in respect of exclusive dealing, market restrictions and tied selling.

Between this time and October 16 it is evident that the minister and Mr. Stevens came to terms, because on the day the bill was given Third Reading Mr. Ouellet was "ready to accept the amendment . . . proposed by the Honourable member for York-Simcoe (Mr. Stevens) but with a further amendment which will clarify and qualify certain aspects of franchise operations."[125] These limited the exemption to multi-product, multi-supplier franchises such as Canadian Tire or IGA. Is it too strong to suggest the aptness of the old saying "the squeaky wheel gets the grease?" Mr. Stevens said that more than thirty briefs had expressed concern with the sections of Stage I dealing with market restrictions and exclusive dealing. In speaking for them. Mr. Stevens, partly through his tactics in the House committee, was able to effect an amendment clearly designed to benefit specific business interests.

The day after the bill received final approval by the House committee, on June 3, 1975 the Canadian Press noted "much of the bill was approved during a morning and afternoon session, while leading opposition critic Sinclair Stevens (PC, York-Simcoe) was absent."[127] On the final day the committee met three times and approved nearly one-half the bill as well as rejecting virtually all of the opposition amendments. Earlier, however, the opposition members, led by John Rodriguez (NDP, Nicket Belt), were able to convince the committee to increase the penalties for misleading advertising, pyramid and referral selling. For conviction on indictment the penalties were increased from a fine at the discretion of the court and/or up to two years' imprisonment to a fine at the discretion of the court and/or up to five years' imprisonment. For summary convictions the maximum penalty of $10,000 and/or one year imprisonment was raised to $25,000 and/or one year imprisonment.

On June 5, 1975 the Commons committee made its final report to the House. Debate on C-2, as amended, resumed on June 10. There had been no debate on the bill since October 28, 1974 when it had been referred to the House committee. The only substantive debate that occurred between the committee's report and the adjournment of Parliament on July 30 took place on June 10 — filling thirty pages of Hansard.

After the summer break debate resumed on October 15, 1975. Some seven pages of Hansard were consumed on minor amendments and discussions regarding the wording of the penalties provision of the version of C-2 reported by the House committee. Then John Rodriguez introduced a series of amendments. The one dealing with loss leader selling was designed to help small businessmen. It was defeated after about seven pages of Hansard was filled with debate. His second amendment was designed "to expand areas of the bill covering false advertising."[127] Another seven or so pages were added before debate was adjourned until October 16. Three pages later it too was defeated. Mr. Rodriguez's third amendment would have prohibited promotional contests involving chance and skill. After a brief debate (approximately two pages) it too was defeated. The next amendment offered by the NDP member also dealt with misleading advertising and was apparently inspired by the investigations of the Food Prices Review Board. It would have required unit pricing, prohibited the artificial enhancement of the appearance and colour of products, prohibited the obstruction of cash register windows and also prohibited the distribution of redeemable coupons or stamps. Three and one-half pages of debate ensued before the amendment was defeated. Apparently the patience of the House was being strained for on his next amendment Mr. Rodriguez was the only speaker. It was aimed at eliminating a loophole, said Mr. Rodriguez, "through which an elephant could crawl," in S.38. He argued, "Surely, the way to sidestep the provision forbidding the suggested retail price is by printing the price on the container or product at the factory."[128] Mr. Rodriguez's desire to eliminate this exception was to remain unsatisfied.

The minister then offered an amendment, partly incorporating a motion put forward by Conservative M.P. Sinclair Stevens. It had the effect of extending the bottlers and fast food exemption contained in S.31.4(7) to multi-product, multiple supplier franchise operations such as Canadian Tire or IGA. These types of businesses were to be exempted from any order of the RTPC regarding exclusive dealing, market restriction or tied selling. In order to introduce his amendment, Mr. Ouellet had to obtain the unanimous consent of the House to waive the rule requiring twenty-four-hours notice of an amendment. His motion passed without any discussion excluding the minister's brief analysis of the amendment. Following this amendment debate continued over the issue of whether the new act could correctly grant criminal jurisdiction to the Federal Court. The motion of Sinclair Stevens to refer this section of the bill to the Supreme Court for a ruling on its constitutionality before it would come into force was ruled out of order.[129] Mr. Stevens did not appear in the House for the evening session to speak to the motion.[130] Shortly before 10 p.m. on October 16, 1975 the House gave Third Reading to the amended Bill C-2 representing Stage I of Canada's new competition policy. The final passage of the bill was not subject to a recorded vote.

Following Third Reading in the House, the Senate referred the set of amendments to the Combines Investigation Act, as amended by the House committee to the Standing Senate Committee on Banking, Trade and Finance. This committee held further hearings on November 5, 13, 19, 27 and on December 3.[131] On December 10, 1975 it presented its final report in which it reported the bill unamended to the Senate. With exception of the application of S.32 to services, the amended Combines Investigation Act came into force on January 1, 1976.

NOTES

[1]*Commons Debates*, July 18, 1973, p. 5745.

[2]*Sun* (Vancouver), November 6, 1973.

[3]This point is most cogently made by Professor Michael J. Trebilcock: "Consumer concerns are diffused across the 50,000 or so products and services each one typically consumes in his lifetime. An individual's interest in any one product will often be so small that it will not be worth his while registering his dissatisfaction to business, government or a government's regulatory agencies. However, business interests concerned with the manufacturing or merchandising of that product have a sufficiently concentrated stake in any prospective regulation of it to make their views known very forcefully to government" ("United We Stand: Initiatives in Consumer Advocacy," *Canadian Consumer*, August 1974, p. 16).

[4]Of particular note are the two merger decisions in 1960: R. v. Canadian Breweries Ltd. [1960] O.R. 601; 33 C.R. 1; 126 C.C.C. 133 and R. v. British Columbia Sugar Refining Limited et al. (1960) 32 W.W.R. (N.S) 577; 29 C.C.C. 7; (1962) 38 C.P.R. 177. More recently the Supreme Court of Canada appears to have foreclosed successful prosecutions in both merger and monopoly cases in R. v. K. C. Irving Ltd. et al. (Unreported Judgment, Supreme Court of Canada, November 16, 1976, Bureau of Competition Policy mimeo 136-5).

[5]The basic reference from which this summary is taken is *Proposals for a New Competition Policy for Canada*, First Stage, Bill C-227, November 1973, Ottawa, Department of Consumer and Corporate Affairs, 1973. This volume is often described as the "Bluebook."

[6]Not until the spring of 1975 did the Department of Consumer and Corporate Affairs commission L. A. Skeoch and B. C. McDonald, together with a committee of two senior businessmen and a lawyer associated with small business to prepare a report incorporating draft legislation on these issues (excluding class actions). Their report was published on May 31, 1976. See L. A. Skeoch and B. C. McDonald, in consultation with M. Belanger, R. M. Bromstein and W. O. Twaits, *Dynamic Change and Accountability in a Canadian Market Economy*, Ottawa, Supply and Services Canada, 1976. Professor Neil J. Williams was asked to prepare a report and draft legislation on consumer class actions. See his "Damages Class Action Under the Combines Investigation Act," in *A Proposal for Class Actions Under Competition Policy Legislation*, Ottawa, Information Canada, 1976, pp.1-195.

[7]Ronald Anderson, "Deft footwork," *Globe and Mail* (Toronto), November 14, 1973. The disorienting effects of rapid social and economic change are now better known since Alvin Toffler's *Future Shock* (New York, Bantam Books, 1971, Chapters 15, 16).

[8]November 6, 1973.

[9]*Financial Post*, November 10, 1973 Maurice Cutler writing in *Canadian Electronics Engineering* (December 1973) argued that the "principal beneficiaries" of the Stage I legislation were the consumer and the small businessman. The evolution of the federation is described in Alexander Ross, "How to Join the March to the New Politics," *Quest* February, 1975, pp. 40-42, 44, 46-48.

[10]November 6, 1973.

[11]November 7, 1973.

[12]*Ibid.*

[13]*Ibid.*

[14]November 8, 1973.

[15]*Ibid.*

[16]*Province* (Vancouver), November 6, 1973, p. 5.

[17]*Citizen* (Ottawa), November 6, 1973.

[18]November 7, 1973.

[19]*Star* (Montreal), November 7, 1973. For the technical evidence on the importance of economies of scale in Canada, see Paul K. Gorecki, *Economies of Scale and Efficient Plant Size in Canadian Manufacturing Industries*, Ottawa, Department of Consumer and Corporate Affairs, 1976.

[20]The *Star* (Toronto) made the same point when it said, "As nobody but a crook or a cad can possibly be in favour of misleading advertising, fraudulent sales practices and selling young hockey players into professional bondage, there is not likely to be much objection in principle to the new competition policy introduced in the Commons" (as reprinted in the *Times-Journal* (St. Thomas), November 13, 1973).

[21]November 17, 1973.

[22]Vincent Egan, "Competition Bill Passage Needed," *Free Press* (Nanaimo), November 8, 1973.

[23]November 12, 1973.

[24]Toronto *Star* editorial as reprinted in the *Times-Journal* (St. Thomas), November 13, 1973.

[25]*Financial Post*, april 27, 1974, p. C-1.

[26]John Meyer, "Fudged!" *Journal* (Ottawa), March 30, 1974. Mr. Meyer made the same points in an article in the *Gazette* (Montreal), April 4, 1974 and in one in *Executive* in May 1974.

[27]April 1, 1974. The *Star* (Toronto) repeated its views in a very similar editorial April 2, 1974.

[28]Michael Barkway, "Restrictive Trade Commission Feared as Powers 'Undefined'," *Herald* (Calgary), March 26, 1974. Mr. Barkway's and the *Financial Times* views on the earlier legislation are contained in *Financial Times of Canada Guide to the Competition Act*, Toronto, 1971, 12 pp.

[29]March 25, 1974.

[30]*Globe and Mail* (Toronto), April 3, 1974 ("The Case Against Trial by Tribunal in Combines Law").

[31]*Globe and Mail* (Toronto), April 16, 1974. With the specification of standards and the clarification of the route of appeal from the decisions of the RTPC the *Evening Free Press* (London) argued that "business interests in Canada should take a second look at the bill. Otherwise the idea could take hold that big business opposes any kind of anti-monopoly legislation no matter how reasonable. And that could eventually lead to more severe measures" (April 19, 1974).

[32]Unfortunately these misstatements were reproduced with approval in a *Free Press* (Winnipeg) editorial April 8, 1974. The same confusion can be found in an editorial in the *Canadian Jeweller*, May 1974, p. 58. The editor advocated a "grass roots" approach to rectifying these problems in the draft legislation: "Jewellers should make a point of outlining to their local candidates and party headquarters how they feel about the implications of this proposed legislation."
    One might be cynical about Mr. Macdonald's very active role in opposing both Bill C-256 and the Stage I amendments. As a partner in a major Toronto law firm (McMillan, Binch) he had a potential pecuniary interest in creating fears and anxiety in the business community which might be channelled into the representation of business's views to the minister and the relevant House and Senate committees by his own firm. One might argue that well-publicized opposition to government policy represents a form of advertising by the lawyers or consultants involved. Mr. Macdonald even carried his message to academics in a paper presented at the annual meeting of the Canadian Association of Administrative Sciences, Edmonton, June 2, 1975, 13 pp. (mimeo).

[33]R. v. *Canadian Breweries* [1960] O.R. 601; 33 C.R. 1; 126 C.C.C. 133. R. v. *British Columbia Sugar Refining Company Limited et al.* (1960) 32 W.W.R. (N.S.) 577; 129 C.C.C. 7; (1962) 38 C.P.R. 177.
    See more generally W. T. Stanbury, "The 1975 Amendments to the Combines Investigation Act: Analysis of the Provisions Relating to Virtual Monopoly, Bid Rigging and New Penalties," in W. T. Stanbury (ed.), *Papers on the 1975 Amendments to the Combines Investigation Act*, Vancouver, University of British Columbia, Faculty of Commerce and Business Administrative, 1976, pp. 57-62.

[34]*Daily Times* (Brampton), April 19, 1974.

[35]Clair Balfour, "Why Business Dislikes C-7," *Financial Times*, April 15, 1974, p. 23. The members of the group were: Abitibi Paper Co. Ltd., Algoma Steel Corp. Ltd., Canada

Packers Ltd., Cominco Ltd., Eaton's, John Labatt Ltd., MacMillan Bloedel Ltd., Molson Companies Ltd., Moore Corp. Ltd., Noranda Mines Ltd., Power Corp. of Canada Ltd. Simpsons Ltd. and Steel Co. of Canada Ltd.

The Stelco Group's brief on Bill C-256 in 1972 was signed by Dominion Foundaries and Steel Ltd. but did not include the Molson Companies Ltd. Said to be associated with the group was Toronto Star Ltd. (*Financial Times*, April 5, 1974).

The Canadian Construction Association in its concern over the bid rigging section of the Stage I amendments had a meeting on March 14, 1974 with the minister. The association's president, Henry de Puyjalon, ws concerned that the section "would go beyond the intentions of the department and include pretender conferences." Mr. de Puyjalon stated that bid rigging was "repugnant" to the association but that he wanted "to make sure that not everything gets labelled as bid rigging." He was also concerned about the legality of joint ventures, a fairly common thing in the construction industry for large projects (Clair Balfour, "Will the Competition Act Keep Us Honest?" *Engineering and Contract Record*, April 1974, pp. 60-61).

[36]*Financial Post*, april 27, 1974, p. C-5.

[37]Mr. Steele's views on the earlier legislation can be found in G. G. E. Steele, "Problems and Policy in Distribution with Special Reference to Price Discrimination," in L. A. Skeoch (ed.), *Canadian Competition Policy*, Kingston, Queen's University, Industrial Relations Centre, pp. 35-49.

[38]*Star* (Toronto), April 4, 1974.

[39]*Ibid.*

[40]*Senate Debates*, March 17, 1974, p. 190.

[41]*Ibid.*, April 2, 1974, p. 217.

[42]*Ibid.*, p. 218.

[43]*Ibid.*

[44]Henry Aubin, "Monopoly Power," *Gazette* (Montreal), January 9, 1975, p. 8.

[45]*Ibid.* Another article stated that the twenty-two members of the Senate committee held 75 percent of the reported corporate directorships in the Senate. See Phil Gibson, "Will Party Fund Reform Affect Competition Policy?" *Gazette* (Montreal), March 27, 1975, p. 9.

[46]When incorporated in 1939 to acquire a predecessor company, originally incorporated in 1926 the firm was known as Acadia Sugar Refining Company Limited. In 1945 the name was changed to Acadia-Atlantic Sugar Refineries Limited and in 1962 to Atlantic Sugar Refineries Company Limited. In June 1973 Atlantic Sugar became part of Jannock Corporation Limited. MacKay J. in *R. v. Atlantic Sugar Refineries co. Ltd. et al.* indicates that Senator Hayden was a vice-president and director throughout the period covered by the indictment in that case, January 1960 to May 1973.

[47]Restrictive Trade Practices Commission, *Report Concerning the Sugar Industry in Eastern Canada*, Ottawa, 1960, p. 4.

[48]*Ibid.*, p. 312.

[49]*Ibid.*, p. 9.

[50]*R. v. Atlantic Sugar Refineries Co. Ltd. et al.* judgment of MacKay J., Superior Court of Quebec (Criminal Division) Dec. 19, 1975, as yet unreported (Bureau of Competition Policy mimeo p. 80).

In 1966 Steinberg's Limited obtained control of Cartier and Robin Austin, the founder of the company, was removed as president.

[51]Richard Cleroux, "Competition Act Study Raises Conflict Issue," *Globe and Mail* (Toronto), Feb. 12, 1975.

[52]*Ibid.* The experience argument was put by senators Flynn, Walker, and Desruisseaux on October 28 and 29, 1975 in the Senate debate on C-2.

[53]*Senate Debates*, October 29, 1975, p. 131.

[54]Quoted in Richard Cleroux, *op.cit.* This article also points out that Senator Croll had

clashed with Hayden repeatedly over the issues before — notably over Croll's truth-in-lending legislation in 1962.

[55]*Senate Debates,* October 29, 1975, p. 1318.

[56]"Statistics Find Senators Big in Business," *Sun* (Vancouver), October 9, 1973, p. 23.

[57]*Ibid.*

[58]*Ibid.*

[59]*Ibid.*

[60]*Ibid.*

[61]Stephen Duncan, "Debate May Focus on 'Concentration'," *Financial Post,* August 28, 1976, p. 4.

[62]*Ibid.*

[63]"Banking Chairman Hangs On," *Sun* (Vancouver), November 2, 1976. The senators were Hartland Molson, Sidney Buckwold, Harry Hays, Paul Desruisseux and Ernest Manning.

[64]*Ibid.*

[65]*Ibid.*

[66]Geoffrey Stevens, "The Blue-Ribbon Committee," *Globe and Mail* (Toronto), June 25, 1976, p. 6.

[67]*Senate Debates,* October 22, 1975, p. 1294.

[68]*Ibid.,* October 28, 1975, p. 1308.

[69]*Ibid.,* p. 1309.

[70]*Ibid.,* October 29, 1975, p. 1315.

[71]*Ibid.*

[72]*Members of Parliament and Conflict of Interest,* Ottawa, Information Canada, p. 28 (Proposal No. 3).

[73]*Votes and Proceedings of the House of Commons,* June 10, 1975, pp. 615-622.

[74]*Minutes of the Proceedings of the Senate,* No. 207, June 29, 1976, pp. 939-942.

[75]Useful brief discussions of the House and Senate committee reports can be found in Doug Small, "Senate Defends Links to Firms on Government Work," *Citizen* (Ottawa), June 20, 1976, p. 42; Geoffrey Stevens, "They Grind Exceedingly Slow," *Globe and Mail* (Toronto), June 30, 1976, p. 6; "Senators Move to Soften Proposed Conflict Rules," *Globe and Mail* (Toronto), June 30, 1976, p. 8.

[76]May 2, 1974.

[77]*Ibid.*

[78]Letter to the *Financial Post,* May 25, 1974, p. 7.

[79]*Financial Post,* September 14, 1974.

[80]George Radwanski, "Gray: Fast Slide Down Ottawa's Razor Blade," *Gazette* (Montreal), September 26, 1974.

[81]"Mr. Trudeau, Cabinetmaker," August 12, 1974.

[82]Maurice Cutler, "Gray Shock and Ouellet Surprise," *Marketing,* August 19, 1974. In an article in the *Globe and Mail* (Toronto), February 1, 1975, M.P. Yvon Pinard (L, Drummond) is quoted as saying, "In ten years of political life he has never made a mistake, never made a faux pas." M. Pinard was a classmate of Mr. Ouellet at the University of Sherbrooke Law School. Another M.P., Monique Begin (L, St. Michel) said of Ouellet, "He is young in age but he's an old politician. . . . Andre has politics in his blood. He's a political animal" (William Johnson, "The Rising Power of Andre Ouellet," p. 2).

[83]August 17, 1974.

[84]George Radwanski, "Ouellet Takes Cabinet Hotseat," *Gazette* (Montreal), September 24, 1974.

85*Ibid.*

86September 14, 1974. The anti-profiteering bill went into legislative and bureaucratic orbit. In an interview in French on January 23, 1975, Mr. Ouellet said that the new bill would not be aimed at profits, but rather at prices and business would have to justify its price increases.
On April 21, 1975 Andre Ouellet indicated that a prices justification bill was in an advanced stage of preparation. It would create a prices tribunal to investigate high prices and with the power to order business to cut prices and even give refunds to consumers (Peter Cook, "Price and Wage Guidelines, Ottawa Program Will Have Teeth," *Financial Times,* April 21, 1975).
Three weeks later a *Globe and Mail* (Toronto) editorial wondered if Mr. Ouellet was trying to sell Ottawa's wage and price restraints program or simply get out ahead of Finance Minister John Turner in the next Liberal leadership race (May 9, 1975). In a radio interview (CJAD) on May 10 the minister stated the price justification bill "was not delayed in any way" but that there was a great deal of other legislation before Parliament. He indicated that the government was trying to effect a program of voluntary restraints. The headline story in the *Gazette* (Montreal) on May 16 described the situation at that time: "Liberals Anti-Profiteering Bill Still in Limbo." Because of its low priority the bill did not return to the Cabinet for consideration until June. On October 14, 1975 it became superfluous with the announcement of mandatory wage and price controls.

87October 7, 1974.

88*Record* (Kitchener-Waterloo), October 17, 1974.

89October 21, 1974.

90Paul Jackson, "David and Goliath Role No Easy Task," *Herald* (Calgary), October 29, 1974.

91William Johnson, "Proposed Competition Law Winning No Friends," *Globe and Mail* (Toronto), March 24, 1975.

92*Star* (Montreal), November 9, 1974.

93Ottawa, Canadian Press wire service, November 14, 1974.

94*Ibid.*

95*Star* (Toronto), November 21, 1974.

96*Globe and Mail* (Toronto), November 14, 1974.

97Sheldon Gordon, "Don't Tell Him Former Ministers Are Supposed to be Seen and Not Heard," *Financial Post,* November 16, 1974.

98*Ibid.*

99Bruce Garvey, "Bounced to the Backbench, the New Herb Gray Speaks Out," *Star* (Toronto), November 12, 1974, p. B-3.

100*Ibid.*

101*Globe and Mail* (Toronto), November 15, 1974 and CBC Radio, "The World at Six," 6:00 p.m., November 14, 1974.

102*Globe and Mail* (Toronto), November 16, 1974, p. 6, italics in the original.

103*Ibid.*

104Nicholas Cotter, "Clarification of Present Advertising Laws Held Reason for Combines Act Revision Plans," *Globe and Mail* (Toronto), November 27, 1974.

105"Ouellet: A Hint of a Not-So-Hard Approach," *Marketing,* December 2, 1974, p. 1.

106*Ibid.*

107*Canadian Grocer,* November 1974, p. 28.

108Glenn Sommerville, "Industry Planning to Review New Competition Amendments," *Journal* (Ottawa), December 5, 1974, p. 9.

109*Citizen* (Ottawa), December 4, 1974, p. 10.

110*Globe and Mail* (Toronto), December 6, 1974, p. B-4.

111*Ibid.,* December 19, 1974, p. B-3.

[112]John Meyer, "Ouellet Calls It Anti-Profiteering But It Looks Like Price Controls," *Executive,* December 1974, p. 15.

[1134]John Meyer,"Pressure for Quick Competition Act Passage?" *Gazette* (Montreal), January 7, 1975.

[114]"Competition Bill May Be Answer to Cuban Deal," *Citizen* (Ottawa), December 26, 1974, p. 3.

[115]Quoted by Henry Aubin, "Monopoly Power," *Gazette* (Montreal), January 9, 1974, p. 9. It should be pointed out that Mr. Huntington's business may not be that large in absolute terms, but it was described as controlling 56 percent of the dried fruit market in western Canada.

[116]*Gazette* (Montreal), January 9, 1975.

[117]January 18, 1975.

[118]*Ibid.*

[119]February 5, 1975. The strong representations of the Canadian Daily Newspapers Publishers' Association and the Ontario Press Council requesting removal of the exception pressed on the House committee reviewing the legislation were unsuccessful. However, the government did introduce its own amendment which would prohibit "a discriminatory restriction directed against a member of the media," i.e., a group boycott. The Publishers' Association meeting with the minister was reported in the *Star* (Toronto), January 31, 1975, p. A3. The general manager of the Publishers' Association said that with the government's amendment "advertisers annoyed at what a newspaper was writing could take thousands of dollars worth of advertising from the newspaper and as long as they left a $5 classified ad, they wouldn't be 'boycotting' the newspaper" (*Marketing,* April 28, 1975, p. 10).

[120]January 21, 1975.

[121]Sheldon E. Gordon, "Combines Law May Clobber Small Firms," *Financial Post,* March 1, 1975, p. 1. The due diligence defence for all persons accused of misleading advertising was recommended by the Senate committee reviewing the legislation in its interim report of March 19, 1975.

[122]Angela Barnes, "June Passage Is Seen for Competition Bill," *Globe and Mail* (Toronto), May 9, 1975, p. B-3.

[123]*Sun* (Vancouver), May 21, 1975, p. 6. Mr. Ouellet was frustrated by a ninety-five-minute wrangle in the committee over the fact that the hearing began on time but opposition members not present when the Liberal chairman apparently called a quorum for voting on amendments. Both Mr. Stevens and Mr. Rodriguez (NDP, Nickel-Belt) later left the meeting in protest (Canadian Press wire service, Ottawa, May 22, 1975). Apparently a week earlier the chairman had "waved government committee members from the room deliberately so a quorum could not be present for a vote while Opposition members had a majority" (Canadian Press wire service, Ottawa, May 23, 1975).

[124]Canadian Press wire service, Ottawa, May 23, 1975.

[125]*Commons Debates,* October 16, 1975, p. 8278.

[126]*Journal* (Ottawa), June 4, 1975, p. 33.

[127]*Common Debates,* October 15, 1975, p. 8244.

[128]*Ibid.,* October 16, 1975, p. 8277.

[129]*Ibid.,* p. 8290.

[130]Mr. Stevens was at this time a candidate for the leadership of the Progressive Conservative Party. He may have been away campaigning.

[131]The Minister and the Director of Investigation and Research appeared on November 13, 19 and 27.

Chapter 10

The Product of the Business-Government Interaction: What Did Business Gain?

What concessions, amendments or administrative changes was business as an interest group able to obtain through its interaction with the government following the introduction of the Competition Act in June 1971? Very shortly after the Stage I amendments were introduced in November 1973, Professor Donald N. Thompson made the following observation:

> One of the rare abilities in this world is that of taking a good but controversial idea a lot of people find objectionable, and revising, rewording and reintroducing it so that it says exactly what it said before but is now embraced as being both desirable and different from what it was.[1]

Thompson argued that not only did Stage I say or promise what C-256 did but that it also went beyond it to cover professional sports, foreign laws applied in Canada and minor issues such as double ticketing. The important thing, he stated, is that "it [said] it in a way that opposition M.P.s and the media have applauded."

Perhaps because he was writing less than two weeks after Stage I was made public, Thompson did not have the opportunity to observe the full flowering of business' opposition to a number of the amendments, e.g., the civil procedures of the RTPC regarding the list of "reviewable matters." As we shall try to point out, Stage I as introduced in November 1973 represented a major improvement over C-256 from business' point of view. In addition, business was able to obtain amendments to the original Stage I proposals which further lessened the impact of the new competition policy. We shall begin by listing the "gains" by business and then we shall try to identify those proposals for change which business did *not* succeed in altering significantly.

CHANGE OF MINISTERS

Pressure by business clearly contributed to the replacement of Mr. Basford as Minister of Consumer and Corporate Affairs by Mr. Andras just six months after Bill C-256 was introduced in the House of Commons. Mr. Basford was viewed as a strong advocate for the Competition Act and for the consumer interest. His aggressive defence of a bill which was an anathema, combined with a perceived unwillingness to accomodate business concerns in the dual role of his department, made Mr. Basford the visible symbol of all that was wrong with the policy. As one executive put it, "If you talk to Basford face to face, he makes no bones about his sincere desire to protect the consumer . . . but shows no concern for the position of business."[2] The reaction by the representations of business interest groups that have already been cited make it clear that Mr. Basford's "lateral arabesque" was seen as a victory for business.

Mr. Basford was perceived by consumers, the Consumers' Association of Canada in particular, as a good Minister of Consumer and Corporate Affairs. He introduced a number of significant consumer-oriented bills in his three and one-half years in office. The fact that business was able to have him removed could be seen as a salutary lesson for any of his successors who might be similarly inclined. In fact, subsequent ministers were much less identified with the consumer interest and went out of their way not only to be "reasonable" but also to appear to be "reasonable" to producer interests. Both Andras and Gray were in Ottawa during business' assault on the Competition Act and had a chance directly to observe the fate of Basford, who, if he was not personally popular, was respected as a hard-working, thorough and conscientious politician. Even after Basford was removed, the business community continued to press their attack on Bill C-256. Mr. Andras's assurances of significant modifications not withstanding, until two clear signals were received in the spring of 1973, business continued to press for a weakening of the legislation. With the appointment of the Director of Investigation and Research, D. H. W. Henry, to the Ontario Supreme Court in February and Mr. Gray's statement in May (formally confirmed in the House in July) that the new legislation would be broken into two parts and introduced in the form of amendments to the existing legislation, business interests realized that their representations and protests were having the desired effect. It is an interesting commentary on the identification of Basford with the consumer interest that five years after he was removed as minister, businessmen and consumers still addressed mail to him as Minister of Consumer and Corporate Affairs.

THE PROCESS OF POLICY REFORM

Business reaction to Bill C-256 strongly influenced the subsequent process of policy change. First, the reforms were split into two stages. Business had complained about the length and complexity of the

Competition Act. They said it would have too large an impact if all of the changes proposed were implemented simultaneously. The omnibus nature of the bill, they argued, meant it was impossible for business to respond realistically to what the government proposed. By bringing the changes in two smaller packages, what was a large indigestible lump became smaller "bite-size" pieces.

Second, the government dropped the idea of a completely new act and introduced its proposals as amendments to the existing statute. Familiarity with the words, administration and judicial decisions associated with the Combines Investigation Act reduced the uncertainty associated with the changes. Incrementalism was demonstrably preferred to a larger discontinuity — no matter how "rational" the changes may have been. Third, business reaction combined with twenty months of minority government and a high turnover of Ministers of Consumer and Corporate Affairs resulted in a significant *delay* in the enactment of new legislation. Had these factors not been present, Bill C-256, introduced in June 1971, could reasonably have been expected to become law by mid-1973. What we have is Stage I, the less controversial set of amendments, effective January 1, 1976[3] while Stage II was not brought before Parliament until March 16, 1977. It is unlikely that they will come into force before mid-1978. Part of the legislation was delayed about two and one-half years and the other part about five years. If business views the new provisions as a "tax" on its potential profitability, then a tax deferred is more acceptable than one immediately implemented.

Fourth, by stretching out the policy change/legislative process business was able to engage in more "consultation" with both elected and appointed officials. They had more time to make their case. Given that the resources of business are far larger than those of consumer interest groups or academics, a longer campaign benefits the business interest groups because they have superior staying power. They may win by the exhaustion of their opponents. After a long enough period theirs is the only voice the policy maker hears. This is the burden of Edelman's point when he states:

> . . . the most effective way to make a public official act as an interest wishes him to, is to assure by institutional means that he will become thoroughly acquainted with its problems as the adherents of the interest see them.[4]

In the final analysis, the business groups opposing all or part of the legislation did not want compromise; they wanted total victory. The public servants, portrayed as intransigent, were often persuaded by business' explanations of some of the untoward consequences of the original draft legislation. They were willing to change quite a number of aspects of the legislation to make it work smoothly. They "gave," by argument or by pressure, far more than did business. To the end, many business leaders continued to see no virtue in the entire set of amendments.

Business efforts aimed at slowing down progress of the legislation through the parliamentary machinery can be reinforced by the dynamics of the legislation process itself. The minister is faced with a fight for House time, with opposition threats to filibuster (often to achieve victories in other areas) and the emotional drain of committee hearings in both the House and Senate. Toward the end of each session the inter-ministerial manoeuvering for time becomes fierce. In almost all these circumstances compromise to get the bill through, particularly in view of the total amount of time taken by the legislation in its earlier form, becomes increasingly attractive. As the total time in process lengthens, the ability to maintain intellectual and emotional commitment is reduced. After the "pressure cooker" atmosphere and exhaustion have taken their toll, the ardent advocates of reform may not recognize what has been wrought by compromise.

"UNDULY" RESTORED IN S.32

A key substantive victory for business was the reinsertion of the word "unduly" in the section dealing with conspiracies. S.16 of the Competition Act, which was to replace S.32 of the Combines Investigation Act, had eliminated the qualifying word "unduly." The *Explanatory Notes* accompanying Bill C-256 stated, "The new provisions clearly outlaw specified kinds of agreements without examining the degree of market control."[5] The effect would be to move to the U.S. approach in which price-fixing and related conspiracies are illegal per se. The decisions under the Combines Act and the Criminal Code had clearly established that price-fixing agreements were not illegal — only those which went so far as to restrict competition "unduly." In practice, the judges adopted a fairly high threshold, in terms of extensive control of the market, before holding an agreement to be illegal. In 1967, Mr. Justice Gibson in R. v. *Canadian Cost and Apron Supply* pointed out that the Canadian cases can be divided into two categories:[6]

1. Situations where the object of the conspiracy, or agreement contemplated that competition be completely or virtually eliminated i.e., *Weidman* v. *Shragge, Stinson-Reeb, Container Materials* and *Howard Smith*.
2. Cases in which the object contemplated was something less than virtual monopoly, but in which on the respective facts of which cases, the courts are able to reach a conclusion of undue interference with competition in violation of the statutory provision, i.e., *Electrical Contractors, Abitibi*.

While it is true that the Crown has obtained convictions in over four-fifths of the conspiracy cases it has brought, the significance of "unduly" lies in the screening of investigations before they are sent to the Department of Justice for prosecution. Unless at least one-half of the relevant market has been subject to the conspiracy, there is no point in taking the case to court. In most cases the conspirators collectively accounted for over three-quarters of the market. As two participants at the Seventh McGill Government-Industry Conference in 1972 remarked, "the argument that the 'undueness' test should be retained is a complete denial of the need for reform."[7] In the same vein Professor Milton Moore has asserted, "price agreements should be subject to a per se ban [as] . . . a necessary condition of an effective compeition policy."[8]

In addition to restoring "unduly" in S.32, the ten types of agreements or arrangements specifically prohibited by S.16 of the Competition Act were dropped and the more general wording of the existing S.32 of the Combines Act was retained. While it seems clear that S.16 was too broadly drawn, the retention of "unduly" together with the previously existing wording of S.32 represent a substantial gain for business and a defeat for consumers and others interested in an effective competition policy in Canada.

THE TRIBUNAL IS SCRAPPED

The fiercely criticized Competitive Practices Tribunal (CPT) was not found in Stage I of the amendments although it is found in both the consultants' report for Stage II and the Stage II proposed legislation, Bill C-42.[9] The CPT represented an attempt to utilize civil procedures in what, traditionally, had been a strictly criminal approach. "The Compeition Act envisage(d) the transfer from [the] courts to the Competitive Practices Tribunal of all but the matters that are prohibited outright."[10] The tribunal was to deal with mergers, specialization, franchise and export agreements, price discrimination, promotional allowances, exclusive dealing and tying arrangements and refusal to deal. These were described as "important matters requiring sophisticated economic and business analysis."[11] Elements of the CPT and its civil procedures can be found in the matters reviewable by the existing Restrictive Trade Practices Commission upon the application of the Director of Investigation and Research.[12] The Competition Act would have permitted any person materially affected by practices under the jurisdiction of the tribunal to take his case directly to that body without first obtaining the permission of the commissioner (i.e., the renamed Director). Under the Stage I amendments, only the Director may initiate cases before the RTPC.

The reviewable matters which may be brought before the RTPC

are: refusal to sell, consignment selling, exclusive dealing, tied selling, market restrictions and the application of foreign judgments, laws or directives which are contrary to the Canadian public interest. The commission is empowered to issue cease and desist orders when it makes an adverse finding. The constitutionality of this section of the ameded act is likely to be challenged before long.[13] If the RTPC is ruled to be constitutionally valid, or at least not challenged, and if it is given jurisdiction over mergers, monopolies, price discrimination and export and specialization agreements as part of the Stage II amendments, then it would appear that the government obtained many of the main elements of the CPT in a different form. If this occurs, Thompson's observation quoted above will be valid for this part of competition policy at least.

THE STING OF PRIVATE CIVIL ACTIONS IS REDUCED

S.55 of the Competition Act provided that persons who suffered loss or damage as a result of a violation of the act or a failure to obey an order of the tribunal could sue for an amount equal to *double* the damage proved to have been suffered by them. As well, S.80 permitted the court to award double damages, upon application of those injured, in addition to the usual criminal penalties. Pressure by business resulted in S.31.1 of the amended Combines Investigation Act, which provides for single damages plus costs in private *civil actions only*. The potential penalty to business for violating the law was thus significantly reduced.[14] We should point out that the amended act does provide that the record of successful criminal proceedings and any evidence given in such proceedings is evidence in the civil suit. The Senate Committee on Banking, Trade and Commerce in its *Interim Report* proposed that Stage I should be amended "to make it clear that 'record of proceedings' is not to include transcripts of testimony given or documents or other exhibits produced in the criminal proceedings."[15] Fortunately, this was not done for it would have effectively vitiated the provision.

"CREDULOUS MAN" TEST ELIMINATED

Business was able to obtain the removal of the "credulous man" test in misleading advertising offences proposed in Bill C-256 [S.20(5)]. While the "credulous man" test had been accepted in at least one case,[16] it represented an obvious example of over-reaching in Bill C-256. Philosophically hard to defend, it was a needless irritation to the business community. Business did not succeed in eliminating the words "materially misleading representation," the "general impression" test, and the broadened concept of "deemed representation" to the public, which includes the salesperon's oral representations. Many of these concepts are already part of provincial consumer protection or trade practices legislation, e.g., the B.C. Trade Practices Act.

BID-RIGGING PROVISION WEAKENED, IDENTICAL TENDERS DROPPED

S.16(2) of the Competition Act provided that evidence of identical tenders was evidence of price fixing which, in turn, was declared to be illegal per se. This very useful provision, under the pressure of business, was eliminated in favour of a much more modest one relating to bid rigging alone.

S.32.2 makes bid rigging an indictable offence and subject to a fine at the discretion of the court and/or imprisonment for up to five years. Bid rigging is defined to be (a) an agreement among potential bidders for one or more of them not to submit a bid, or (b) an agreement to submit bids arrived at by collusion. Two exceptions are made: (a) and (b) are not illegal if such agreements are made known to the person (firm) calling for bids, or if the agreement not to bid or as to the amount of the bid is between affiliated companies as defined in the act [S.38.7 and 38.7(1)].

The most important implication of 32.2 is that bid rigging becomes an offence per se, and is not subject to the qualifying word "unduly" of S.32. This removes the necessity to define "the market" and to prove that the conspirators in the bid-rigging scheme had sufficient control to establish that competition had been lessened unduly. It is also important to interpret 32.2 in conjunction with the fact that *services* are now within the orbit of the act, unless they are specifically regulated by a provincial schedule. In the *Beamish*[17] case, for example, the Crown failed to sustain its case because the Ontario Court of Appeal ruled that the rigged tenders for the supply and installation of road surfacing materials (sand, gravel, stone chips and asphalt) were predominately contracts for work and labour. As services, such contracts were not within the purview of the Combines Investigation Act. In a similar case a few years later, the Crown did not prosecute following an RTPC report.[18]

As enacted, the provisions relating to bid rigging represent an improvement over the previous state of affairs if one uses the argument that "half a loaf is better than none." However, 32.2 represents a substantial retreat from what was proposed in the Competition Act in 1971. S.16(2) of Bill C-256 provided that the existence of *identical tenders* was evidence of price fixing, which in turn was declared to be illegal per se. S.32.2 does not really attack the problems of identical tenders — unless the Crown can show that the identical bids were arrived at by collusion. This is a difficult task. Seldom does the evidence of collusion accompany the submission of tenders and fall out of one of the bidder's envelopes[19] nor is it apparent that all bids were typed on the same typewriter.[20] By far the largest number of cases of identical bids do not occur as a result of overt collusion.[21] Instead, they occur in the context of a highly concentrated industry producing a homogeneous product, usually sold to a fairly small number of buyers. In addition, it is frequently the case that the flow of transactions is "lumpy," i.e., a few major purchases each year (often by tender) account for a good proportion to total industry volume. This problem has long been recognized by the Director of Investigation and Research.[22]

When he appeared before the House of Commons Standing Committee on Public Accounts on December 6 and 9, 1963, the Director observed that identical tenders were common in chemicals, construction materials, electrical equipment and supplies, iron and steel products, paper and paper products, petroleum products and a wide variety of other products purchased by federal, provincial, and local governments and their agencies.[23]

S.32.2 does nothing to ameliorate this problem, nor does any other element in the Stage I amendments. Apparently, non-collusive tendering can have some credulity-straining results. In 1963 Hydro Quebec received six identical bids of $14,394,537.12 for 4,800 miles of aluminum cable steel reinforced. Because he could not prove collusion, the Director discontinued this inquiry and others relating to numerous cases of identical bids in the wire and cable industry.[24]

In summary then, S.32.2 advances a modest behavioural remedy for what is fundamentally a structural problem. Only inept conspirators are likely to get caught while the basic problem remains. The change from S.16(2) of the Competition Act to S.32.2 must be classed as a victory for producer interests over consumers.

INDUSTRY AMENDMENTS

As Stage I moved through the parliamentary committees, specific industries were able to insert amendments beneficial to their interests. S.31.4(5)(c) has been described as "the Canadian Tire amendment." It prevents the application of orders by the RTPC in respect of exclusive dealing, market restrictions or tied selling to multiple product "franchise" operations such as Canadian Tire, Shoppers Drug Mart, Becker Milk Stores, McDonald's, IGA grocery stores and others. The key phrase in the section is "multiplicity of products obtained from competing sources of supply and a multiplicity of suppliers." The section does not, therefore, exempt the national oil companies operating through a large number of service station lessees.[25]

S.31.4(7) prevents the application of orders made by the RTPC in regard to market restriction agreements of franchise bottlers or franchise food outlets. The pressure for this amendment, referred to as "the bottlers amendment," came from the Canadian Soft Drink Bottlers' Association which presented its brief to every member of Parliament. Most of the bottlers are local businessmen who hold an exclusive territorial franchise for a brand name product.

The effect of the bottlers amendment will be to preserve local or regional monopolies for the brand name soft-drink bottlers, e.g., Coca-Cola, Canada Dry and Pepsi Cola. While competition, primarily of the non-price variety, will continue to exist between the brand name bottlers, the effect of the amendment will be to reduce the total number of direct competitors in any given market. This will make oligopolistic coordination on price and other variables easier. The final result is most unlikely to benefit consumers.

The real estate industry, through the Canadian Real Estate Association was able to have S.32(6) inserted into the act. It provides that "the court will not convict the accused if it finds that the conspiracy combination, agreement or arrangement [under S.32] relates only to a service and to standards of competence and integrity that are reasonably necessary for the protection of the public. . . ." This amendment, which applies to all service industries, could be used to establish significant barriers to entry — typically in the form of exaggerated educational requirements.[27] The result could well be a restriction in number of competitors and in the range of quality/price combinations available to the public. The effect of most professions or would-be professions is to over-protect the public in the name of ethical standards and professional competence for which the proxy used is formal education. Over-protection occurs when the poorer members of society are prevented from purchasing lower price/lower quality services which, in fact, would meet their needs wholly or in part.

Security dealers and underwriters were able to extend the scope of S.4.1 from that first proposed in the Stage I amendments to what was enacted. Originally, the exemptions from S.32 and S.38 applied only to syndicates formed by security dealers to underwrite new issues. As enacted, it permits agreements between the issuer and those involved in the primary distribution and extends to secondary distribution "where such agreement or arrangement has a reasonable relationship to the underwriting of a specific security." This qualification is likely to be interpreted broadly, thus potentially reducing competition among dealers in the secondary market. No doubt S.4.1 will be a boon to the members of the Investment Dealers' Association who worked so hard to have the government accept this amendment.

S.18 of the Competition Act proposed to strengthen greatly the prohibition of resale price maintenance in the Canadian law. Subsection 4 specifically prohibited "the placing by a producer or a supplier . . . of a price or suggested price on the commodity or its container by direct application or by attaching thereto a ticket . . . unless, in the case of suggested retail price, the suggested price is so expressed as to make it clear to any person to whose attention it comes, that it is a suggested price only and that the commodity may be sold at a lesser price." In the Stage I legislation the prohibitions against suggested resale prices, "unless it is clear . . ." etc., "do not apply to a price that is affixed or applied to a product or its package or contained" per S.38(5). The reasons for this exemption were given by George Orr, a senior official of the Department of Consumer and Corporate Affairs:

> There were representations from people who had pre-pricing done for them on the articles they wanted to sell, such as products sold by rack jobbers. This can be much more efficiently done in the factory. If the change had not been made, it would have been impossible to do that sort of thing.[28]

Conservative M.P. Bill Kempling recognized the benefit of permitting the practice.

> The manufacturer cannot direct the selling price. All he is suggesting is that this is a retail price, and in fact it is very useful in retail selling and in wholesale selling as well where the suggested retail price is used as a basis for discounts.[29]

With this amendment we can chalk one up for producers able to pre-ticket their merchandise. The power of suggested resale prices is not to be underestimated. Many merchants, particularly small ones, will sell at the pre-ticketed or suggested price. Resale price maintenance will be fostered.

Newspaper publishers were successful in having S.32(2)(f) inserted in the final bill. It permits agreements among competitors to restrict advertising or promotion "other than a discriminatory restriction directed against a member of the mass media." The minister admitted that the amendment modifying a section in the previous act "follows numerous representations designed to prevent its utilization against one or many information media."[30] Mr. Kempling wanted to be sure "this is as a result of the newspaper people's brief. . . ."[31] Mr. Ouellet assured him it was.

REFUSAL TO DEAL DEFENCES REINSTATED

S.18 of the Competition Act would have eliminated the four defences to a charge of refusal to deal (to enforce resale price maintenance), which had been inserted in the act in 1960 by the Conservative government of John Diefenbaker. The defences were not to be found in the Stage I amendments as introduced in Parliament on November 6, 1973. Nor were they part of the thirty amendments proposed by the Minister of

Consumer and Corporate Affairs on December 3, 1974. The four defences, which became S.38(9) (loss leader selling, bait-and-switch, misleading advertising and inadequate level of servicing) were restored by the House Committee on Finance, Trade and Economic Affairs in its final report to the House on June 5, 1975. The defences were reinserted into the Combines Act upon the motion of Norman Cafik, parliamentary secretary to the minister and a member of the committee, on the final day and evening of hearings on June 3, 1975. Speaking to the amendment, the Minister, Mr. Ouellet stated, "This is something that had been suggested by various groups, more particularly by the Senate committee, and we feel that it would be a constructive amendment."[32] Asked by a committee member if the amendment was in reply to requests from various groups of small wholesalers, the minister pointed out that loss leader selling was an issue which would be in the Stage II legislation. He went on to say, "However, since there is already in the act this S.38(5), which deals partly with this matter as one of the means of defence, we thought it might perhaps be better not to interfere with the act for the time being. Therefore, although we are not doing all we could to favour these wholesalers who are asking for a more basic revision of the act, we are at least not changing the existing act."[33]

By this action, Mr. Ouellet converted what could have been a gratifying victory into a defeat for the forces of competition.

REFUSAL TO DEAL: THE CHOICE OF ADJECTIVES AND THE EXEMPTION OF SPECIFIC BRAND NAMES

Refusal to deal is one of the reviewable matters subject to civil procedures by the Restrictive Trade Practices Commission. In the Stage I legislation as originally proposed, S.31.2 read in part

> where, on application by the Director, the Commission finds that (a) a person is *adversely affected* in his business or is precluded from carrying on business due to his inability to obtain adequate supplies of a product anywhere in a market on usual trade terms . . . [the Commission may recommend the removal or reduction in the relevant tariffs or it may make an order a supplier to accept the firm as a customer].

In his list of thirty amendments, the minister amended the italicized words to read "substantialy affected," saying it was done "with the intention of clarifying the threshold below which the section would have no possible application."[34] What he meant was that the threshold for an offence to be created was being raised. This will give producers using periodic refusal to supply as device to discipline their customers into resale price maintenance more room with which to employ their weapon without committing an offence. This change was recommended by the

Senate committee in its *Interim Report,*[35] but the Senate wanted to go even further by deleting the words "or is precluded from carrying on business" so that the section would not be vailable to those who had never been in business.

In the *Interim Report* of the Senate committee studying the Stage I legislation Senator Hayden noted, "there has been considerable debate as to whether the Commission should make an order under the refusal to deal provisions with respect to a particular brand name product."[36] The minister included as one of his amendments S.31.2(2), which provides that failure to obtain supplies of a single brand name product would not constitute grounds for an order under these provisions unless that particular brand name was so dominant in the market that failure to obtain it would substantially affect the ability of the person to carry on business in that class of articles. In supporting his amendment, Mr. Ouellet said, "There is only a very small number of sectors where one firm so dominates his industry that, without supplies of his branded lines, a dealer cannot stay in business."[37] One can think of cases where a firm's business could be substantially affected, yet the producer engaging in refusal to deal does not have an "article so differentiated [that it] occupies such a dominant position in that market. . . ." Consider the case of Kodak colour film; it is clearly the leading brand name. While there are competitors, e.g., Fuji, Ilford, GAF, a photo dealer's inability to obtain Kodak film could seriously affect his film sales and overall viability.

S.31.2 was further weakened with the addition of ss.(3) which defined trade terms as "terms in respect of payment, units of purchases and reasonable technical and servicing requirements." The first two aspects can be determined objectively by examination of purchase/sales records. The latter two, being much more subjective, might well be used as a successful defence to refusal to deal. Although the minister, in proposing this amendment, said, "This change makes clear that the commission will not order supply where the would-be buyer fails to meet such reasonable standards as are imposed on competing dealers in respect of the matters mentioned,"[38] the "gateway," at face value, is broader than he indicated.

ABUSE OF INTELLECTUAL AND INDUSTRIAL PROPERTY

As introduced on November 3, 1973 the Stage I legislation contained a provision which would have included copyrights and registered industrial designs in S.29 which prohibits and provides remedies for the abuse of patents and trademarks. The minister's amendments returned the section to *status quo ante.* The justification was that when Stage I was introduced the anticipated revision of the Patent Act and the Trade

Marks Act was "some considerable distance off." Because of the delay in passing Stage I, the amendments to the other acts were not far off, "it appears to be more appropriate to amend the underlying legislation first before amending the abuse provisions of the Combines Act."[39] The minister also pointed out that all statutory monopolies would be reviewed in Stage II under the issue of monopolization. Canadian business was no doubt pleased to hear the minister say that, "one of the consequences of the delay, however, is that the Combines Act will continue to have no direct application to copyright or registered industrial design."[40]

PYRAMID AND REFERRAL SELLING

In the original Stage I legislation both pyramid and referral selling schemes were banned outright. The minister, in his amendments, softened these provisions by inserting S.36.3(4) and 36.4(4), which exempted from the prohibition schemes "licenced or otherwise permitted by or pursuant to an act of the legislature of a province."

DUE DILIGENCE DEFENCE

In response to pressure from business interests the strict liability for misleading advertising representations in S.36 and 36.1 was dropped and S.37.3(2), the "due diligence" defence, inserted.

THE CORPORATE VEIL RESTORED

While they extol individualism and personal responsibility for success and failure, Canadian executives do not like to be charged with combines offences. In this the Crown has been most accommodating, seldom laying charges against individuals if there is a corporate entity available to "take the rap." S.73(7) and (8) of the Competition Act proposed to pierce the corporate veil and to recognize the fact that corporations are merely legal entities and that only natural persons are capable of conspiring to fix prices, engaging in resale price maintenance, arranging mergers and ordering the publication of misleading advertising messages. These sections provided:

> (7) Where a company has been convicted of an offence under this section
> (a) every director of the company, and
> (b) every officer, servant or agent of the company who was in whole or in part responsible for the conduct of that part of the business of the company that gave rise to the offence,

is a party to the offence unless he satisfies a court that he had no knowledge of any of the acts constituting the offence and could not reasonably be expected to have had such knowledge and that he exercised reasonable diligence to prevent the commission of such an offence.

(8) Where an offence under this section is committed by a person who, in respect of the business in the course of which the offence was committed and at the time the offence was committed, was the servant or agent of another person, that other person is a party to the offence unless he satisfies a court that he had no knowledge of the acts constituting the offence and could not reasonably be expected to have had such knowledge and that he exercised reasonable diligence to prevent the commission of such an offence.

Not surprisingly business executives were not anxious to be subject to these strictures. Their protests were loud, sufficiently so that the government conveniently omitted any provision relating to the legal responsibility of officers and/or directors for acts "committed by their corporations" in the Stage I amendments. In doing so, the government continued to support the myth that corporations, not individuals, commit illegal restraints of trade.

Let us now look at the results of the business-government interaction over competition policy up to and including the Stage I amendments as passed by Parliament from a different perspective. What did business as an interest group *not* succeed in eliminating?

THE GAINS FOR CONSUMERS DEPEND UPON STAGE II

As much as they may have wished to stay with the *status quo ante,* business could not persuade the government that no additional competition legislation was required. There are some gains in Stage I but the delivery of real benefits to consumers will depend upon the constitutionality of the civil damages provisions and the civil procedures inherent in the matters reviewable by the RTPC and the effectiveness of the administration and enforcement of the legislation. For example, even a large increase in the number of convictions for misleading advertising, if they result in fines of $100, $200 or $500, will hardly disprove the proposition that "crime pays."[41]

Just how far the government was able to move in spite of the strong opposition of business will also depend a great deal on what is enacted in Stage II. What is proposed in the Skeoch-McDonald report would represent a desirable improvement in the existing policies toward mergers, monopolization, and administration and enforcement. In this author's opinion, however, what is proposed does not go far enough.[42] The proposals by Neil J. Williams[43] with respect to consumer class actions are highly desirable. The reform of the existing merger section is absolutely imperative. The decisions in *Canadian Breweries*[44] and *B.C.*

Sugar[45] had the effect of allowing the Crown to attack successfully (perhaps), only the merger of the last two firms in an industry. The Supreme Court's unanimous decision in November 1976 in the K. C. *Irving* case[46] has totally nullified the merger and monopoly provisions of the existing Combines Investigation Act.[47]

The Director's attempt to operate a "jaw bone" anti-merger policy through his stated position on merger law and his program of compliance (with respect to mergers) are admissions of the fact that Crown could not wield the statutory provisions with any effect.[48]

CIVIL PROCEDURES

As we have noted above, some elements of the civil procedures have been introduced in the form of matters reviewable by the RTPC. However, they may only be placed before the commission by the Director, not by persons directly affected by one of the restrictive practices as contemplated in Bill C-256. The commission's powers are modest. It can only issue cease and desist orders. The effectiveness of such orders, like the Prohibition Orders now obtainable under S.30 of the act, depend upon the ability of the Director and his staff to enforce them. Single-damage civil actions by affected persons will assist the Director when an order has not been obeyed. But while the number of cease and desist orders will pile up, the enforcement capabilities of the Bureau of Competition Policy will not likely grow apace. The Director should publish a list of firms already subject to prohibition orders to permit firms and individuals to, in effect, assist him in the enforcement of the act. Unless the cost of committing combines offences is vastly increased, rational, profit seeking executives will knowingly violate the act.

AN INCREASE IN MAXIMUM PENALTIES

The maximum penalties in the form of fines and imprisonment have been increased for misleading advertising. For proceedings by indictment the penalties are unchanged — a fine at the discretion of the court or five years' imprisonment or both. For proceedings by summary conviction (except in the case of double ticketing) the ceiling on fines is increased to $25,000 and the ceiling on imprisonment to one year.

Misleading advertising fines have been increasing in the last few years, but they only infrequently have exceeded $5,000. An analysos of the cases decided in 1974/75 indicated that the total fine (all counts) in S.36 cases (misleading price advertising) was $200 or less in eleven of the seventeen cases. In four cases it was in the $201-$400 range and in two it was between $401 and $1,000. Of the sixty-four S.36 cases (false advertising), in twenty the total fine was $400 or less, in twenty-nine it was between $401 and $1,000. In only six cases was the fine $5,000 or more. There were four fines of $5,000, one of $8,000 and one of $20,000, the last being two counts at $10,000 each. The largest fine on record was levied on Benson and Hedges in March 1973.[41] Reversing the usual order, the judge fined them $2,500 on the first count and $25,000 on the second. As Table 10-1 indicates, the average fine in misleading advertising cases has been low. For S.36 offences it was only $229 in 1973, rising to $296 in 1975. For S.37 offences, the average was $1,347 in 1973 (raised significantly by the Benson and Hedges case), but in 1975 it had fallen to $1,081.

In the case of conspiracies (S.32) the government proposed a $1,000,000 maximum fine in place of a fine at the discretion of the court and this was enacted. How this could be an improvement from the Crown's point of view is hard to see. It has been suggested that indicating a seven-figure maximum fine may have a desirable psychological effect on Canadian judges. The largest fine until april 1977, on a single count, was $125,000. On april 13, 1977 Canadian General Electric was fined $300,000, Westinghouse Canada $150,000 and GTE Sylvania $100,000 in the *Large Lamp* case.[50]

The average fine per firm in eight bonspiracy cases decided between 1970 and 1975 was only $13,758. If the two cases with the largest fines are removed, the average falls to $8,149 — just slightly more than the average fine per firm in the twenty-one cases decided between 1960 and 1969.[51]

Business was able to eliminate the provision of a maximum fine of $2,000,000 and/or imprisonment for up to five years for second or subsequent S.32 convictions from the amendments as enacted. Bill C-256 had also provided that previous convictions under S.32 or S.411 or 498 of the Criminal Code would count in determining the number of previous convictions.

CONSTITUTIONALITY NOT TESTED

Despite repeated requests, business interest groups did not succeed in their attempts to have Bill C-256 or the Stage I amendments referred to the Supreme Court of Canada for a ruling on their constitutional validity. In the House committee, Conservative M.P. Sinclair Stevens pressed the minister very hard[52] for an amendment which would have required the government refer S.31.1 and Part IV.1 of the legislation (the provisiosn for private civil actions and all civil procedures before the RTPC) to the Supreme Court of Canada to test their constitutionality.[53] The amendment also provided the sections affected would not come into force until ruled *intra vires* by the Supreme Court.

A study by S. G. M. Grange (since appointed to the Supreme Court

TABLE 10-1

Disposition of Misleading Advertising Cases, Calendar 1973, 1974 and 1975

	S.36 1973	1974	1975	S.37 1973	1974	1975
Charges laid	26	40	15	69	102	70
Acquittals	6	10	3	15	30	17
Convictions	20	30	12	54	72	53
Average fine – per case[1]	$ 229	$ 262	$ 296	$ 1,347[2]	$ 1,160	$ 1,081
Average fine/all counts	$ 191	$ 207	$ 254	$ 836[2]	$ 739	$ 486
Average fine/first count only						
• Corporations	$ 247	$ 293	$ 311	$ 888	$ 1,124	$ 1,272
• Individuals	$ 44	$ 212	$ 183	$ 532	$ 316	$ 193
• Both	$ 204[3]	$ 242[4]	$ 279	$ 711[5]	$ 890[6]	$ 807[7]
Total fines in the year	$4,575	$7,852	$3,550	$72,725	$83,525	$57,295
Prohibition orders	2	2	–	11	5	5
Other (jail only, discharge, restitution)	–	3	–	–	3	2

NOTES:

[1] Incorporates multiple counts and both individuals and corporations.

[2] In the Benson and Hedges case the firm was fined $2,500 on the first count and $25,000 on the second.

[3] Based on nineteen first count convictions.

[4] In three cases, sentences were suspended, hence there were no fines.

[5] Fines imposed in lump sum against four accused have been averaged to determine fines by count, i.e., $500 total on four counts has been treated as $125 fine first count, etc.

[6] Bases on sixty-nine first count convictions in three of which no fine was imposed.

[7] Based on fifty-one first count convictions on two of which no fine was imposed.

SOURCE:

Ms. Tandy Muir-Warden, Bureau of Competition Policy, Department of Consumer and Corporate Affairs, Ottawa.

of Ontario), published by the C. D. Howe Research Institute, casts doubt on the constitutionality of the legislation, but two other reviews of it see the legislation as within the powers of the federal government.[54]

INCLUSION OF SERVICES

One of the major elements of the Competition Act did get enacted in the 1975 amendments. That was the placing of services (including the professions) within the orbit of the Combines Investigation Act. This was done in the face of severe pressure by such groups as the Canadian Real Estate Association. To give the service industries time "to clean up their act," the application of S.32 was held up until July 1, 1976, six months after the rest of the amendments came into effect. The real impact of this amendment will depend on the extent to which the purveyors of services are able to find shelter under the umbrella of provincial regulation and remain "safe and dry" beyond the reach of the Combines Act. Until now at least, the Director has accepted the dictum of McRuer C.J.H.C. laid down in *Canadian Breweries.*

> When a Provincial Legislature has conferred on a Commission or Board the power to regulate an industry and fix prices, and the power has been exercised, the Court must assume that the power is exercised in the public interest. In such cases, in order to succeed in a prosecution laid under the Combines Act with respect to the operation of a combine, I think it must be shown that the combine has operated, or is likely to operate, so as to hinder or prevent the Provincial body from effectively exercising the powers given to it to protect the public interest. If the evidence shows that by reason of a merger the accused is given a substantial monopoly in the market, this onus, in my opinion, would be discharged.[55]

Should he successfully challenge this ruling, the Director would sharply enlarge the coverage of the act.

IMPROVED MISLEADING ADVERTISING AND DECEPTIVE PRACTICES PROVISIONS

By and large, the government succeeded in getting on the books its proposals for reform in the area of misleading advertising and deceptive practices. The "credulous man" disappeared but the injunctions against pyramid selling, referral selling, bait-and-switch, sales above advertised prices, and promotional contests moved into law. As we have pointed out, the concept of "deemed representation" was broadened, and a "general impression" test instituted.[56] The previously existing provisions, which date effectively from 1960 and mid-1969,[57] resulted in an explosion of complaints, investigation and prosecutions. For example, only 104 non-misleading advertising cases were launched between April

1960 and March 1976 while in 681 misleading advertising cases charges were laid in the same period. Some 591 of these occurred in the last six years (1970-71 to 1975-76). If a similar result follows from the new legislation, the enforcement activities of the Bureau of Competition Policy may become over-weighted by misleading advertising/deceptive practices cases at the expense of larger structural cases involving price fixing, mergers and monopolies. In the 1960s this is what occurred in the U.S. Federal Trade Commission, where the resources absorbed by the larger number of small cases involving the labelling of textiles and furs resulted in a very low level of activity in terms of significant anti-trust cases.[58]

ELIMINATION OF THE "VIRTUAL MONOPOLY" TEST

While producer interests were able to restore "unduly" to the conspiracy section, 32, the reformers did succeed in inserting S.32.1.1 into the amended act. This section extinguishes the "virtual monopoly" test in conspiracy cases which had been raised by Cartwright J. in the *Howard Smith* case decided in 1957.[59] Cartwright's view that a virtual monopoly was required before competition was restricted unduly was *not* the dominant view *before* he expressed it or without challenge *after* he stated it in 1957. For example, Manson J. in *Crown Zellerbach,* upheld on appeal, stated in 1955 that "there are no words in the statute which put the Crown under the onus of proving a monopoly or virtual monopoly."[60] In a 1960 decision, Batshaw J., in the *Abitibi* case,[61] specifically rejected the virtual monopoly concept expressed by Cartwright J., which was put before him by the defence counsel.

Manson's words were specifically adopted by Laidlaw J. A. in the Ontario Court of Appeal in the *Electrical Contractors Association of Ontario* case in 1961.[62] More recently the virtual monopoly doctrine was also rejected in *R. v. Aetna Insurance* (1975) by MacDonald J. A. (Cooper J. A. concurring) in the Appeal Division of the Supreme Court of Nova Scotia.[63] Despite this record, we find all three judges (in a decision written by Houlden J. A.) in the Ontario Court of Appeal in *R. v. Armco Canada Ltd. et al.* endorsing Cartwright J's words.[64]

In conclusion, it appears that the elimination of the virtual monopoly doctrine represents a useful, but fairly minor, victory for the pro-competition forces. The benefits of S.32.1.1 depend upon the ability of the Crown to get judges to label as "undue" conspiracies involving a smaller percentage of the relevant market than have previously been the case. The real importance of Cartwright's virtual monopoly criterion was found not so much in conspiracy cases as it was in *merger* cases.[65]

EXTRATERRITORIALITY

Finally, in response to a long history of the extraterritorial application of U.S. laws in Canada, principally the antitrust and trading-with-the-enemy laws, officials in the Bureau of Competition Policy were able to insert, in Stage I, amendments concerning the implementation of foreign judgments and the application of foreign laws and government and corporate directives in Canada (S.31.5 and 31.6). These sections were not in C-256 when it was introduced in 1971. The inclusion of these sections resulted in consumer and corporate affairs receiving the support of the

Department of Industry, Trade and Commerce — for these sections at least. The extent of the benefits of these sections is hard to predict, but they should insure that the Canadian subsidiaries of U.S. multinationals will be somewhat more responsive to the Canadian policy environment.

STRENGTHENED PRICE MAINTENANCE PROVISIONS, PROBLEMS OF ENFORCEMENT

Perhaps because they did not recognize its potential, business did not make as much noise as might be expected about the change in S.38 dealing with price maintenance.[66] The keys are the words "by agreement, threat, promise or any like means, *attempt to influence upwards* or to discourage the reduction of, the price at which any other person . . . supplies . . . or advertises a product . . ." (emphasis added). Depending on the interpretation by the courts, this section could be used to attack a wide variety of activities unassailable under S.32 (conspiracies). If applied only to the usual resale price maintenance schemes, the section will not realize its full potential. The impact of the section will depend, in the first instance, on the aggressiveness with which the officials in the Bureau of Competition Policy try to use the section in a wider domain. Despite their best efforts and willingness to bring cases, they could be hamstrung by the unwillingness of the Department of Justice to prosecute cases using this line of attack. Fundamentally, the Bureau of Competition Policy is a research and investigation agency. It can only recommend prosecution of a case; it cannot proceed to the courts on its own volition. This is in sharp contrast to the United States, where the Assistant General of the Antitrust Division, Department of Justice, who also performs the investigation and research functions, can go to court on his own initiative. In Canada, the monopoly enjoyed by the Department of Justice over all federal prosecutions represents an important filter or decision point between investigation and prosecution.

In the past it is safe to say that officials in the Office of the Director of Investigation and Research have been frustrated by the diffidence and delay on the part of the Department of Justice in pressing cases.[67] Combines work forms a very small proportion of the Department of Justice's total workload. The small absolute number of such cases (excluding misleading advertising cases) in a given year means that few Crown prosecutors have much knowledge in the area or much sympathy for such prosecutions. As combines cases are often complex and involve protracted litigation, they reduce the apparent output of the Crown attorneys assigned to them.

Having to to court, a major hurdle remains — convincing a judge to apply a new interpretation of the law. Canadian judges, particularly in the area of combines law, have generally been conservative legalists. For example, in the application of economoc theory to such cases they have largely accepted the dictum, "our lady, the Common Law, is not a professed economist."[68] On this point, as with the others outlined above, the final outcome will depend most importantly on the accumulation of judicial decisions. Unfavourable decisions, if Canadian history is a guide, will remain undisturbed by remedial legislation for many years. The emasculation of the merger section of the Combines Investigation Act, which took place in 1960, with the *Beer* and *Sugar* decisions will not be remedied until at least 1978. The slow pace of reform favours the existing concentrations of social and economic power.

NOTES

[1]Donald N. Thompson, "New Competition Bill Pleases 1971 Critics," *Globe and Mail,* (Toronto) November 17, 1973.

Thompson's detailed analysis of Bill C-256 can be found in his "Competition Policy and Marketing Regulation," in Donald N. Thompson and David S. R. Leighton (eds.), *Canadian Marketing: Problems and Prospects,* Toronto, Wiley, 1973, pp. 13-43. His analysis of the Stage I amendments can be found in Donald N. Thompson, "Canada's New Competition Policy: Status and Outlook," *California Management Review,* Vol. 16, No. 4, Summer 1974, pp. 93-103.

[2]Anthony Pengelly, chairman of the Association of Canadian Advertisers quoted in the *Globe and Mail* (Toronto), October 20, 1971, p. B5.

[3]The application of S.32 to the service industries did not begin until July 1, 1976.

[4]Murray Edelman, "Governmental Organization and Public Policy," *Public Administration Review,* Vol. XII, Autumn 1952.

[5]Department of Consumer and Corporate Affairs, *The Competition Act, Explanatory Notes,* Ottawa, 1971 (mimeo) p. 76.

[6]R. v. *Canadian Coat and Apron Supply Limited et al.,* [1967] 2 Ex C.R. 53; 52 C.P.R. 189; 2 C.R.N.S. 62 at p. 80.

[7]*Competition Policy in the Context of A Canadian Industrial Strategy,* Seventh McGill Government-Industry Conference, Montreal, McGill University, Faculty of Management, 1973, p. 17, footnote 17.

[8]A. Milton Moore, "Mergers and Price Agreements," in *Canada's Competition Policy,* Ottawa, Conference Board in Canada, 1972, p. 22.

[9]L. A. Skeoch and B. C. McDonald, in consultation with M. Belanger, R. M. Bromstein, and W. O. Twaits, *Dyanmic Change and Accountability in a Canadian Market Economy,* Ottawa, Supply and Services Canada, 1976; Department of Consumer and Corporate Affairs, *Proposals for a New Competition Policy for Canada, Second Stage,* Ottawa, Supply and Services Canada, 1977, 251 pp.

[10]*Explanatory Notes, op.cit.,* p. 28.

[11]*Ibid.*

[12]See J. J. Quinlan, "The Restrictive Trade Practices Commission: Its Functions and Duties," paper presented before the Anti-trust Law Section of the American Bar Association, Montreal, August 12, 1975, mimeo, 27 pp; R. S. MacLellan. "The New Quasi-Judicial Powers of the Restrictive Trade Practices Commission Contained in the Proposed Amendments to the Combines Investigation Act — Bill C-2," paper presented to the Consumer and the Law Conference, University of Montreal, September 27, 1975, mimeo, 18 pp; and Gordon E. Kaiser, "The New Competition Law: Stage One," *Canadian Business Law Journal,* Vol. 1, No. 2, 1976, pp. 147-196.

[13]Discussions on the constitutionality of the legislation can be found in S. G. M. Grange, Q.C., *The Constitutionality of Federal Intervention in the Marketplace — The Competition Case,* Montral, C. D. Howe Research Institute, 1976; Peter W. Hogg and Warren Grover, "The Constitution the Competition Bill," *Canadian Business Law Journal,* Vol. 1, No. 2, 1976, pp. 197-228; and Robert Reid "The New Role of the Restrictive Trade Practices Commission: A Constitutional and Administrative Viewpoint," in W. T. Stanbury (ed.), *Papers on the 1975 Amendements to the Combines Investigation Act,* Vancouver, University of British Columbia, Faculty of Commerce and Business Administration, 1976, pp. 157-187.

[14]For a discussion of the importance of private civil actions in combines penalties and remedies, see W. T. Stanbury, "Penalties and Remedies Under the Combines Investigation Act, 1889-1976," *Osgoode Hall Law Journal,* Vol. 14, No. 3, 1976, pp 571-631.

[15]*Debates of the Senate,* 1st Session, 30th Parliament, Vol. 123, No. 64, March 19, 1975, p. 678.

[16]R. v. *Imperial Tobacco Products Limited* (1970), 64 C.P.R. 3; 2 C.C.C. (2d) 533; 16 D.L.R. (3d) 470 (Trial). Upon appeal the verdict was reversed, see [1971] 5 W.W.R. 409; 4 C.C.C. (2d) 423; 22 D.L.R. (3d) 51; 3 C.P.R. (2d) 178. Brief descriptions are contained in *Annual Report of the Director of Investigation and Research, Combines Investigation Act* for the year ended March 31, 1971 Ottawa, Queen's Printer 1971, pp. 63-64 and *Annual Report of the Director, . . .* year ended March 31, 1972, pp. 41-43.

[17]R. v. *K. J. Beamish Construction Company Limited et al.,* [1968] 2 C.C.C. 5.

[18]Restrictive Trade Practices Commission, *Report in the Matter of an Inquiry Relating to the Supply and Transportation of Asphalt Paving Materials in The Province of Ontario,* Ottawa, Queen's Printer, 1970.

[19]Restrictive Trade Practices Commission, *Report Relating to the Supply, Transportation and Application of Asphalt Mixes used in the Paving and Repair of Municipal Streets in the Cities of Ottawa and Eastview, Ontario and Hull, Quebec,* Ottawa, Queen's Printer, 1965.

[20]Restrictive Trade Practices Commission, *Report on an Alleged Combine in the Matter of a Call for Tenders by the Town of Duvernay for the Construction of Sewers and Water Mains,* Ottawa, Queen's Printer, 1964.

[21]For a most useful discussion see James Sherbaniuk, "Identical Bids Usually Result of Market Forces," *Financial Post,* May 5, 1973, pp. C-1 and C-2.

[22]*Annual Report of the Director of Investigation and Research, Combines Investigation Act* for the year ended March 21, 1961, Ottawa, Queen's Printer, 1961, pp. 23-24.

[23]*Ibid.,* March 31, 1974, Ottawa, Queen's Printer, 1964, pp. 11-12.

24*Ibid.,* March 31, 1968, Ottawa, Queen's Printer, 1968, pp. 43-46.

25This amendment was avidly sought by Conservative M.P. Sinclair Stevens. However, Mr. Stevens did not get all he asked for. As the minister pointed out in his testimony before the House Committee on Finance, Trade and Economic Affairs on June 3, 1975, Mr. Stevens amendment as originally proposed, "while considering very carefully whether or not it was feasible to exclude franchises from application of the section [S.34.4], the fact is that acceptance of this exclusion will cut the heart out of the proposed section" (*Minutes of Proceedings and Evidence of the Standing Committee on Finance, Trade and Economic Affairs,* Issue No. 55, June 3, 1975, p. 90).

26The chairman of the House committee, Robert Kaplan, referred to it as "the soft drink amendment" (*Minutes,* June 3, 1975, p. 86). Earlier in proposing the amendment, the minister said, "Representations have been received to the effect that investment made in soft drink bottling industries may be jeopardized by subsection 31.4(3) in their unique case" (*Minutes,* April 8, 1975, p. 5).

27See the discussion in the *Minutes,* June 2, 1975, pp. 10-19, where many of the comments were framed in terms of "codes of ethics" established by professional or industry bodies.

28*Minutes,* June 3, 1975, p. 57.

29*Ibid.,* p. 58.

30*Ibid.,* June 2, 1975, p. 10.

31*Ibid.*

32*Ibid.,* June 3, 1975, p. 61.

33*Ibid.*

34"Amendments and Comments to Bill C-2, An Act to Amend the Combines Investigation Act," December 3, 1974, mimeo, clause 12, p. 3. S.31.4(2) dealing with exclusive dealing or tied selling was also weakened by the insertion of the words "lessen competition substantially" which raised the threshold before the RTPC could make an order with respect to these practices.

35*Debates of the Senate,* March 19, 1975, p. 679.

36*Ibid.*

37"Amendments and Comments to Bill C-2" *op.cit.,* clause 12, pp.6-7.

38*Ibid.,* p. 7.

39*Ibid.,* clause 10, pp. 1-2.

40*Ibid.,* clause 10, p. 2.

41See W. T. Stanbury "Penalties and Remedies Under the Combines Investigation Act, 1889-1976," *Osgoode Hall Law Journal,* Vol. 14, No. 3, 1976, pp. 571-631.

42See W. T. Stanbury, "Dynamic Change and Accountability in a Canadian Market Economy: Summary and Critique," *Osgoode Hall Law Journal,* Vol. 15, No. 1, 1977 pp. 1-50. A discussion of the Stage II legislation and Bill C-42 itself can be found in the second reference in footnote 9.

43Neil J. Williams, "Damages Class Action Under the Combines Investigation Act," in *A Proposal for Class Action Under Competition Policy Legislation,* Ottawa, Information Canada, 1976, pp. 1-195.

44*R.* v. *Canadian Breweries Ltd.,* [1960] O.R. 601; 33 C.R. 1; 126 C.C.C. 133.

45*R.* v. *British Columbia Sugar Refining Company Limited et al.* (1960), 32 W.W.R. (N.S.) 577; 129 C.C.C. 7; (1962) 38 C.P.R. 177.

46*R.* v. *K. C. Irving Ltd. et al.* Unreported judgement, Supreme Court of Canada, November 16, 1976, Bureau of Competition Policy, mimeo 136-5.

47See G. B. Reschenthaler and W. T. Stanbury, "Benign Monopoly: Canadian Merger Policy and the K. C. Irving Case,", *Canadian Business Law Journal,* 1977, forthcoming.

48The Director's position on merger law is outlined in *Annual Report of the Director of Investigation and Research, Combines Investigation Act,* year ended March 31, 1966, Ottawa,

Queen's Printer, 1966, pp. 18-22. The program of compliance is outlined in every *Annual Report* beginning in 1964-65.

[49]See *Annual Report of the Director*, year ended March 31, 1973, p. 94.

[50]In the following cases, fines of $125,000 were levied for a single count: R. v. *Ocean Construction Supplies Ltd. et al.* (1975), 18 C.P.R. (2d) 166 and R. v. *Armco Canada Ltd. et al.* (1975), 6 O.R. (2d) 521; 21 C.C.C. (2d) 129; 17 C.P.R. (2d) 211. The fines in the *Large Lamp* conspiracy were reported in the *Star* (Toronto) April 14, 1977, p. 12.

[51]Per note 41, Table 5.

[52]*Minutes*, June 3, 1975, pp. 78-86.

[53]*Ibid.*, June 2, 1975, p. 3 for the wording of the amendment.

[54]See note 13.

[55]R. v. *Canadian Breweries Ltd.* [1960] O.R. 601 at 629-530.

[56]See Ronald I. Cohen "Bill C-7: Its Proposed Amendments to the Law of False Advertising," 13 C.P.R. (2d) 197 and Jacob S. Ziegel, "Legal and Managerial Problems in Implementing the Consumer Aspects of the Combines Amendment Bill; Bill C-7," 17 C.P.R. (2d) 182.

[57]S.33C (later S.36) misleading advertising with respect to price was brought into the Combines Act in 1960. S.33D (later S.37) dealing with deceptive or misleading advertising more generally was formerly S.306 of the Criminal Code before it was transferred to the Combines Act in mid-1969. Under the Criminal Code it existed in one form or another since 1917, but there was only one reported prosecution. See R. I. Cohen, "False Advertising in Canada: An Overview of Sections 33C and 33D," in McGill University, Faculty of Law, *Five Lectures on Combines Law and Policy, False Advertising in Canada, Consumer Protection*, W. C. J. Meredith Memorial Lectures, 1971, Montreal, Wilson and Lefleur, 1971, p. 118.

[58]American Bar Association, *Report of the ABA Commission to Study the Federal Trade Commission*, 1969 (including the "Separate Statement of Richard A. Posner"); E. Cox, R. Fellmeth, J. Schultz, *The Nader Report on the Federal Trade Commission*, New York, Grossman, 1969; Mark J. Green *et al.*, *The Closed Enterprise System*, New York, Bantam Books, 1972, Chapters 10-14.

[59]*Howard Smith Paper Mills Ltd. et al.* v. *The Queen*, [1957] S.C.R. 403 at p. 426.

[60]R. v. *Crown Zellerbach Ltd. et al.* (1955) 113 C.C.C. 201 at p. 219.

[61]R. v. *Abitibi Power and Paper Company Limited et al.* (1961) 131 C.C.C. 201 at p. 251.

[62]R. v. *Electrical Contractors Association of Ontario and Dent*, (1961) 37 C.P.R. 1 at p. 37.

[63]R. v. *Aetna Insurance Company and 72 Other Corporations*, (1975) 22 C.C.C. (2d) 513 at pp. 546-550.

[64]R. v. *Armco Canada Limited et al.*, Ontario Court of Appeal unreported judgment of February 2, 1976, Bureau of Competition Policy mimeo 221-3, p. 23.

[65]See W. T. Stanbury, "The 1975 Amendments to the Combines Investigation Act: Analysis of the Provisions Relating to Virtual Monopoly, Bid Rigging and New Penalties," in W. T. Stanbury (ed.), *Papers on the 1975 Amendments to Combines Investigation Act*, Vancouver, University of British Columbia, Faculty of Commerce and Business Administration, 1976, pp. 60-62.

[66]In addition to the point outlined in the text, we should note that in the amendments to Stage I public officials were able to obtain the inclusion of credit cards in the purview of S.38. This could be a potentially valuable gain for consumers.

[67]See Paul K. Gorecki and W. T. Stanbury, *"Canada's Combines Investigation Act: Public Law Enforcement,"* paper presented at the National Conference on Competition Policy sponsored by the University of Toronto, Toronto, May 12 & 13, 1977.

[68]Sir Frederick Pollock, *The Genius of the Common Law*, New York, Columbia University Press, 1912, p. 94.

Chapter 11

Summary and Conclusions

We shall not use this chapter to systematically summarize the major points made in each of the preceeding ones. Rather, it will be used to provide a sort of gestalt of the entire study. These, then, are our lingering impressions at the end of detailed analysis of a single case study of business-government interaction over a major issue of federal policy — competition legislation.

NEITHER TOTAL VICTORY NOR TOTAL DEFEAT

There can be no doubt that the collective efforts of many business firms and trade associations over the period 1971-1975 changed significantly the competition policy legislation put forward by the Department of Consumer and Corporate Affairs first in June 1971 and again in November 1973. Business as a pressure group was able to delay the legislation, split it into pieces and make it more amenable to its interests and less protective of consumer interests. At the same time, business did not succeed in preventing new competition legislation which must be rated as an improvement over the pre-existing provisions. When one views the Stage I amendments as incorporated into the Combines Investigation Act in relation to the act as it existed before those amendments, one notes the following changes which, from the point of view of consumers and citizens generally interested in an effective competition policy, must rank as improvements:

- The inclusion of services (although subject to provincial legislation which may exempt them from the provisions of the act).
- Strengthened misleading advertising provisions and a broadened list of prohibited deceptive practices.
- Strengthened resale price maintenance provisions.
- Provision for private civil actions for combines offences.
- Provision for civil procedures for certain reviewable matters (including five restrictive trade practices).
- Increased maximum penalties for most offences.
- Prevention of the application of the "virtual monopoly" doctrine in conspiracy cases.

- Provision for bid rigging as a per se offence.
- Provision for the Director to intervene in federal regulatory proceedings.

However, if one compares these amendments as enacted to what was proposed in the Competition Act of 1971, the improvements in Canada's competition legislation are much more modest. Conversely, the difference between what was proposed and what was actually attained four and one-half years later is a measure of business' success in lobbying the government. It may be useful to indicate, briefly but necessarily incompletely, what business was ale to *prevent* from becoming part of our competition law:

- A wide variety of conspiracies in restraint of trade including price fixing) did not become illegal per se but remain illegal only if they restrain competition "unduly."
- The extent of civil procedures is limited to five restrictive practices and a few other matters; there is no tribunal, but rather these matters come before the existing RTPC, which had its responsibilities enlarged.
- As of January 1, 1976 there were no new provisions with respect to mergers, monopoly and monopolization, price discrimination, rationalization and specialization agreements, interlocking directorates, abuse of intellectual and industrial property, loss leader selling and delivered pricing schemes. All were dealt with in the proposed Competition Act in a way that would have a positive effect on competition and almost certainly benefit consumers. The final verdict on these matters depends upon the Stage II amendments as enacted.
- Successful private civil actions cannot result in double damages (only single damages) nor can the courts award double damages to those injured in addition to the usual criminal penalties as proposed in Bill C-256.
- The existence of identical tenders does not constitute an offence per se as proposed in Bill C-256.
- Franchise operations are now excluded from the scope of civil orders in respect of exclusive dealing, market restriction or tied selling arrangements.
- Resale price maintenance prohibitions were not extended to pre-ticketed goods.
- The four defences for refusal to deal, which were eliminated in Bill C-256, were reinstated in the Stage I amendments. The provision making brand name products subject to the prohibition of refusal to deal was also eliminated in Stage I.
- Copyrights and registered industrial designs, which were made

subject to abuse of the statutory monopoly provisions along with patents and trademarks, were eliminated from the proposed Stage I amendments.

Directors and officers were made personally liable for combines offences when a company was convicted; this provision of Bill-256 was eliminated from the Stage I amendments.

Seen from the vantage point of what the very ambitious Competition Act promised, business interests surely scored more than a modest victory. But the final outcome is yet to be determined. It hinges on what the government can get into law with the Stage II amendments. If the merger and monopoly provisions remain completely ineffectual, as indicated by the decision in the *K. C. Irving case*,[1] the magnitude of business victory will be great indeed.

Assuming that the Stage II amendments do constitute at least a modest improvement over the existing legislation, both the business interests which opposed the Competition Act and the Stage I amendments and the government which sought to greatly strengthen Canada's competition legislation can find something in the final result to cheer about. Neither group won a complete victory nor suffered a complete defeat.

TACTICAL ERRORS?

Did the minister and the government commit a tactical error in introducing the Competition Act as an "exposure draft" before detailed private consultations with business? Second was the timing of Bill C-256 inappropriate in light of (1) the number of pieces of legislation which preceeded it which had a significant impact on business and (2) the state of the economy in mid-1971?

The first point was raised by Gordon Sharwood, then president of Acres Limited, in a speech in January of 1972 when he said:

> Trudeau has . . . adopted a curious method of introducing new policy. A minister (such as Basford, with his Competition Act, or Benson, with his tax policy, or Herb Gray, with his foreign ownership report, or Kierans, with Communications) is invited to initiate a program, is given no obvious support by Cabinet or Prime Minister and is sent out to "play in the street." If he comes back alive, we have a massive new government initiative; if he does not, Trudeau withdraws the initiative and the minister concerned may not survive.
>
> Even if we disregard the question of fairness to the minister involved, this method of introducing policy warrants criticism for its failure to involve major interest groups in the early stages of policy formation. A small task force is delegated with the responsibility of preparing a report with recommendations for the inception of new policy.

The resulting proposals have often turned out to be impractical, illiberal and immoderate. Regardless of the extent to which concessions are granted before final legislation is passed, the climate of hostility that invariably follows such proposals is not conducive to cooperation. It also has a disturbing impact on the market mechanism.[2]

When Bill C-256 was introduced for First Reading in the Commons, the minister stressed it was an "exposure draft" and that no final legislation would be enacted without widespread public discussion and consultation with the affected interest groups. In the months of debate following the introduction of the bill, the minister repeated that he was willing to change the bill and that C-256 did not represent the government's final position. On September 28, 1971, in a speech to the annual meeting of the Canadian Chamber of Commerce, Mr. Basford said:

> I want to voice the government's conviction that policy so fundamental to the workings of our economy cannot be determined without the understanding and cooperation of the business community. It is the government's responsibility to put forward sound and effective legislation; but in doing so we fully recognize the value and necessity of utilizing the practical knowledge and experience of business in framing this legislation.
>
> In this context, it is my hope that we will soon be receiving your views on the proposals contained in Bill C-256, either through your respective firms or associations, or through the Chamber of Commerce directly.[3]

Later in his speech Mr. Basford argued that "business should welcome and support an effective policy on competition because no other group in the community has such a direct interest in the success of the policy."[4] He went on to say that Bill C-256 was not a radical departure from the Economic Council's *Interim Report*[5]. Near the end of his address the minister restated his desire to receive and consider the views of business: "It is our intention that every opportunity will be given to interested parties to study the bill and to have their views considered before it passes into law."[6] He indicated that representations "that make a persuasive case for better or more effective ways to reach our policy objectives will be very closely considered."[7] The minister added, "I would hope that [Bill C-256] will be amended to reflect constructive suggestions from interested parties."[8] However, in the next paragraph he indicated, "the government is firmly committed to the principles laid down in the Competition Act and the objectives it is designed to fulfill. We are satisfied that the bill as presently written answers these principles in all important respects."[9]

Having reaffirmed both his and the government's firm commitment to the principles which underlay the bill, Mr. Basford went on to say, "I assure you we do not have closed minds when it comes to listening to better ideas or more effective methods. We ask for your comments because we sincerely want them and need them."[10]

Mr. Basford's theme of a clear commitment to the principles embodied in the Competition Act, combined with flexibility as to how to draft the specific language to achieve the given objectives, was repeated in a series of speeches across the country in the next couple of months.[11]

Businessmen may have been receiving mixed signals about the extent of the government's flexibility in respect to the bill. For example, at a conference on the Bill in September 1971, the Director of Investigation and Research, Mr. Henry, stated, "The new bill is a statement of government policy quite unlike, for example, a White Paper. This is a bill which the government has introduced into Parliament."[12]

This point was re-emphasized in the discussion following Mr. Henry's speech when the vice-president and secretary of Westinghouse Canada Limited said, "You say this is a matter of government policy. I take it that you are saying that this is to be presumed by the fact that this bill has been laid before the House." Mr. Henry replied, "Yes."[13]

Yet at the same conference the Westinghouse executive asserted, "one cannot be sure if Bill C-256 is to be regarded as an expression of government policy." Later in the day Mr. Henry stated:

> The Minister is sponsoring the Bill. He has introduced it in Parliament and, of course, the introduction of the Bill is a decision of the Government collectively, and that is the only point to my remarks. The Minister has also indicated that he is prepared to listen to reasonable arguments as to how the Bill should be revised.[14]

Business interests were not alone in their criticism of the way the government went about the process of reforming the nation's competition policy. The Edmonton *Journal* made the point that as draft legislation the government's proposal "tends to reduce the maneuverability of the minister in charge to make significant changes."[15] An Ottawa *Citizen* editorial was also critical of the tactical approach of the government with respect to the Competition Act.

> The manner of introducing this legislation has been unfortunate. Putting out a bill in half-cooked state and withdrawing it under fire with the plea that it was only draft legislation has become a trademark of the Trudeau administration.[16]

Mr. Basford's offer to review the proposed legislation was seen as inadequate by the Toronto *Globe and Mail* which wrote:

> What the bill needs is not a review; it is a complete rethinking. Until Mr. Basford is prepared to offer individuals and businesses assurances that they will be dealt with equitably, fairly and

predictably, he needn't bother worrying about reintroducing the bill. It will remain unacceptable.[17]

At the same time the government was praised for the way it handled the process. D. Gordon Blair, , prominent Ottawa lawyer and Liberal M.P., argued:

> One of the beneficial results of procedural reform in the House of Commons has been to make it possible for legislative proposals to be given First Reading and published without debate and having to spill an awful lot of parliamentary blood in the process. I think, increasingly we will benefit, as a country, by having complicated legislation of this kind published well in advance of detailed parliamentary debate and enactment. It is now possible for it to be studied and reviewed in detail by people who are interested. Subsequent parliamentary discussion will benefit from, and the ultimate form of the legislation will reflect, this study and participation.[18]

Some editorials stressed the theme of public participation in redrafting Bill C-256 and the necessity for the bill to be acceptable to a broad spectrum of Canadians. As the Edmonton *Journal* put it,

> Unless Mr. Basford receives the feedback from as many Canadians as possible who have gone to the trouble of informing themselves about all facets of the act, its scope and implications, the legislation won't enjoy the consensus it requires to be workable and effective. For their own sake, it is to be hoped that Canadians individually and collectively as members of specialist groups will rediscover their passion for participatory democracy.[19]

The Regina *Leader Post* stated that, "The minister and his advisors in Ottawa should face up to the fact that a general foundation of consent, reluctant or otherwise, must be found before the legislation is enacted. . . ."[20] But there is no fine line between consulting with interested parties at the formative stages of legislation and having the interest groups control what is put before Parliament. In its submission on C-256, the Canadian Chamber of Commerce asked for direct discussions between departmental officials and members of the business community. The Lethbridge *Herald* questioned how far such discussions should properly go. It said the chamber's request "that discussions continue throughout the redrafting period, at least until the best possible understandings have been effected . . . means that the business community wants the privilege of telling the drafters what to put in the bill and what to leave out." The editors thought that discussion with the officials was legitimate but not to the point of "seeking to decide [the] final form" of the new bill.[21]

A Windsor *Star* editorial praised the government for stating it would allow C-256 to die on the order paper and introduce a revised bill in the next session. It saw the move as "a recognition by the government of the principle of allowing proposed legislation to be scrutinized by those who will be affected. . . ." The editorial was critical of the drafting of the bill, saying it "offers no recommendation for the Canadian civil service . . . the loopholes and uncertainties . . . were far more than could be excused . . ." by the complicated nature of the legislation.[22]

The clash over the process of policy reform occurred for a number of reasons. Despite his repeated statements that he was anxious to hear from the practical men of business and to make changes in Bill C-256, Basford was perceived as inflexible,[23] anti-business and too consumer-oriented. A review of Basford's public statements in the fall of 1971 indicates he was strongly committed to the principles underlying the legislation. What was "negotiable" were the specifics of implementation, not the basic objectives. This point is also made clearly in the *Explanatory Notes* which accompanied the bill.

> . . . the Government's commitment is to the central policy objective of producing an efficient and competitive economy fully responsive to the needs and desires of all citizens, rather than to any or all of the specific provisions contained in the new Bill. In this context, any submissions and suggestions that can aid in achieving this objective are invited.[24]

Yet it was precisely the basic objectives that so infuriated the business and producer interests. As we have discussed, historically there has been almost no business support for the proposition that effectrive competition is desirable both for the attainment of productive efficiency and the dispersion of economic power. A statute which was going to declare price fixing and market sharing agreements to be illegal per se, require that mergers be registered and required that merged firms pass on to consumers in the form of lower prices the efficiency benefits of the merger was bound to create both fear and loathing in the minds of Canadian businessmen.

The length of time the policy formation process had already taken by 1971 constituted a pressure on the minister to bring forth his legislative proposals. By mid-1971 it had been five years since the Economic Council had been asked to review Canada's competition policy and it had been two years since its *Report* had been published. The Liberal government, elected in mid-1968, had used up three years of its mandate by June 1971. For practical purposes the Liberals had one or two years remaining before another general election would be called. Because of business' strong adverse reaction to Finance Minister Benson's White Paper on tax reform, Mr. Basford realized that all he could get out of the Cabinet — divided as it was on the desirability of a major overhaul in competition policy — was a *draft* bill which would have to be modified in light of business inputs. With the business and legal communities forming the organizational and financial bases of the Liberal party, Mr. Basford would have had to have been startlingly naive not to realize that these two groups would have to accede to any change in combines legislation if the party was to stay in power. What the minister did not anticipate, despite his experience with the drug manufacturers' lobby in 1968-69,[25] was the extreme hostility the Competition Act engendered. Facts were grossly distorted, personal attacks on the minister were made and "gut reactions" came to the fore. Basford's plea for a rational debate on the issues was either never heard or simply rejected. He could not have foreseen the very skillful use of the media, principally newspaper and the trade press, which reported in detail on business criticisms of the bill and found little space for its supporters.[26]

However, the minister can be criticized for his failure to try to build support for Bill C-256 during the period of its gestation. Between November 1969 and early June 1971 Mr. Basford did not give a single speech stressing the need for comprehensive reform of competition policy. The total inadequacy of the merger legislation as interpreted by the courts, might alone have created a positive environment (at least as far as consumers and small business was concerned) in which to launch what was a very ambitious bill. The Competition Act was introduced in Parliament just before the summer hiatus and after a brief flurry of briefings for the press in Ottawa and four other major cities it was not the subject of the department's communication effort until September. As we have noted in Chapter 8, the minister was criticized for having his senior officials brief reporters and editors in their tour to explain the bill.

There is no doubt the government made extensive efforts to disseminate information on the Competition Act and to assure members of the business and legal communities that their inputs were welcome and would be utilized in amending the legislation. For example, a Department of Consumer and Corporate Affairs memoradum written in January of 1972 lists the following steps taken "to communicate with members of the public, including businessmen affected by the Bill:[27]

- A professionally staffed Information Secretariat was established and ready to function on the day the Bill was introduced.
- More than 4,000 copies of the Bill and a 136-page set of *Explanatory Notes* have been sent out.[28]
- The Minister attended with his senior officials at a Press Conference in Ottawa where all this policy was emphasized.
- Four additional seminars were held in mid-Summer for the press Montreal, Toronto, Vancouver, and Winnipeg. These were attended by the Deputy Minister and senior officials.
- Nine seminars with over 200 legal counsel of various Canadian companies, trade and professional associations were held in October and November 1971 and the Minister and his senior advisors attended them.

- Some 50 meetings were held by the Minister and his officials with the officials of various companies, trade associations and consumer groups.[29]
- Two seminars were held at universities (University of Alberta and University of British Columbia).
- The Minister gave eight speeches dealing with various provisions of the proposed Competition Act to carefully selected audiences across the country."

The memorandum went on to indicate that by mid-January 1972 a total of 217 briefs or proposals for amendments had been received. "These have been carefully considered and their constructive proposals for change are being reflected in a revised bill to be introduced in Parliament. Many of the representations from business are critical of detailed provisions, many were favourable to the underlying philosophy of the bill, many were fundamentally opposed."[30]

With the best public relations effort in the world, it is unlikely that the department and the government would have been able to elicit anything but a negative response from business, given the extensiveness and direction of the legislation and the larger circumstances under which it was introduced. The Competition Act came on the heels of a number of major places of legislation, each having a potentially significant impact on business. It also came at a time of worsening economic conditions.

It seems fair to say that business was already suffering from "new legislation overload" in mid-1971 when the Competition Act was introduced. In the few years before or contemporaneously with Bill C-256, business was faced with:

- The White Paper on taxation (*Proposals for Tax Reform*) following the Carter Commission.
- Significant amendments to the Canada Labour Code and later the new Public Service Staff Relation Act.
- A new Unemployment Insurance Act.
- A new Canada Corporations Act.
- A number of consumer protection bills from the Department of Consumer and Corporate Affairs. These dealt with hazardous products, textile labelling, toys, T.V. advertising aimed at children, unit pricing and packaging and labelling.
- The great debate over foreign ownership which was to lead to legislation in 1973.

In addition, a number of provincial governments were becoming more active in the field of consumer protection.

Economic conditions were deteriorating during 1971.[31] Unemployment, which averaged less than 4 percent of the labour force between 1965 and 1967, had risen steadily. It was 4.8 percent in 1968, 4.7 percent in 1969, 5.9 percent in 1970 and 6.4 percent in 1971. At the same time, the rate of inflation was rising. By the end of 1971 the Consumer Price Index was rising at an annual rate higher than at any time during the 1960s. It continued to climb at even faster rates in the next few years. From business' viewpoint, government transfer payments to persons were rising at an alarming rate: they increased 13.4 percent in 1970, 18.3 percent in 1971 and 19.7 percent in 1972. Fixed investment expenditures were lagging, rising only 0.3 percent in 1970, 7.9 percent in 1971 and 5.3 percent in 1972. Productivity growth was relatively low. Output per person employed in Canada increased by 1.2 percent in 1970, 3.3 percent in 1971 and 2.0 percent in 1972. More important than the increase in domestic prices was the deterioration of Canada's price position relative to her trading partners throughout 1971 and 1972. During 1971, 1972 and 1973 imports were growing much more rapidly than exports. In summary, business had reason to be relatively pessimistic about its economic position in the period 1971-1973. This mood, when coupled with cumulative effect of many other pieces of federal and provincial legislation having a potentially significant effect on business, resulted in the Competition Act is being the focal point for business' frustrations with the economy and the government.

LESSONS TO BE LEARNED?

One might ask the question, "Was the success of business and producer interest in delaying and watering down the competition legislation proposed by the government preordained?" There are a number of good reasons for answering yes to this question. First, business interests are organized and strongly motivated to protect their existing stake in the system or to increase their economic benefits through group action. Their interests are intense (government legislation may affect a significant proportion of the income of firms and/or managers) and they are narrowly defined. In contrast, consumers who, in the aggregate, stand to benefit a great deal from an effective competition policy, are not organized for lobbying activity with the exception of the Consumer's Association of Canada. The consumer interest is broad (we are all consumers) but it is diffuse. For example, price-fixing conspiracies or mergers resulting in very high levels of concentration which raise prices above competitive levels reduce the real income of an individual consumer by only a small absolute and very small relative amount. Because of the public good[32] characteristics of consumer interest representation or advocacy, it does not pay an individual consumer to contribute anything toward a lobbying effort on his or her behalf.

The Canadian Chamber of Commerce in the mid-1970s had more

business enterprise members (125,000) than the Canadian Association of Consumers had individual memberships (about 100,000). The Retail Merchants' Association of Canada currently represents 10,000 independent retailers. The president of the association notes that Statistics Canada data indicate that 50 percent of retail volume in Canada is handled by independent retailers or, as he prefers to call them, "the little guys."[33] The Canadian Manufacturers' Association has 9,000 members who jointly account for $85 billion in business.[34] A 1972 article indicates that the CMA represents 80 percent of Canada's industrial capacity and that 1,200 of its members serve on one or more of its many committees.[35] These are just a few examples of extent of the organization of business interests in Canada.

The Investment Dealers' Association of Canada spent $150,000 on association activities in 1974-75 fighting "a rearguard battle to keep government at bay." Some $25,000 was spent on briefs and submissions regarding the Competition Act. "Actual costs could be three times this amount if the IDA were to cost staff salaries and time donated free of charge by staffs of member firms."[36] The CMA's salary bill for its full time staff of fifty in its headquarters must exceed $1 million per year. In contrast, the Consumers' Association is a "hand-to-mouth" operation dependent upon membership fees of $5 per year (which includes the subscription to its *Canadian Consumer* magazine) and grants from the Department of Consumer and Corporate Affairs for about one-half its total budget.[37] With the exception of a special grant for consumer advocacy before federal regulatory bodies, only a very small percentage of the CAC's budget is employed on lobbying activities. This is at a time of "the growing power and influence of the anonymous lobbyists who have in recent years become one of the capital's new growth industries."[38]

Business interest or pressure groups can and do spend a great deal of money on the preparation of briefs, on public relations efforts and on personal contacts with key policy makers. They can call upon the expertise of numerous Toronto lawyers — well versed both in making the best possible case and in treading the corridors of power in Ottawa. The present Minister of Consumer and Corporate Affairs was appointed President of the Retail Council of Canada in 1971. A few years later he became an M.P., and in September 1976 he was appointed minister. Having participated in preparing the council's brief in respect of the Competition Act, four years later Mr. Abbott as an M.P. was able to examine the representatives of the council when they appeared before the House of Commons committee examining the Stage I amendments. It is fair to say that Mr. Abbott, on becoming the Minister, was familiar with business' views on competition policy legislation.

It is true that the Consumers' Association of Canada has been able, from time to time, to call upon academic experts to assist them in the preparation and presentation of briefs. The problem is that theCAC's brief is often the only one in support of stronger and effective competition legislation. Beside it, in the case of the Stage I amendments, were over one hundred briefs from business firms, trade associations, lawyers and professional associations decrying the legislation. When M.P.s examine the pros and cons as expressed in the briefs and representations before them, the cons have it by an enormous margin. When they also realize that the Canadian Chamber of Commerce has more member firms than the CAC has individual members, and that the chamber's members provide the contributions which fuel both major political parties, they become realists. The interests of business are accommodated as far as possible without totally destroying the legislation. In the bluntest terms, consumer interests are politically ineffectual; business or producer interests are not.[39] That the ambitious Competition Act was proposed in 1971 and that a number of desirable amendments to the Combines Investigation Act were made in 1975 in spite of the massive attack by business are facts that are not the result of the counterpressure of consumer interest groups such as the CAC, but rather of the efforts of a handful of senior officials in the Bureau of Competition Policy in the Department of Consumer and Corporate Affairs. They kept the flame burning. It is hard to overestimate their importance to the maintenance of any form of competition policy in this country. Both within the bureaucracy and in the wider policy arena, they operate in an environment almost unflaggingly hostile to the virtues of competition and the consumer interest.

During the period it faced the most difficult tests over competition policy, the Department of Consumer and Corporate Affairs had to withstand a large number of changes in its leadership, both politial and administrative. Table 11-1 sets out the changes in the three most senior positions in the department from the point of view of competition policy. Between April 1967 and April 1977 seven different men held the post of minister. During the six-year period the new policy was being drafted in the department, introduced as the Competition Act, changed into the form of the Stage I amendments and passed into law, the Department was headed by four different men. These figures must constitute the highest turnover of any federal ministry during the indicated time periods.

In the decade 1967-1977 the department was under the direction of four different deputy ministers. In addition, there were two periods of four or five months, during the time the new legislation was under attack, when the administrative head was an acting deputy minister.

The early part of the policy formulation process and introduction of Bill-C256 was overseen by D. H. W. Henry who was Director of

TABLE 11-1

Turnover of Senior Personnel, Department of Consumer and
Corporate Affairs, 1967-1977, By Date of Appointment

Minister	Deputy Minister	Director of Investigation and Research
April 1967,[1] John Turner	December 1967,[1] J. F. Grandy	September 1960 to February 1973, D. H. W. Henry
July 1968, Ron Basford	October 1971, D. H. W. Henry (acting deputy minister)	
January 1972, Robert Andras	March 1972, G. F. Osbaldeston	February 1973, J. J. Quinlan (acting director)
November 1972, Herb Gray	March 1973, Michael Pitfield	May 1974, R. J. Bertrand
August 1974, Andre Ouellet	October 1974, Blair Seaborn (acting deputy minister)	
March 1976, Marc Lalonde and Bryce Mackasey (acting ministers)	February 1975, Sylvia Ostry	
April 1976, Bryce Mackasey		
September 1976, Anthony Abbott		

[1]In December 1967 Royal Assent was given to the statute which transformed the Department of the Registrar General into the Department of Consumer and Corporate Affairs.

Investigation and Research from September 1960 to February 1973. For over a year following Mr. Henry's appointment to the Ontario Supreme Court, J. J. Quinlan (who for years had been the deputy director) became the Acting Director of Investigation and Research. R. J. Bertrand who became the director in May of 1974 had the responsibility for getting the Stage I amendments through the House and Senate committees as well as to start the policy wheels turning on Stage II. He had to do so without the assistance of J. J. Quinlan, one of the most experienced and respected combines officials, who was appointed chairman of the Restrictive Practices Commission when Bertrand became Director.

When one reviews in Table 11-1, the total set of changes in the "top management" of competition policy during the period of intensive efforts at policy reform (1970 through 1975), it is difficult to imagine a situation less conducive to the successful implementation of an effective policy. While each of the changes can probably be "explained" in terms of factors peculiar to itself, the cumulative and interactive effects of the extensive turnover was to make it more difficult to withstand the intense pressures generated by business interests in opposition to the reform of competition legislation. While the department may not have been divided (united we stand, divided they conquer!), its political leadership and top administrative management was fragmented by executive turnover.

The pluralist argument that interest groups will become organized to represent all significant groups in the society effectively is false. This is nowhere more evident than with the case of the interests of consumers. The idea that government will represent the unrepresented is also at variance with reality. Professor Milton Rakove of the University of Illinois has remarked:

> The theory of democratic politics is that people are elected to deal with public interests. But once they get into office, they realize that the only way to stay there is by appealing to private interests at the expense of public interests.[40]

The reality of pressure groups and lobbying is unlikely to change in a democratic system which is concerned with representativeness and participation in public policy formation. As Marjorie Nichols has pointed out,

> Lobbying is (or can be) an honourable profession. It is often useful to the lawmakers to solicit expert information and opinion from [lobbyists].
> The difficulty is that there is a reluctance on the part of this government to concede that Ottawa has a lobby industry and that, given the influence over the operations of government by these lobbies, perhaps some effort should be made to identify them.[41]

Although desirable, the registration of lobbyists is clearly insufficient.

The U.S. experience should disabuse us of the idea that this would be an effective way to combat the untoward effects of interest groups. Registration will not counteract the important informal process of influence. As T. F. Causey et al. have put it;

> If the American way of getting things done is one of dramatic overstatement, the ideal Canadian way of making arrangements [between governments and business] has been one of elegant understatement; the politics of keeping things pleasant, dull and controlled. Influence comes from very private meetings with very important people. Public displays of power and verbal abuse are vulgar and should be avoided.[42]

Before he came to head the Federation of Independent Business in 1971, John Bullock organized the Canadian Council on Fair Taxation to lobby for changes in the proposed tax reform legislation in 1969 and 1970. In doing so, Bullock learned how the policy process operated in Ottawa.

> I began to see how the system is stacked in favour of those who own all the lawyers. I found out that the big corporations, without being conspiratorial, control the knowledge factory in this country. All the positions that government takes are the results of conversations, the chinwags, that go on between the experts who are owned by the major corporations and the trade unions, and the experts who work for government. It's a mandarin-to-mandarin process.[43]

After documenting some of the successes enjoyed by the Federation of Independent Business, Alexander Ross indicated the moral of the story.

> You don't win concessions . . . from government without a solid power base, and the Federation has built one. Its mandate is based on federal constituencies, which makes M.P.s highly responsive to Federation appeals. A Federation column on small business appears in more than 150 weekly newspapers. The Federation is spending $25,000 on advertising this year, and building a $1 million war chest.[44]

From the point of view of protecting and advancing consumer interests, what is needed is an effective counterpressure to the manifest organizational strength of business and producer interest.

> To cope with the problem of government by pressue groups, of which business is the strongest, requires the development of stronger democratic institutions than are now at hand. It is necessary to even up, to equalize, the unequal pressures to which government is subjected.[45]

An adequate consumer interest group will need financial resources to research the current and potential issues, to publish and publicize its point of view and to participate actively in the lobbying and influence process — both formal and informal. For technical reasons, consumer interest groups cannot raise sufficient funds from their own constituents. Such funds must come from government. This and related issues have been discussed in considerable detail elsewhere,[46] but we will conclude with following points. The agency should not be another stem in the mushrooming government bureaucracy (at all levels). The danger of bureaucratic "ossification," "capture" by client groups and goal displacement are too well known. By keeping consumer representation agencies outside government, there is less danger they will be compromised. Because the consumer interest is not homogenous, the government should fund a number of consumer interest agencies. A monopoly on the representation of the consumer interest should not be permitted. Unlike the business and producer interest groups they seek to counter, publicly financed consumer interest agencies should be subject to period review to determine if they are doing their job. If competition in economic markets is desirable, it is even more desirable that there be competition in the market for ideas and the representation of interests.

NOTES:

[1]R. v. K. C. Irving Ltd. et al. Unreported judgment of the Supreme Court of Canada, November 16, 1976, Bureau of Competition Policy mimeo 136-5. See also G. B. Reschenthaler and W. T. Stanbury, "Benign Monopoly: Canadian Merger Policy and the K. C. Irving Case," *Canadian Business Law Journal*, 1977, forthcoming.

[2]Gordon R. Sharwood, "Some Comments on Canadian Government Economic Policies During Recent Liberal Administration," notes for a speech given to the St. Paul's Riding Liberal Association Annual Meeting, January 22, 1972.

[3]"Notes for a Speech by the Honourable Ron Basford, Minister of Consumer and Corporate Affairs to the Annual Meeting of the Canadian Chamber of Commerce, Quebec City, September 28, 1971," p. 2.

[4]*Ibid.*, p. 6.

[5]*Ibid.*, p. 7.

[6]*Ibid.*, p. 12.

[7]*Ibid.*, p. 13.

[8]*Ibid.*

[9]*Ibid.*

[10]*Ibid.*

[11]October 5, 1971, Annual Meeting of the Canadian Better Business Bureau, Toronto; October 25, 1971, National Automotive Trades' Association, Vancouver; October 26, 1971, Central Canada Broadcasters' Association, Ottawa; November 17, 1971, Seminar on the Competition Act, Edmonton; November 19, 1971, Seminar on the Competition Act, Vancouver; November 21, 1971, Federation of Automobile Dealer Associations of Canada, Montreal; November 30, 1971 Canadian Manufacturers' Association, Montreal.

[12]David H. W. Henry, "The Competition Bill — Background and Perspective," in *Canada's Competition Policy*, Ottawa, The Conference Board in Canada, 1972, p. 5.

[13]*Ibid.*, p. 13.

[14]*Canada's Competition Policy, op.cit.*, p. 44.

[15]August 19, 1971.

[16]As reprinted in the *Herald*, (Prince Albert) February 7, 1972.

[17]*Globe and Mail*, (Toronto) October 4, 1971.

[18]D. Gordon Blair, "Procedure," in *Canada's Competition Policy, op.cit.*, pp.66-67.

[19]*Journal*, Edmonton September 16, 1971.

[20]November 3, 1971.

[21]*January 6, 1972.*

[22]As reprinted in the *Beacon-Herald*, (Stratford) November 25, 1971.

[23]On all of the major bills he had sponsored as Minister of Consumer and Corporate Affairs, Basford had sponsored amendments reflecting the concerns of the business community. For example, in respect of the Hazardous Products Act, over the objections of his departmental officials, he had permitted the use of "add-one stickers" for a period of six months for products already on the shelves instead of the more strict requirements of the new bill.

[24]*The Competition Act — Explanatory Notes*, Ottawa, Department of Consumer and Corporate Affairs, 1971, mimeo, p. 4.

[25]See Ronald W. Lang, *The Politics of Drugs*, Lexington, Mass., Saxon House, D. C. Heath Ltd., 1974.

[26]It is alleged, for example, that the *Globe and Mail* (Toronto) declined to print a story by one or two of its reporters attending a speech given by the minister to an organization of service station operators after which the members of the audience cheered the minister and his legislation.

[27]"Bill C-256 — The Competition Act," Department of Consumer and Corporate Affairs memorandum, January, 1972, pp. 2-3.

[28]The memorandum notes that a copy of the bill and *Explanatory Notes* was sent to over three hundred members of the press and senior business executives when the bill was introduced in Parliament. It also pointed out the *Notes* called for all interested parties to make their views known to the government.

[29]The memorandum stated that, while not all firms were able to obtain interviews, "certain key companies were seen and the others were represented by . . . trade associations."

[30]The subsequent discussion is drawn from Economic Council of Canada Eleventh Annual Review, *Economics Targets and Social Indicators*, Ottawa, Information Canada, 1974, Chapters 2, 7.

[32]As defined in Chapter 3.

[33]Patricia Anderson, "Those 'Little Guys' Sell Big," *Financial Post*, May 15, 1976, p. 38.

[34]*Star*, (Toronto) June 1, 1976.

[35]*Globe and Mail*, (Toronto) October 7, 1972, p. 39.

[36]*Financial Post*, June 21, 1975, p. 5.

[37]See Sheldon E. Gordon, "CAC Soul-Searching Precedes a New Crusade," *Financial Post*, July 3, 1976, p. 5.

[38]Marjorie Nichols, "Lobbying: Ottawa's Growth Industry," *Sun*, (Vancouver) January 29, 1977, p. 4.

[39]An excellent example of this proposition can be seen in the ability of Canada's dairy farmers to raise the guaranteed price of manufacturing milk at a time of enormous surpluses (300 million pounds of skim milk powder in early 1976) "The government's recent decision to help bail out surplus-burdened milk farmers through higher taxpayer and consumer costs again illustrates the political strength of the relatively tiny dairy

industry. . . . the federal cabinet, worried about the declining number of milk farmers and under pressure from rural M.P.s from all parties, agreed to pull the industry out of its jam by increasing butter and skim milk powder costs to consumers and the guaranteed price for manufacturing milk to producers." The Minister of Agriculture told farmers it would cost taxpayers $40 million to get rid of the surplus. Before the price increase, skim milk powder sold for 68¢ per pound versus 20¢ on export markets. See *Sun*, (Vancouver)

[40]Quoted in William Grieder, "A Little Bit of Money Makes the Politics Go Down," *Sun*, (Vancouver) January 4, 1977, p. 5.

[41]*Ibid.*, See also note 38.

[42]T. F. Causey, *et al.*, *Managing the Political Regulatory Environment: A Study of Business Response to the A.I.B.*, London, Ontario, Research and Publication Division, School of Business Administration University of Western Ontario, 1986, p. 89.

[43]Alexander Ross, "How to Join the March to the New Politics," *Quest*, February 1977, p. 47.

[44]*Ibid.*, pp. 47-48.

[45]Donald C. Blaisdell, assisted by Jane Greverus, *Economic Power and Political Pressures*, TNEC Monograph No. 26, Washington, D.C., 1941, p. 10.

[46]See Michael J. Trebilock, *The Case for a Consumer Advocate*, Ottawa, Canadian Consumer Council, 1972; W. T. Stanbury, "The Consumer Interest and the Regulated Industries: Diagnosis and Prescription," in K. M. Ruppenthal and W. T. Stanbury (eds.), *Transportation Policy: Regulation, Competition and the Public Interest*, Vancouver, Centre for Transportation Studies, 1976, pp. 109-155; Michael J. Trebilcock, "Winners and Losers in the Modern Regulatory System: Must the Consumer Always Lose?" *Osgoode Hall Law Journal*, Vol. 13, No. 3, 1975, pp. 619-647.

Appendix A

Chronology: The Development of Competition Policy in Canada 1966-1977

July 22, 1966 — Economic Council of Canada asked to prepare a report on the responsibilities of the Department of the Registrar General, which was established by the Government Organization Act, given royal assent on June 16, 1966. The Office of the Director of Investigation and Research was located in the Department of the Registrar General. The Government Organization Act was proclaimed on October 1, 1966.

April 4, 1967 — John N. Turner, formerly Minister without Portfolio, appointed Registrar General of Canada.

July 1967 — Publication of the Economic Council of Canada's *Interim Report: Consumer Affairs and the Department of the Registrar General* (Ottawa, Queen's Printer).

December 21, 1967 — Royal assent given to the statute which transformed the Department of the Registrar General into the Department of Consumer and Corporate Affairs.

June 25, 1968 — The Liberal government of Pierre Trudeau returned to office in the federal general election with 155 seats to the Conservatives' 72.

July 1968 — Mr. Ron Basford appointed Minister of Consumer and Corporate Affairs.

June 27, 1969 — The Patent Act and the Trade Mark Act amended permitting the compulsory licensing of pharmaceuticals. The process by which this legislation was arrived at is described in Ronald W. Lang, *The Politics of Drugs*, Lexington, Mass., Lexington Books, 1974.

July 13, 1969 — S.306 of the Criminal Code dealing with false and misleading advertising transferred to the Combines Investigation Act as S.33D and proclaimed July 31, 1969.

July, 1969 — Publication of the Economic Council's *Interim Report on Competition Policy* (Ottawa, Queen's Printer).

mid-1969 — The legal positions in the Department of Consumer and Corporate Affairs transferred to the Department of Justice. What was the legal branch in the Office of the Director of Investigation and Research became the legal branch for the entire Department of Consumer and Corporate Affairs.

November 3, 1969 — Joint statement by Honourable Ron Basford and U.S. Attorney General John N. Mitchell confirming and extending the Fulton-Rogers understanding of 1959, the Antitrust Notification and Consultation Procedure.

December, 1969 — Publication of the Royal Commission on Farm Machinery's *Special Report on Prices of Tractors and Combines in Canada and Other Countries* (Ottawa, Queen's Printer).

December, 1970 — Publication of the *Report of the Special Senate Committee on Mass Media* in 3 volumes (Ottawa, Queen's Printer).

December, 1970 — Publication of Milton Moore's *How Much Price Competition? The Prerequisites of an Effective Canadian Competition Policy* (Montreal, McGill-Queen's Press, 1970). This work was originally prepared as a background study for the Economic Council's *Interim Report on Competition Policy* (1969).

January, 1971 — Publication of the Economic Council's *Report on Intellectual and Industrial Property* (Ottawa, Information Canada).

March, 1971 — Publication of the *Report of the Royal Commission on Farm Machinery* (Ottawa, Information Canada).

May, 1971 — Publication of the study by the Department of Consumer and Corporate Affairs, *Concentration in the Manufacturing Industries of Canada* (Ottawa, Information Canada).

June 29, 1971 — Bill C-256, The Competition Act, introduced in the House of Commons and given First Reading. Accompanying the 106-page act are the *Explanatory Notes*, 137 pages (mimeo).

July 15, 1971 — The 1970 edition of the Revised Statutes of Canada incorporated the various revisions of the Combines Investigation Act since 1952. A number of section numers were changed, i.e., S.33A, 33B, 33C, 33D and 34 became, Sec 34, 35, 36, 37 and 38 respectively.

September 1971 — Symposium on Bill C-256 held by the Conference Board in Canada in Ottawa — later published as *Canada's Competition Policy*, Ottawa, The Conference Board in Canada, 1972.

October 1, 1971 — Mr. J. F. Grandy, Deputy Minister of Consumer and Corporate Affairs, promoted to the same position in the Department of Industry, Trade and Commerce. No replacement was named until March 1, 1972.

October and November 1971 — Series of nine seminars for businessmen and lawyers on the Competition Act in major Canadian cities by senior officials of the Office of the Director of Investigation and Research.

January 20-21, 1972 — Conference at Queen's University on Bill C-256, the Competition Act — later published as L. A. Skeoch (ed.), *Canadian Competition Policy*, Kingston, Queen's University Industrial Relations Centre, 1972.

January, 1972 — Bill C-256 is allowed to die on the Order Paper as planned.

January 25, 1972 — Robert K. Andras, formerly Minister of State for Urban Affairs, became Minister of Consumer and Corporate Affairs. Mr. Basford moved from Consumer and Corporate Affairs to Urban Affairs.

March 1, 1972 — Mr. Gordon F. Osbaldeston appointed Deputy Minister of Consumer and Corporate Affairs.

March 17, 1972 — The Minister of Consumer and Corporate Affairs, Mr. Andras, announced that a revised bill would be reintroduced incorporating substantial changes. He indicated that a series of seminars would be held for the public and businessmen and that the provinces will be consulted. Mr. Andras indicates that the new bill will not be ready until the autumn of 1972.

March and April 1972 — Series of seminars by departmental officials on revisions to Bill C-256 confined to the legal advisors of business, labour and consumer groups.

October 30, 1972 — A federal general election, and a minority Liberal government is returned with 109 seats to the Conservatives' 107. The NDP holds the balance of power.

November 27, 1972 — Mr. Herb Gray, formerly Minister of National Revenue, appointed Minister of Consumer and Corporate Affairs. Mr. Andras became Minister of Manpower and Immigration.

February 15, 1973 — Mr. D. H. W. Henry, the Director of Investigation and Research since September 1960, appointed to the Supreme Court of Ontario. J. J. Quinlan, the deputy director, becomes the acting director.

March 1, 1973 — Michael Pitfield appointed Deputy Minister of Consumer and Corporate Affairs, succeeding G. F. Osbaldeston who moved to the Treasury Board.

March and April 1973 — Hearings by the House of Commons Special Committee on Trends in Food Prices. Includes testimony by the Minister of Consumer and Corporate Affairs, Mr. Gray.

July 18, 1973 — Honourable Herb Gray, in reply to a question in the House indicated that, "Instead of bringing forward legislation concerning competition policy in a single complex bill, the government has decided to implement this policy in stages. It is our aim to introduce the first stage during this session of Parliament" (*Hansard* p. 5745).

November 6, 1973 — Honourable Herb Gray introduced Bill C-227, an act to amend the Combines Investigation Act, as Stage I of the new competition policy. The Department of Consumer and Corporate Affairs published *Proposals for a New Competition Policy for Canada, First Stage, 1973* incorporating the amendments, a detailed discussion of the amendments and considerable historical material.

December 12, 1973 — The Foreign Investment Review Act is enacted, the first phase to become effective April 9, 1974. The second phase was to become effective October 15, 1975.

January 1974 — Department of Consumer and Corporate Affairs releases its *Working Paper on Trade Marks Law Revision* (Ottawa, Information Canada, 1974).

March 11, 1974 — Bill C-7, identical to C-227 is introduced and is given Second Reading March 13.

March 27, 1974 — Senator Salter A. Hayden, chairman of the Standing Senate Committee on Banking, Trade and Commerce seeks authorization to examine and report on the proposed Stage I amendments to the Combines Investigation Act. The committee is given authorization a week later.

April 1, 1974 — Bill C-7 is referred to the House Standing Committee on Finance, Trade and Economic Affairs.

April 29, 1974 — Bill C-29, amendments to the Combines Investigation Act regarding profiteering practices, is given First Reading in the House of Commons. It is given Second Reading on May 1, 1974. It dies on the Order Paper when Parliament is dissolved a week later.

May 1, 1974 — The Standing Senate Committee on Banking, Trade and Commerce holds its first day of hearings on the Stage I amendments. The first witnesses are from the Canadian Manufacturers' Association.

May 1, 1974 — R. S. MacLellan and F. R. Roseman appointed to the Restrictive Trade Practices Commission. Mr. A. S. Whitely had retired as a member on December 29, 1973.

May 8, 1974 — J. J. Quinlan, Acting Director of Investigation and Research appointed chairman of the RTPC. Mr. R. J. Bertrand appointed Director of Investigation and Research.

May 8, 1974 — The minority Liberal government is defeated on a want of confidence motion. Parliament is dissolved the next day.

July 8, 1974 — In the federal general election the Liberals are returned with 141 seats to the Conservatives' 95.

August 8, 1974 — M. Andre Ouellet, formerly Postmaster General of Canada, appointed Minister of Consumer and Corporate Affairs. Herb Gray was dropped from the Cabinet.

October 2, 1974 — Bill C-2, identical to C-7 and before that C-227, reintroduced in the House of Commons and given First Reading. It is given Second Reading on October 22 and is referred to the House Standing Committee on Finance, Trade and Economic Affairs on October 28, 1974.

December 3, 1974 — Honourable Andre Ouellet, Minister of Consumer and Corporate Affairs, presents his amendments to Bill C-2 to the House Standing Committee on Finance, Trade and Economic Affairs.

February 19, 1975 — Dr. Sylvia Ostry appointed Deputy Minister of Consumer and Corporate Affairs. Michael Pitfield became Clerk of the Privy Council and Secretary to the Cabinet.

March 18, 1975 — Standing Senate Committee on Banking Trade and Commerce presents its first *Interim Report* on the Stage I amendments to the Senate.

April 1, 1975 — The reorganization of the Bureau of Competition Policy from an "offence basis" to a sectoral basis becomes effective.

April 22, 1975 — Prime Minister Trudeau announces the establishment of the Royal Commission on Corporate Concentration to be headed by the former Deputy Minister of Finance, R. B. Bryce.

June 5, 1975 — Final Report on the Stage I amendments of the House Committee on Finance, Trade and Economic Affairs presented to the House.

October 16, 1975 — Bill C-2, as amended, received Third Reading in the House of Commons. These amendments to the Combines Investigation Act become effective January 1, 1976 with the exception of S.32 as applied to services which was to become effective July 1, 1976.

December 9, 1975 — Bill C-2, as amended, passed the Senate without further amendment.

January 1, 1976 — Stage I amendments to the Combines Investigation Act become law with the exception of S.32 as applied to the service industries which was to become effective July 1, 1976.

January 27, 1976 — Andre Ouellet, Minister of Consumer and Corporate Affairs, convicted of contempt of court for his comments on the decision of Mr. Justice K. Mckay in the Sugar case. Two days later Mr. Ouellet announced he would appeal the decision.

March 16, 1976 — Andre Ouellet resigns as Minister of Consumer and Corporate Affairs. In January he had been convicted of contempt of court in regard to his remarks regarding the judgment of Mr. Justice K. Mckay on December 19, 1975 in the sugar case (*R. v. Atlantic Sugar Refineries et al*). At that time Mr. Ouellet stated: "I find this judgment completely unacceptable. I think it is a silly decision. I just cannot understand how a sane judge could give such a verdict. It is a complete shock and I find it a complete disgrace." Mr. Ouellet's resignation prompted by the "judges affair" (see *Maclean's Magazine*, March 22, 1976, pp. 18-19) in which it was revealed that C. M. Drury, Minister of Public Works called Mr. Justice James Hugessen, who was to hear the Ouellet contempt case and asked whether it would be possible for Mr. Ouellet to make a formal apology and thereby end the case. He also asked if the judge was aware of the view in some quarters in Ottawa that the proceedings against Mr. Ouellet constituted a "ganging up" of the English-speaking establishment against prominent French-speaking persons. When he resigned, Mr. Ouellet indicated he did so because the publicity associated with the "judge's affair" made it impossible for him to function as a minister. Both Marc Lalonde, Minister of National Health and Welfare and Bryce Mackasey, Postmaster General were named Acting Minister of Consumer and Corporate Affairs.

April 9, 1976 — Bryce Mackasey was named Minister of Consumer and Corporate Affairs, also retaining his post as Postmaster General.

May 31, 1976 — The proposals for the Stage II amendments to the Combines Investigation Act were released. See Lawrence A. Skeoch with Bruce C. McDonald, in consultation with Michel Belanger, Reuben M. Bromstein and William O. Twaits, *Dynamic Change and Accountability in a Canadian Market Economy*, Ottawa, Supply and Services Canada, 1976; Neil J. Williams, "Damages Class Action Under the Combines Investigation Act," and Jennifer Whybrow, "The Case for Class Actions in Canadian Competition Policy: An Economist's Viewpoint," in *A Proposal for Class Actions Under Competition Policy Legislation*, Ottawa, Information Canada, 1976.

June 8, 1976 — Additional studies prepared for Stage II amendments were released. See R. I. Cohen and J. S. Ziegel, *The Political and Constitutional Basis of a New Trade Practices Act*, Ottawa, Information Canada, 1976; M. J. Trebilcock *et al.*, *Proposed Policy Directions for the Reform of the Regulation of Unfair Trade Practices in Canada*, 2 Volumes, Ottawa, Information Canada, 1976; Corwin D. Edwards, *Studies of Foreign Competition Policy and Practice, Vol. I The United States*, Ottawa, Supply and Services Canada, 1976; T. D. MacDonald *et al., Studies of Foreign Competition Policy and Practice, Vol. II,* Ottawa, Supply and Services Canada, 1976.

June, 1976 — Department of Consumer and Corporate Affairs releases its *Working Paper on Patent Law Revision* (Ottawa, Supply and Services Canada, 1976) and *Proposed Patent Law* (Ottawa, Supply and Services Canada, 1976).

September 16, 1976 — Anthony C. Abbott becomes Minister of Consumer and Corporate Affairs after Bryce Mackasey resigned both as Minister of Consumer and Corporate Affairs and as Postmaster General.

October 21, 1976 — The appeal of Andre Ouellet against his contempt conviction is unsuccessful in a decision written by Chief Justice Lucien Tremblay. The Court ruled that the Trial Court's order to pay a $500 legal fee, incurred by the Crown, should stand as a fine, but that Mr. Ouellet did not have to make a public apology to Mr. Justice MacKay as ordered by the Trial Court (or serve a three-month probation). Shortly thereafter, Mr. Ouellet was again appointed to the Cabinet as Minister of Urban Affairs.

March 16, 1977 — The Stage II amendments to the Combines Investigation Act (to be renamed the Competition Act) are given First Reading in the House of Commons as Bill C-42. See *Proposals for a New Competition Policy for Canada, Second Stage* Ottawa, Department of Consumer and Corporate Affairs, March, 1977.

March 25, 1977 — Bill C-42 was referred to the House of Commons Standing Committee on Finance, Trade and Economic Affairs chaired by Norman Cafik, formerly Parliamentary Secretary to Minister of Consumer and Corporate Affairs Andre Ouellet.

April 4, 1977 — The Minister of Consumer and Corporate Affairs announced that Bill C-42 was being withdrawn from the House of Commons agenda. Rather, after the House Committee held it's hearings in June and submitted its report, the Government would revise the bill and submit it again to Parliament in October 1977 when Parliament begins a new session after the summer break.

May 20, 1977 — Deadline for the submission of briefs on Bill C-42 to the House of Commons Standing Committee on Finance, Trade and Economic Affairs.

June, 1977 — House of Commons Standing Committee on Finance, Trade and Economic Affairs holds hearings on Bill C-42. (The Stage II amendments).

Summary of the Contents of Bill C-227, the Stage I Amendments to the Combines Investigation Act, Introduced in the House of Commons on November 6, 1973

Principal amendments to the Combines Investigation Act contained in the bill are:

1. A series of prohibitions against particular trade practices harmful to the interests of the consumer are included. These provisions create criminal offences or make desirable amendments to existing prohibitions, as follows:

   - The misleading advertising provisions of the present bill are consolidated and clarified so that they apply to all kinds of serious misrepresentation concerning products or services made to the public, rather than merely to published advertisements. Not only the literal meaning of a representation, but also the general impression it conveys is to be taken into account.
   - Untrue or misleading warranties and testimonials are banned.
   - A sale at any price but the lowest of two or more prices is prohibited when goods are double-ticketed.
   - Pyramid selling is conditionally prohibited, and referral selling, as defined, is prohibited.
   - Bait-and-switch selling is prohibited.
   - Selling at higher than advertised prices is prohibited.
   - Promotional contests are prohibited unless they meet certain rules.
   - The prohibition of resale price maintenance is strengthened.

2. The Restrictive Trade Practices Commission on application of the Director of Investigation and Research, is authorized to:

   - Review instances of refusal to sell and, after according full opportunity to be heard, to order a supplier to supply or to recommend tariff changes.

- Review instances where consignment sales are used to control a dealer's prices or so as to discriminate in price between competitors and, after according full opportunity to be heard, to order a supplier to cease the practice.

- Review instances where exclusive dealing practices, i.e., the requirement that a purchaser deal in particular products only, are engaged in by major suppliers so as to lessen competition substantially and, after affording reasonable opportunity to be heard, make the necessary remedial order.

- Review instances where tied selling, i.e., the tying of one product to the sale of another, is engaged in by major suppliers so as to lessen competition substantially and, after affording reasonable opportunity to be heard, make the necessary remedial order.

- Review instances where market restriction, i.e., where the supplier, as a condition of sale, imposes restrictions as to the market in which his customer may trade, is engaged in by major suppliers, so as to lessen competition substantially and, after affording reasonable opportunity to be heard, make the necessary remedial order.

- Review instances where foreign judgments, foreign laws or directives from foreign managers are contrary to the Canadian public interest and, after according full opportunity to be heard, to make orders forbidding their implementation in Canada.

3. The prohibitions of the act against combinations, mergers and monopolies, which now are largely restricted to production and trade in articles or commodities, are extended to apply to all services and service industries. There already exists well-established jurisprudence which makes it clear that the prohibitions of the act do not apply where the restrictive situations and trade practices are authorized specifically under valid federal or provincial legislation.

4. It is made clear than in order for a restrictive agreement to qualify as one that violates the act because it lessens competition unduly, it is not necessary to prove that its effects would be to completely or virtually eliminate competition.

5. It creates the following additional new offences:

- A company in business in Canada may not implement a foreign directive giving effect to an agreement contrary to the act.

- Bid rigging.

- Unreasonable agreements concerning participation in amateur and professional sport.

- Failure to comply with an order of the Restrictive Trade Practices Commission.

6. Provision is made for authorizing and facilitating civil suits for recovery of loss or damages resulting from conduct contrary to the act, up to the full amount incurred plus costs of investigation and proceedings.

7. S.32(2) already provides that a court shall not convict if an agreement is found to relate only to certain specified matters set out in that clause. The bill would add to these matters agreements about the size and shape of containers, the adoption of the metric system and measures to protect the environment.

8. The bill contains new provisions making admissible in evidence official statistics which are not already privileged by reason of other federal or provincial statutes and prescribing the method of their preparation and introduction.

9. Provision is also made, under prescribed conditions, for statistics collected by sampling methods to be admissible in evidence.

10. The bill incorporates into the act the policy towards British Columbia fishermen and associations of buyers from them, which was enacted in a series of annual statutory extensions culminating in the extension of indefinite length found in the act to amend an act to amend the Combines Investigation Act, being Chapter 23 of the Statutes of 1966-67. At the same time the bill extends this policy to all other fishermen and buyers associations throughout Canada.

11. The bill provides that the minister may order a research inquiry into any matter which he certifies to be related to the policy and objectives of the act.

12. The bill provides for the Director of Investigation and Research to appear before any federal board to make representations concerning the maintenance of competition, at the request of the board, on his own initiative or upon direction by the minister.

13. The bill provides for interim injunctions to prevent serious damage being done to competition or to a person when it appears than an offence has been or is about to be committed, but has not yet reached the prosecution stage.

14. Finally, the bill prohibits, by amendment to the Bank Act, agreements among the chartered banks of Canada to fix the rates of service charges and the amount and kind of a loan to a customer.

SOURCE:
Proposals for a New Competition Policy for Canada, First Stage, Bill C-227, November 1973, Ottawa, Department of Consumer and Corporate Affairs, 1973, pp. 5-9.